Advance Praise for
The Science of Selling

"A crisp, unmissable guide. . . . Hoffeld's deft guidebook is a must-read for salespeople unsatisfied with anecdotal data and hungry for real data to improve their techniques."
—*Publishers Weekly*

"A terrific book! Sales trainer David Hoffeld has built his selling methods on a solid foundation of science. Let his research-based insights into why people buy help you increase sales and retain loyal customers."
—Dan Pink, bestselling author of *To Sell Is Human*

"David Hoffeld provides strong, clear, and practical advice about selling, supported by the relevant research and not just one-off anecdotes. Sales reps and sales managers are wasting their time with the vast majority of blogs and books and training 'tips' offered to them. But they should read and study *The Science of Selling*: It's perhaps the best discussion yet of the core essentials about this key business, and life, activity."
—Frank Cespedes, Harvard Business School; author of *Aligning Strategy and Sales*

"Is selling an art or science? David Hoffeld proves conclusively it is a science rooted in universal buyer behaviors that yield predictable, repeatable results—and in *The Science of Selling*, he explains precisely how you can apply that science to produce far greater sales results. Grab your yellow highlighter and be prepared to use it on every page."
—Stu Heinecke, author of *How to Get a Meeting with Anyone*

"This book is a breath of fresh air. While most sales books are based on the author's experience, every chapter in this superbly well-written book is rooted in science. The Six Whys formula is a great tool any sales organization can use to increase their chances for selling more and accelerating their sales cycle."
—Gerhard Gschwandtner, CEO of Selling Power

"This book is a must-read if you would like to excel in the game of influencing others! What David has pulled together in this masterpiece will surely advance your career or business. A science-based approach to selling that is revolutionary."
—Chris Spurvey, vice president, KPMG Canada; author of *It's Time to Sell*

"This is a refreshingly different kind of sales book. In it, David takes an almost shockingly different approach. He looks deeply at the science behind what happens during the sale, assesses the causes and effects, and serves up his conclusions in a way that translates to actionable awareness for sales reps and their managers. This book is a must-read."
　　　　　—Dave Stein, principal, DaveStein.biz; author of *Beyond the Sales Process*

"Can science and selling come together? YES, and in a powerful way—just read this book! *The Science of Selling* is as good as it gets—fantastic and really usable. I have already given it to my sales team to read."
　　　　　—David Horsager, CEO, Trust Edge Leadership Institute; bestselling author

"Many believe that sales is just a numbers game, but David Hoffeld has proven that there is actually a science to it. In *The Science of Selling*, he elevates sales from a robotic process to one rooted in recognizing behaviors and triggers and applying proven strategies that result in sales success. Hoffeld proves that selling is a skill that can be developed and perfected. A fascinating book."
　　　　　—Donna Serdula, founder and president,
　　　　　Vision Board Media & Linkedin-Makeover.com

"David has done a great job separating the science from the art of selling. It's refreshing to see research-backed methods and practices versus guesswork and theory around how influence really works. Hats off to Mr. Hoffeld for advancing our understanding around how to turn the practice of selling into a true profession."
　　　　　—Marc Miller, bestselling author of *Selling Is Dead* and *A Seat at the Table*

"*The Science of Selling* is outstanding; I haven't been able to put it down. It's helped me reexamine and rethink how I sell. Scientifically, I now understand the best way to present options, how to make my sales stick, and how to better use stories. In short, *The Science of Selling* eliminates guessing and common sales myths. It has my highest recommendation."
　　　　　—Ed Tate, principal, Ed Tate & Associates; World Champion of Public Speaking

"*The Science of Selling* is buttressed by extensive studies on 'how people buy,' along with David's real-world applications. I can't recommend this book enough!"
　　　　　—Victor Antonio, Sellinger Group

"For many years, we have been taught that salespeople are successful because they are either born with a natural ability to influence others, have outgoing personalities, or are just good with people. But we no longer have to rely on anecdotal methods like these. David Hoffeld uses scientific data to reveal why many salespeople underperform (and why the select few who succeed do) and shows you and your sales team how to implement his well-defined, repeatable sales strategies that are scientifically proven to improve your results. *The Science of Selling* is the future of selling!"　　—Ray Reyes, managing director, Globalize Localization Solutions

"Finally, you can get inside your buyer's head and this book is your blueprint. David Hoffeld unpacks the science behind what makes us choose, purchase, and trust those we buy from—essential insights for any sales professional wanting to become even more effective."
—Leary Gates, venture coach and founder,
Lumina Consulting Group and StrategicCEO.com

"Following on from the science behind selling that Dan Pink introduced in *To Sell Is Human*, Hoffeld dives deeper into how to use scientifically proven ways to build rapport, influence with ease, and pass through the skepticism that's inherent in the selling process. If you believe successful sales pros are made and not born, this book was written for you."
—Mary Poul, founder, *Sales Mastery Magazine*

"In the world of educational leadership, we know that the most effective leaders are those who do so through the utilization of research-based best practices. David Hoffeld provides an incredible resource of research-based strategies for influencing others—effective not only for meeting the needs of the salesperson, but for anyone who is in leadership or aspires to leadership."
—Toby Travis, International Head of School and educational consultant/trainer

"David Hoffeld believes that 'selling is too important to be based on anything other than proven science.' In *The Science of Selling*, he engages the reader in a fast-paced and fact-filled analysis of the sales process in which he demonstrates how scientific principles of influence and decision making can improve sales effectiveness. He focuses on how potential customers formulate buying decisions and teaches how sales success can be achieved by aligning sales strategies with how the brain is influenced. You will have a much deeper understanding of the sales process and how you can be more effective after reading his book."　　—David Fairbarn, president, Kinney & Lange

"A groundbreaking book that lays the foundation for a new way to approach the study and execution of sales. Based on the latest understanding of cognitive science, David provides sales professionals with a scientifically based framework to replace the sales methodology 'du-jour' for one that sales professionals can rely on throughout their entire professional careers. The book also provides insightful examples that will facilitate the sales professional to improve their productivity right away."
—Juan Carlos Cerrutti, managing partner, LinkIT Latam

"Finally . . . a book on selling that is based on scientific evidence. *The Science of Selling* is an engaging journey that bridges the gap between cutting-edge science and the realities of the modern marketplace. It's a must-read for anyone who wants to become more influential and increase their sales effectiveness."
—Ron Friedman, Ph.D., author of *The Best Place to Work: The Art and Science of Creating an Extraordinary Workplace*

"Of the thousands of sales books that are published each year only a few are groundbreaking. *The Science of Selling* is one of these. This book draws on the explosion of recent research around the world to challenge many traditional sales practices—and identify the most effective way to sell. You will learn how to transform the way they sell to enable a much higher level of success."
—John Smibert, Strategic Selling Group

"*The Science of Selling* is a tour de force of scientific research spanning a whole range of critical selling behaviors. Sales in general is going through a transitional period where some traditional skills are more important than ever, some are becoming obsolete, and of course, there are a host of new skills that are needed to address the twenty-first-century buyer. This book has done the hard work of identifying what they are and explaining clearly where to focus and how to adopt them. I highly recommend this book to anyone interested in sales success both now and in the future."
—John Golden, CSO, Pipelinersales; bestselling author of *Winning the Battle for Sales*

THE
SCIENCE
OF SELLING

PROVEN STRATEGIES TO MAKE
YOUR PITCH, INFLUENCE DECISIONS,
AND CLOSE THE DEAL

DAVID HOFFELD

A TarcherPerigee Book

tarcherperigee

An imprint of Penguin Random House LLC
375 Hudson Street
New York, New York 10014

Most TarcherPerigee books are available at special quantity discounts for
bulk purchase for sales promotions, premiums, fund-raising, and educational needs.
Special books or book excerpts also can be created to fit specific needs.
For details, write: SpecialMarkets@penguinrandomhouse.com.

Library of Congress Cataloging-in-Publication Data

Names: Hoffeld, David, (Economist), author.
Title: The science of selling : proving strategies to make your pitch, influence decisions,
and close the deal / David Hoffeld.
Description: New York : TarcherPerigee, 2016.
Identifiers: LCCN 2016023463 (print) | LCCN 2016033072 (ebook) |
ISBN 9780143129325 (hardback) | ISBN 9781101993187.
Subjects: LCSH: Selling. | Consumer behavior. | BISAC: BUSINESS & ECONOMICS / Motivational.
| BUSINESS & ECONOMICS / Sales & Selling. | BUSINESS & ECONOMICS / Skills.
Classification: LCC HF5438.25 .H6254 2016 (print) | LCC HF5438.25 (ebook) |
DDC 658.85—dc23

Printed in the United States of America
1   3   5   7   9   10   8   6   4   2

Book design by Elke Sigal

To my children, Jolene and David,
who seem to be able to sell me just about anything.

And to Sarah,
who read, encouraged, and never doubted.

CONTENTS

Why Use Science to Sell?

We are in the midst of a scientific revolution. Over the past few decades, there has been an explosion of research on how the human brain makes choices and which factors influence what we say, how we act, and what we decide to buy. All of us can benefit from this deeper understanding of what makes us tick. But for one group in particular, these scientific breakthroughs can lead to indescribable success and even revolutionize that entire profession—*if* they know how to use them.

That group is salespeople. One out of every nine employees in the United States works in sales, making it the second-largest occupation in the country.[1] (And that's not counting the millions of other people who do indirect selling every day and don't even realize it—like presenting a new idea to a boss or encouraging a friend to adopt a healthier habit.) However, in spite of the large community of people working in sales, the profession is in turmoil. Reports from the research firm CSO Insights reveal that up to half of all salespeople fail to meet their quota.[2] Even more alarming is the reason why: many of the most common sales techniques actually drive down performance. One study found that the majority of behaviors salespeople engage in hinder the likelihood of the sale.[3] (Throughout this book, I will call your attention to these destructive behaviors and what you should replace them with.)

What's more, potential customers now have easy access to information online that allows them to learn about all the sellers offering a product or service and to pick and choose as they want, rather than relying on one trusted source for their purchases. As a result, salespeople are engaging buyers later in the buying cycle than ever before—after buyers have already identified those who are offering similar products or services. These and other factors have created a hypercompetitive marketplace where salespeople must battle stiff competition for every sale.

The problem is that the marketplace has changed, but our methods for selling have not. Sales reps, managers, and business leaders generally agree that the old strategies are no longer working. Those in the sales community are wondering what to do and where to find new, effective solutions.

I encountered this issue during a conversation with an old colleague (we'll call him Bill) about the development of a new sales training curriculum. As Bill and I chatted, we turned to the topic of how salespeople can cultivate rapport with buyers. I recommended a particular strategy that I'd found very successful at strengthening relationships. To my surprise, he disagreed.

Bill insisted my approach was unreliable, simply an old sales gimmick. Undeterred, I explained how I had personally used it to increase rapport. He responded by sharing how in the past he had also applied the strategy, but had not experienced any positive outcomes. I quickly countered by launching into some examples of salespeople I had trained who had employed the strategy and had testified that it had helped them enhance rapport with buyers. He told me that early in his career he too had taught others to use it, with dismal results.

I paused, both to avoid escalating an argument I wasn't sure how to win, with a colleague I admired and liked, and because I was perplexed by his refusal to embrace what I had seen with my own eyes was a useful sales tool. At this point in my career, I was a highly successful sales professional who had risen to the top of every sales force I'd been on. Over the years, I had also been a top-producing sales manager, director of sales, and vice president of sales. Surely my success alone should prove my approach worked. Why didn't he believe me? Was I wrong? Could I have been using and teaching sales strategies that were actually hindering sales performance?

But my accolades, of course, didn't mesmerize Bill into submission. After all, he was a productive salesperson as well, who had advanced to become a successful manager and trainer.

Instead, whenever I would reference my record of success as evidence that *I* was right, he would point to *his* achievements as a counterargument.

That's when it hit me: We were each relying on our individual experiences and those of others we knew to prove that we were right and the other person was wrong. Yet neither of our sales methodologies was defensible because they weren't based on factual evidence that could be proven to work again and again. The reason I sold the way I did was rooted in my own anecdotal experience and knowledge. It was the same for Bill and, I slowly realized, for *every salesperson we knew.* Even the training that salespeople receive is commonly based on anecdotal evidence grounded in the experiences of one or a few individuals. No wonder the replicable success rate of any sales approach was so unpredictable; it wasn't based on anything that could be empirically proven to succeed. No one was using science to determine what strategies worked consistently.

I also realized that not being able to verify the most effective way to sell something amplifies your likelihood of failure, because it forces you to guess your way through the sales process. However, in sales, failure is not an option. If you're a salesperson, your capacity to earn sales will affect your job satisfaction, the trajectory of your career, and your income. And if you are a sales manager or business leader, your success is tied to the performance of the salespeople who serve under you.

> Sales ability is not a minor issue because it will determine your career success and, as a result, impact the quality of your life.

Even if you don't work directly in sales, this still applies. For example, if you are going on job interviews, you'll attempt to sell yourself and your skills to a prospective employer. If you are starting a business, your ability to pitch your idea and gain clients will determine whether or not your company survives. Selling is the lifeblood of our society. Directly or indirectly, it influences most aspects of our lives, especially our careers, businesses, and relationships. That's why we all need a proven, research-backed method for successful selling—because it's vital for achieving whatever we want to accomplish in life.

WHY SALESPEOPLE STILL MATTER

Because of the importance of selling, I began searching for real answers, studying different selling systems, hoping to find one that was evidence based. However, as I explored countless methods taught by well-known sales trainers and companies, I became increasingly discouraged. Though each training system promised they were right or "the best!" none offered definitive proof to back up those claims.

After a couple of years sifting through these sales methods, I made a decision that almost seemed crazy at the time. In spite of my own success, I decided to start over and discard every idea I had about selling. I embraced a healthy skepticism by adopting the belief that if I could discover why and how we make a decision to buy something, I could use that as my guide for determining what sales strategies are more effective than others.

As I embarked on what would turn into nearly a decadelong undertaking, it wasn't clear where to look for answers. So I put to use the research skills I had acquired while working on my master's thesis on nonverbal communication and started analyzing the many activities and behaviors that salespeople regularly engage in.

When I deconstructed each activity and behavior, I was struck by the fact that everything salespeople do is for the primary purpose of influencing someone. This was true regardless of whether a salesperson was engaging in precall planning, discovering a buyer's needs, presenting a product or service, or closing the sale. Even when salespeople utilize social media, customer relationship management (CRM) systems, and sales intelligence providers, they do so in the hope that this technology will help them positively influence prospective customers.

It quickly became clear from my research that influence is the foundation of selling. It is what inspires others to take an idea seriously and act on it. Information alone will rarely persuade someone to take action. (If it could, then salespeople would be unnecessary.) Rather, what moves people is *how* that information is presented and *who* presents it to them.

As neuroscientist Gregory Berns explains, "A person can have the greatest idea in the world—completely different and novel—but if that person can't convince enough other people, it doesn't matter."[4]

To be sure, in our technology-saturated world, potential customers are now forming initial impressions about a company, product, or service from information they glean online. But this doesn't negate the importance of salespeople. In fact, it makes them more essential than ever. Buyers rarely make purchases based solely on information provided over the Internet, unless the product or service is a very low-priced, low-risk item. In any other situation, and especially for higher-priced, higher-risk purchases, potential customers need to interact with a salesperson to make an informed and confident decision.

This was clearly shown when the *Journal of Business & Industrial Marketing* published the findings of a survey that asked buyers how the Internet has changed their purchasing behaviors.[5] The survey revealed that they still consider salespeople a more significant source of information than the Internet. As sales thought leaders Ben Shapiro and John J. Sviokla explain, "Despite the tremendous contributions of information and communications technology, selling is still largely a function of interpersonal relations, which are guided by the artful ability to recognize motivations, needs, and perceptions."[6]

In other words, despite the undeniable role that technology plays in selling and buying these days, people still buy from people. Research studies have shown that a persuasive appeal is enhanced when it is done through interpersonal relationships, and salespeople create the relationships that inspire a confident buying decision. This is why salespeople need to know how to guide buyers through the buying process and what evidence-based sales strategies will help their customers make the right choices. That's where this book comes in.

WHY SELLING WITH SCIENCE WILL INCREASE YOUR SALES AND SUCCESS

As I began researching the role of influence in selling, I stumbled on an academic journal that contained studies that revealed how influence occurs.

This experience fueled my research, as I was excited to discover that there is now a consensus in the scientific community about which behaviors specifically support and enable influence. Behavioral scientists Douglas Kenrick, Noah Goldstein, and Sanford Braver affirm, "The study of persuasion no longer exists only as an ethereal art. It is now a science that can reproduce its results. What is more, whoever engages in the scientific process can reproduce its results."[7]

> There have been thousands of scientific studies focused on understanding the behaviors that generate influence. This has transformed the process of influencing others from an art to a proven science.

I pored over academic journals, methodically investigating a variety of scientific disciplines, such as social psychology, which is defined as "the scientific study of how people think about, influence and relate to one another."[8]

I also delved into communication theory, the scientific study of how humans communicate both verbally and nonverbally. This research provided a strong understanding of how certain communicative signals can increase a person's receptiveness to a persuasive appeal or idea.

A third field that offered some valuable insights was neuroscience. I focused specifically on advances in cognitive neuroscience and social neuroscience. I researched how human thought, emotion, and behavior occur and how each are influenced.[9] I also investigated how the brain perceives, learns, and retains information.

Cognitive psychology—which focuses on mental processes such as attention, perception, critical thinking, and problem solving—provided many meaningful insights that guided me in grasping how influence occurs and how buying decisions can be shaped.

Last but not least, I explored behavioral economics, which is the integration of social science and economic theory, to uncover the factors that inspire buying decisions.

As I analyzed the information gathered from my intensive research into these scientific disciplines, the way I approached the act of selling radically changed. No longer was I forced to guess my way to the best solution to clinch the sale. Instead, with this knowledge, I could develop effective sales strategies that could be successfully applied in any situation. In other words, I figured out how to change the way selling is perceived, transforming it from an innate talent some have and some don't to a predictable science that can be learned by anyone.

Now it was time to reenter the world of sales and begin testing what I had learned in real-life situations.

I used myself as the first test case, joining a respected sales team and selling using the scientific principles I'd gleaned. The improvement was instantaneous. I immediately noticed I was able to build trust faster, diagnose buying motivators more accurately, outsell competitors, and guide buyers through the key stages of the sale with little resistance. Within months I became the number-one performing salesperson in the company.

Others noticed the impact too. My colleagues began asking me for advice and the company I was selling for requested that I train their entire sales force. However, unlike my training in the past, this time I was armed with strategies that I knew for a fact would guide those I trained to be consistently successful in their efforts. What happened next shocked me. I figured that when salespeople began utilizing science, there would be a reasonable increase in sales, but I was wrong. There was a *staggering* increase. The company's closing rates increased by 92 percent and their sales revenue grew by 156 percent.

From there, I began to accept invitations to provide training and consulting for various organizations. I formally launched Hoffeld Group, which has grown to be a leading research-based sales training, coaching, and consulting firm, specializing in taking science and applying it to selling. This finally gave me the opportunity on a much larger scale to provide salespeople, managers, business leaders, and CEOs the training, knowledge, and strategies to improve their selling success.

My clients experienced the same dramatic improvement in their sales results I had the first time I deployed my science-backed sales approach. One client raised their average sale size by 34 percent; another experienced rapid sales growth, increasing their overall sales by more than 230 percent. Not only were sales increasing, but so was customer loyalty, as yet another company I conducted training and consulting for lowered their loss of customers by almost 50 percent!

I also noticed that this knowledge could be applied across a variety of selling environments. It didn't matter how long the sales cycle was, or the size of the sale, the methods I developed based on my research improved sales success across the board.

What impressed me most was that not only were salespeople selling more and selling better, but they repeatedly reported that their customers and prospective buyers were *enjoying* being sold to a lot more. It makes sense: when salespeople align their activities and behaviors with the science of influence, they actually sell in the way that human beings are designed to receive messages and make purchasing decisions. This harmony between buyer and seller amplifies the buyer's receptiveness to the salesperson's pitch and increases the likelihood of the sale.

Even though I could now verify that selling with science would make anyone more successful, I still felt that I needed to put my research through one more test. I wanted to step back and critically analyze what I was observing because the results that I and those I had trained were achieving seemed almost too good to be true. So I decided to attend Harvard Business School and further study selling. I also used this opportunity to share my research findings with fellow students and a few of the professors who taught sales and marketing. It was during one particular conversation with a professor that I realized the far-reaching impact selling with science could have. It was what the profession of sales had been waiting for, some fresh air for this industry mired in old ideas and struggling to adapt to the modern sales environment. My research and method had the potential to transform the entire industry of selling.

I also began to conduct some unique research experiments that analyzed things like how the brain makes a buying decision and identified the core components of sales performance enhancement. The findings of this research, which will be shared in this book, led to some revolutionary innovations that have been field tested and implemented by companies and industries across the globe to significantly improve their sales success.

WHAT THIS BOOK WILL TEACH YOU

I've broken the book down into three parts. Part One gives you the knowledge and background that you need to use the strategies you'll learn in Part Two. Part Three discusses the science-based selling movement and how you can set yourself up for continued success into the future.

PART ONE: FOUNDATIONS OF SELLING WITH SCIENCE

In Part One, I reveal a framework you can use to incorporate science into any selling situation. The chapters in this section will uncover the foundational principles that every sales methodology should be built on. Because this part will equip you with the knowledge to begin applying this powerful science to selling situations in your own career and life, I strongly recommend you read the chapters in Part One in the order they're presented.

In Chapter 1, "Why Salespeople Underperform," you will see how the success of salespeople is linked to the overall health of an organization. Yet salespeople are struggling in today's complex marketplace, and thus their careers and their companies are suffering too. This chapter sheds light on the daunting obstacles salespeople face, and exposes why they're struggling and how this trend can be reversed.

Chapter 2, "The Two Methods of Sales Influence," discusses the scientific research that shows the two primary routes of influencing others. Salespeople must utilize both ways to increase their success. Throughout, I've included entertaining stories and real-life examples of how people have put these two methods of persuasion to work. You will also learn numerous practical strategies that will help you generate more influence when selling.

Chapter 3, "How to Sell the Way People Buy," unveils groundbreaking sales research that confirms that when the brain makes a buying decision, that decision is comprised of a series of small, incremental commitments that naturally guide a customer's mind through a progression of consents and into the final commitment to purchase. The Six Whys® are six specific questions that represent the mental steps the brain takes when formulating a buying decision. In this chapter, I will show you how to structure your sales processes to gain a commitment to each of the Six Whys®, so that you are selling the way buyers mentally construct their purchasing choices, and thereby substantially increasing your chance of earning the sale.

Chapter 4, "Selling to Your Buyers' Emotions," explores the science behind how the brain assigns meaning and value through emotions. There is compelling research showing that if potential customers do not become emotionally connected to a product or service, they will not care enough to buy it. That's why emotions are a determining factor in the success of the sale. In this chapter, I disclose the two primary types of emotional states and share numerous strategies that you can use to stimulate your customers' emotions and improve buying behaviors.

PART TWO: THE SALESPERSON'S TOOLKIT

Even experienced salespeople often behave in ways that contradict science and obstruct their ability to generate sales. In Part Two, you will be shown how to apply science to the major parts of the sale so you can avoid these mistakes.

Chapter 5, "The Science of Asking Powerful Questions," tackles the topic of how to ask great questions. Despite the fact that questions are mission critical in creating successful relationships with customers and prospective buyers, many of the ways that salespeople have been trained to formulate questions directly conflict with how the brain discloses information and encourage buyers *not* to share key information. The chapter begins with the scientific evidence that reveals how the brain naturally conveys information. Then I share a practical, easy-to-execute questioning strategy that is aligned with how our brains divulge information, and I demonstrate how to implement it in a variety of scenarios.

In Chapter 6, "Why People Buy," you will explore how to identify the conditions that will cause potential customers to purchase a product or service. These buying triggers are called *primary buying motivators*. Once you determine your buyers' primary buying motivators, you will be able to demonstrate real-world value by tailoring your sales process to what truly matters to your potential customers.

Chapter 7, "Creating Value, Neutralizing Competitors, and Overcoming Objections," delves into how you can apply science to boost your capacity to create value, reduce the influence of your competitors, and overcome challenging objections. This chapter will give you a look inside your buyers' minds and show you how to sell with an understanding of how the brain is wired to positively perceive people, products, and services.

In Chapter 8, "Closing Redefined: Obtaining Strategic Commitments," I demonstrate that the ways most salespeople have been taught to close the sale are antiquated and ineffective. In fact, most closing techniques conflict with how the brain instinctively makes a buying decision and, as a result, inspire negative feelings of pressure and anxiety in the buyer. This chapter is packed with powerful closing strategies that align with the science of decision making and are proven to increase sales results. You will learn that although a positive buying decision may be revealed only at the close of the sale, it must be cultivated throughout the sales process. This ensures that the close is a stress-free event for both parties, which also makes your buyer more likely to buy from you again.

In Chapter 9, "Five Science-Based Sales Presentation Strategies," you'll see what makes one presentation highly persuasive and another fall flat. I will also show you how to apply numerous scientific strategies to improve the effectiveness of *any* sales presentation. By the end of this chapter, your ability to present in ways that will result in buying decisions in your favor will be at an all-time high.

PART THREE: MERGING SCIENCE AND SELLING
The third part of this book consists of the concluding chapter, "The Future of Selling." Here, I explore three significant shifts that will occur as science begins to permeate selling. I'll also describe the five core qualities that enable heightened levels of sales performance and that should guide sales hiring practices. Then you'll learn why merging selling with science will alter the future of sales and how you can be at the forefront of the transformation.

Selling is a noble and necessary activity, a critical endeavor for every organization. I believe that those in the profession of sales, as well as anyone who has to do any kind of indirect selling in their everyday lives (which is all of us), deserve to learn about the science that has the power to enhance their ability to sell successfully. I also believe that selling is too important to be based on anything other than proven science. My hope is that armed with the knowledge and research-backed methods and strategies you will learn from this book, you, your colleagues, and your customers will benefit from long, prosperous business relationships.

So how exactly can you do this? Turn the page and we'll begin by looking at why salespeople underperform and what can be done to make sure *you* succeed.

PART ONE

———

FOUNDATIONS OF SELLING WITH SCIENCE

CHAPTER 1

Why Salespeople Underperform

A study published in the *Harvard Business Review* a few years ago should cause everyone in sales to cringe. Why? When the researchers analyzed the behaviors of eight hundred salespeople on sales calls they found that only "37% of salespeople—were consistently effective. What's more, some of the behaviors of the remaining 63% actually drove down performance."[1] In other words, the way that these salespeople were selling was actually preventing them from making the sale.

Unfortunately, these salespeople are not alone in their struggle. Lack of sales production is a devastating problem. In fact, surveys that measure the sales performance of thousands of companies found that 38 to 49 percent of all salespeople do not make quota every year.[2] This means that roughly four to five out of every ten professional salespeople fail to meet the minimum standard their company has placed on them.

The way that salespeople sell is a mission critical issue, because the behaviors they use when interacting with potential customers is a determining factor in the buying decision. For instance, when the performance measurement firm Chally Group conducted a series of studies examining the buying behaviors of more than 100,000 decision makers, they identified the salesperson as a deciding factor in whether buyers chose to purchase from one vendor or another.[3] In addition, research published by CEB, a leading advisory company, found that 53 percent of customer loyalty—customers choosing to buy from a company repeatedly—is not the result of the product, company, or service, but the behaviors salespeople use when selling.[4] Every day, the fates of careers and companies hinge on salespeople because they serve two imperative functions: creating customers and producing revenue to keep their organization alive. As Peter Drucker, legendary management expert and author of many culture-shifting business books, famously said, "There is only one valid definition of business purpose: to create a customer."[5] That said, there is no doubt that selling has become more challenging than ever. The marketplace is extremely competitive. Potential customers are blitzed by sellers fighting to earn their business. At the same time, buyers are extremely busy and have less time to deal with salespeople. To further complicate the situation, as I mentioned in the introduction, technology allows buyers to research potential solutions online before talking to a seller. As a result, salespeople are entering into the buyer's decision process later than ever before. The data indicates that around 60 percent of the buying cycle is completed before a salesperson is able to engage a potential client. Because of these new realities, salespeople have no room for error. They are selling in an extremely complex and competitive environment where they must battle competitors for every sale.

To make matters worse, these daunting challenges aren't the only reasons salespeople are struggling.

NATURAL ABILITY IS NO LONGER ENOUGH

For years, many in the sales community believed that success in selling is dependent on innate communication skills and a gregarious personality. The assumption has been, if you didn't have "it," you couldn't be taught it. However, a tidal wave of scientific research studying what makes people successful has disproven that idea in recent decades.[6] Though some people do have heightened levels of natural ability, talent is not enough to become a top performing salesperson. Because of the exceptionally crowded marketplace, you must continually improve your knowledge and skills.

> To be successful in sales today, you must sell *beyond* your natural ability.

One fascinating example of this is seen in the work of Carol Dweck, professor of psychology at Stanford University, who has conducted several studies on how one's mentality influences one's performance.[7]

She has found that people tend to embrace one of two common outlooks:

1. Fixed mindset: the belief that you can do little to change your abilities.
2. Growth mindset: the belief that through effort you can improve your abilities.

Below is a short quiz that will help you identify what mindset you have.

QUIZ

Which of the following statements do you believe to be true?

1. Your ability to sell is part of who you are and not something you can change.
2. No matter how good you are at sales, you can always improve.
3. You can learn new selling strategies, but you can't change much about your ability to influence others.
4. Selling is a skill that you can develop, regardless of your natural talent or personality.

Options 1 and 3 are fixed mindset statements, while options 2 and 4 are growth mindset statements.

So do these mindsets influence sales results? Yes, because the outcomes these mentalities produce are radically different. Those who have a growth mindset are far more likely to be successful than those who don't.[8] One of the main reasons a growth mindset drives high achievement is because it alters how the brain perceives failure. Those with fixed mindsets are more prone to see failure as a judgment on themselves. If they fail, they *feel* like failures. In contrast, people with a growth mindset view failure as the feedback that shows them how to adapt and take their abilities to the next level.

Over the years, I have witnessed the vast difference in performance between salespeople who are content to rely on their giftedness to bring in enough sales to squeak by (fixed mindset) and those who work hard to surpass their natural aptitude to achieve or beat their sales goals each year (growth mindset). In fact, this is one of the things I recommend that sales leaders test for when hiring for an open sales position. (We'll talk more about how to do this in Chapter 10.) Those with a growth outlook are more motivated to succeed and, as a result, far more likely to become top performers.

What about you? If you have a growth mindset, great! If you have a fixed mindset, you should address it because it will hinder your ability to achieve the level of success you desire. The good news is that your mindset is *your mindset,* and you can change it. By choosing to embrace the new, empowering belief that your sales skills are like a muscle that needs to be continually strengthened, you will inspire the work ethic necessary to achieve high levels of sales performance.

SALES TRAINING HASN'T BECOME MANDATORY . . . YET

Why do elite salespeople make selling look effortless? It's easy to assume they have always been terrific at selling. But rest assured, they make selling look easy because they have been capably trained. Science has shown that these individuals' brains have been altered by training, and this is what allows them to competently execute selling behaviors. Let me explain.

People used to believe that the human brain was static, remaining unchanged through adulthood. However, neuroscientists have recently demonstrated that the brain contains neurons that are constantly changing based on one's thoughts, behaviors, and experiences.[9] Neuroscientists describe the brain's flexibility as "neuroplasticity."[10]

When you learn any new behavior, your brain changes and new neural pathways are created. The more these neural connections are used the more they develop and, as a result, the more proficient you become at the activity they are associated with.[11]

For example, research published in the *Proceedings of the National Academy of Sciences* analyzed the brains of experienced London taxi drivers who were skilled at navigating the complex streets of London.[12] The researchers identified that the part of the taxi drivers' brains (the hippocampus) that deals with spatial relationships (navigation) had grown in size and contained an elevated number of neural networks. Essentially, these taxi drivers had changed their brains.

In much the same way, when salespeople go through effective training, their brains are being rewired. New clusters of neurons are formed and existing clusters connected with previously learned behaviors are strengthened.

Here are two fascinating examples that illustrate how training reprograms the brain and equips people to perform well beyond their natural abilities.

Behavioral scientist K. Anders Ericsson has led a series of research studies over an almost thirty-year period on how training can produce exceptional levels of performance. In one of his most famous studies, Ericsson and two other researchers studied how memory could be enhanced with continuous training.[13] They recruited a college student (whom they referred to by his initials, S.F.) with a normal IQ and memory; after listening to a sequence of numbers, he could recall around seven digits. After several hundred hours of memory enhancement training, S.F. drastically exceeded the goal of the training (fourteen digits) and was able to memorize eighty-two random digits. Just so you appreciate the impact of this, below are eighty-two random numbers. Read through them and try memorizing all these yourself. It's harder than it looks!

2 4 7 9 3 6 2 5 3 2 6 8 9 1 1 0 3 6 3 2 6 1 7 3 4 6 2 7

9 0 1 4 9 7 8 2 5 2 3 5 1 7 9 2 8 4 5 2 7 9 2 1 4 0 5 9

6 3 7 0 5 2 7 9 5 6 6 8 2 1 7 2 0 8 6 4 8 6 9 5 2 1

The researchers attributed the vast improvement of his memory to his use of mnemonic associations—such as converting random numbers into running times, so 247 became 2 minutes 47 seconds—and relentless training.

The effects of training on memory performance have been replicated many times by numerous researchers and participants.[14] When behavioral scientists from Florida State University analyzed the decades of research in this area they concluded that there is no "evidence that would limit the ability of motivated and healthy adults to achieve exceptional levels of memory performance given access to instruction and supportive training environments."[15] Even more fascinating is that when Ericsson and others analyzed how those in other professions such as business, music, mathematics, and sports become experts capable of superior performances, they found that it was due to continual training.[16]

Another intriguing example of how training can significantly boost skill levels is seen in the work of Betty Edwards, an art teacher who takes people with ordinary abilities and teaches them how to draw impressive self-portraits. She accomplishes this feat not in years, months, or even weeks. She does this within a mere five days. In her book, *The New Drawing on the Right Side of the Brain*, Edwards writes that once a person understands the technical components of drawing, he or she will progress rapidly with focused practice.[17] She emphasizes that most people do not lack drawing skills, but rather *seeing* skills. She maintains that once she shows her students how to perceive things such as edges, spaces, lighting, shadows, and relationships among objects, their ability to draw quickly improves. On the next page are some examples of the self-portraits her students drew on the first day of the class and the same students' drawings on day five.[18]

Likewise, I have witnessed salespeople who were struggling to keep their jobs go through high-quality sales training and transform their careers. Salespeople cannot sell beyond their training. Why? Because the training they receive is what creates their philosophy of selling, which I refer to as "sales truth." These are the core beliefs that govern how they sell, and especially which sales activities, behaviors, strategies, and skills they use or ignore. As professors at the Leavey School of Business James Kouzes and Barry Posner confirm, "the investment in training will pay off in the long term. People can't deliver on what they don't know how to do . . . you have to upgrade capabilities."[19] The way you do that is by training them how to do something better.

What's more, in today's hypercompetitive marketplace, if salespeople do not receive proper training they will fall behind; selling, like any other skill, must be developed. This is why a competent, well-trained sales team is often a company's most significant advantage—and an incompetent one its biggest liability.

As intertwined as sales training is with the success of salespeople, sales leaders, and companies, there is a glaring problem with modern sales training: most of it does not properly equip salespeople to sell in today's challenging business environment.

MODERN SALES TRAINING HAS NOT ADAPTED TO THE NEW SELLING CLIMATE

The marketplace has radically changed, but sales training has not. No longer can salespeople get by using the same old selling strategies that have been used for generations. (I will share some of these antiquated and ineffective strategies with you later in the chapter and throughout this book.) This is why, alarmingly, when salespeople go through sales training, much of it makes little difference in their job performance.

For example, research published by both ES Research Group and CEB has identified that 85 to 90 percent of all sales training has no positive impact after the training.[20] Now, this does not negate the need for competent training, but it does illuminate the fact that modern sales training is failing salespeople.

When you add together the fact that most of sales training makes no impact on the sales results of trainees and the widespread lack of sales production that was discussed at the beginning of this chapter, you start to see the scope of the problem. There is something horribly wrong.

Many in the profession of sales realize this problem exists, but they fail to properly identify the cause. Often, the finger is pointed at a variety of concerns, such as:

- Failing to follow-up and reinforce training
- Ineffectively leveraging technology (social selling)
- Making training an event, not a process

- Improperly assessing sales people before training (thus trying to solve the wrong problem)
- Participants or management not buying in sufficiently
- Not linking the training with the strategic initiatives of the company

To be sure, each of these issues should be addressed, but the evidence points to something much deeper as the reason why sales training and selling is in dire straits.

WHY SELLING SHOULD BE FOCUSED ON BUYING

In the introduction, I admitted that years ago, before I delved into finding and developing a successful sales strategy based on science, the way I sold was completely subjective, and relied on my own opinions and experience. I have since realized that I was not alone in this predicament. Virtually everyone else in business struggles with this issue, because our modern sales training methodologies are not founded on any objective standard, but rather are rooted in conjecture.

That's a bold declaration, I know, so let me demonstrate what I mean. A while ago, I led a Webinar whose audience included salespeople from numerous leading organizations. During my talk, I polled the participants, asking them a multiple-choice question: "In your organization, what are your sales behaviors based on?" In other words, why do you sell the way you do? Here is how they answered:

1. Trial and error (45 percent of participants)
2. Recommendations from experts (45 percent of participants)
3. Wishful thinking (5 percent of participants)
4. Unsure (5 percent of participants)
5. Scientific findings on how the brain formulates a buying decision (0 percent)

These responses mirror those I have received in numerous training seminars and workshops I've conducted over the years. The two most common answers are always trial and error and recommendations from experts. Let's stop for a minute and consider the implications of each.

Trial and error is precarious for two reasons. First, because of the dynamic nature of selling, testing one sales strategy in an effort to validate causation is not an easy task. This is something that even scientists struggle with, and most salespeople and business leaders are unfamiliar with how to carry out this complex process productively. Second, continual testing with trial and error takes time, and revenue generation (sales) is hardly the place to gamble on experimentation.

Recommendations from experts are equally problematic because their advice is usually based on flimsy evidence. These experts will refer to their personal experience or their observation of what elite salespeople do. Yet these ideas typically conflict with the ideas of other trainers, also pointing to their experiences and observations, to suggest that they are right. So which experts should you believe and, more important, why? (This is the same debate with my colleague that I described in the introduction.) Even more concerning is the fact that many of the sales techniques that experts recommend blatantly contradict what science has proven regarding how the brain constructs a buying decision. In other words, the experts are often wrong.

In the poll I shared earlier, the option that no one has *ever* chosen is "the scientific findings on how the brain formulates a buying decision." *This* is the root of the problem in selling. The way most salespeople are taught to sell is grounded in selling, not buying. Salespeople are shown sales activities and behaviors and then taught to make their buyers conform to *their* model of selling. It's the exact opposite of how it should be.

> The way most salespeople are taught to sell is grounded in selling, not buying. Salespeople are shown sales activities and behaviors and then taught to make their buyers conform to *their* model of selling. It's the exact opposite of how it should be.

Think about it: shouldn't selling be focused on how people buy? How can salespeople guide their buyers through the brain's decision-making process when they do not know how it occurs? I know these are deep questions, but nevertheless, they are important ones. If salespeople, managers, and trainers do not know how buyers mentally construct buying decisions, how can they know if a sales behavior is aligned with or violates that process? The obvious answer is *they can't*. Is it any wonder that the majority of the behaviors that salespeople engage in drive down their performance?

But this does not have to be the case. My goal is to make sure that you don't act in ways that hinder your ability to influence others. Yet it is hard to fight against the unknown. So before we can talk about how to correct this, we must first take a quick look at some examples of how conjecture-based sales training leads people astray.

MODERN SALES TRAINING CONFLICTS WITH SCIENCE

How would you feel if you found out that you were regularly using sales strategies and tactics that actually clash with how human beings are wired to be influenced? Unfortunately, you probably are. It is not your fault. Many popular selling strategies have been disproven by science. In fact, in this book you will see that some of the most commonly taught sales ideas on topics such as prospecting, asking questions, presenting value, creating urgency, justifying cost, negotiating, and closing, all conflict with science. This is a serious concern, because science discloses reality. When salespeople sell against science they are inadvertently selling in ways that decrease their effectiveness.

Here are two examples of common sales practices that oppose science:

EXAMPLE #1: ARE EXTROVERTS THE BEST SALESPEOPLE?

Traditional sales wisdom claims that the best salespeople are extroverts, outgoing, social individuals believed to be so naturally gifted they can "sell ice to Eskimos." There is just one problem with this supposition: It's wrong.

Numerous research studies have shattered this myth.[21] One meta-analysis of the findings of thirty-five different studies concluded there is no causal relationship between extraversion and heightened levels of sales performance.[22]

Another study, conducted by Wharton's professor of management Adam Grant, examined the effect of extraversion on sales performance. Grant scrutinized the results of 340 sales representatives over a three-month period.[23] He discovered that the introverted salespeople generated $120.10 per hour, while those who were extraverts sold slightly more, averaging $125.19 per hour. But interestingly enough, the higher they scored for extraversion, the lower their performance fell.

The biggest surprise was that those who were neither introverts nor extraverts, but exactly in between—referred to as ambiverts—had the highest hourly revenue of $208.34!

Extraverts often make poor salespeople because they are so gregarious they have trouble listening to buyers, which hinders them from understanding their buyers' perspectives. This is their downfall, because without ample knowledge of their potential customers they will unintentionally sell in ways that are out of sync with those customers' needs and desires.

The reason the extravert myth has persisted is that there seems to be a bias, especially in sales, toward extraverts, because they engage in outgoing social behaviors traditionally associated with selling. In addition, until recently there had not been any scientific inquiry into this topic, so no one had the data to mount a compelling counterargument. As a result, this notion, like many other false ideas, has lingered in the profession of sales.

EXAMPLE #2: HOW SHOULD YOU BEGIN A SALES CALL?

At the start of a sales call, should you ask buyers how they are feeling? There is widespread agreement from sales trainers that the answer to this question is an emphatic "no." They claim that asking such a question is "salesy" and "adds nothing to the conversation." Yet is that true?

This may seem like a minor issue, but when it comes to influencing others, sometimes a small behavior can make a surprisingly big impact.

This is what social psychologist Daniel Howard found when he conducted a series of psychological studies that demonstrated how this single question significantly increased receptiveness to a persuasive appeal.[24] Howard worked with representatives of the Hunger Relief Committee, who called homeowners and asked if they would be willing to allow someone from the organization to come to their home and sell them baked goods.

Howard analyzed the script that the representatives used when calling. He calculated that when the representatives followed their script, 18 percent of the people they spoke to agreed to the request. After observing the organization's representatives set appointments, Howard asked them to make one change. After introducing themselves, he had them ask the potential customer, "How are you feeling this evening?" When the representatives asked this question, the vast majority responded with a favorable reply. This caused the acceptance rate to nearly double: 32 percent of those contacted agreed to allow a representative into their home!

In spite of the overwhelming success of the study, Howard wanted to further confirm that it was that specific phrase and the person's verbal response to it that had triggered this substantial increase in compliance. So he organized a second research experiment, returning to the Hunger Relief Committee. Once again he had the representatives ask the question, "How are you feeling this evening?" at the beginning of the call. The rate of compliance was nearly identical with the level it had been in the previous experiment. Howard then changed the script and told representatives to stop asking, "How are you feeling this evening?" but instead to state, "I hope you are feeling well this evening." The impact of changing the question to a statement resulted in a drop in agreement to only 15 percent.

After analyzing his research findings, Howard explained, "Before you ask anyone for a donation, you first ask them how they're feeling. After they tell you they're feeling good . . . they'll be more likely to contribute."[25] (The reason for this will be described in Chapter 8.)

The notions that top salespeople are extraverts and that you should never ask buyers how they are feeling at the beginning of a sales call are just two of the many established sales ideas that have been refuted by science.

Now that you understand the problem, let's talk about the solution. The time has come for the profession of sales to look to science as its single source of sales truth. No longer must you guess your way to success. Sales, like almost every other discipline, can now be guided by science.

In the next chapter, we'll begin this journey by looking at the two foundational ways that salespeople can influence buyers—and learning how to use them to increase your sales effectiveness.

CHAPTER 2

The Two Methods of Sales Influence

Let's say you're meeting with buyers to deliver a formal sales presentation, and you know a direct competitor will also be there to make their own pitch. Should you go first or last?

Behavioral scientists Norman Miller and Donald Campbell analyzed the impact that presentation order had on decision making.[1] Their research found that whether you should present before or after your competitors depends on one factor: the time between presentations. If you and the competitor are presenting back-to-back, you should go first, because your presentation will shape buyers' perceptions and create biases that will put your competitor at a disadvantage. This is because of what researchers call the *primacy effect*, which is the brain's tendency to be more influenced by what is presented first than by what is presented later. This is also why first impressions matter. They create strong confirmation biases that effect one's perception of another person, situation, or idea. If you've ever had a tough time shaking a wrong first impression of someone or something, you know what I mean.

However, the research also shows that if the time between the presentations is considerable—more than a week—you should go last. That's because the memory of your competitor will have faded, while your presentation will be fresh in the buyers' minds, increasing the likelihood that you'll be chosen.

This is just one of the many factors that influence the decision-making process we'll examine in this chapter. The process of making buying decisions is no longer a mystery. There is a science to it, and once you know the rules of this science, you can develop an advantage over competitors who do not. In this chapter, I will take this research out of the laboratory and into everyday selling situations, showing you how to leverage it in your favor to sell yourself and your product or service more successfully.

HOW INFLUENCE OCCURS

For decades, scientists have been investigating how influence occurs. Much of this research was initiated by the U. S. government in the middle of the twentieth century in an effort to discover ways to protect its citizens and POWs from enemy propaganda. Building on these federal initiatives and their findings, behavioral scientists Richard Petty and John Cacioppo conducted vigorous research on why some messages were considered more convincing than others.[2] Through various experiments that analyzed how the brain perceives persuasive messages, they were able to do the unthinkable: they deconstructed the process of influence.

Petty and Cacioppo identified that the brain perceives influence in two different ways, the peripheral route (influencers outside of the message) and the central route (the influence of the message). These mental pathways are interconnected as they occur simultaneously, which scientists refer to as parallel processing.[3] Understanding both of the ways that influence occurs is extremely important, because they are what determine how others receive, interpret, and respond to your ideas—and what you can do about it.

These two methods of influence are at the core of an effective sales process, and shape the outcome of every sales call. In fact, for you to become highly successful at selling you must successfully leverage both paths of influence. If you do not use or unknowingly sell against either, your capacity to influence others is severely diminished, which will drive down sales performance.

Let's take a look at what they are and how to apply them when selling.

THE PERIPHERAL ROUTE OF INFLUENCE

The peripheral route of influence refers to factors that are outside of the message itself, but still have considerable sway on how we make decisions. It includes essential elements of selling such as building rapport, compellingly presenting a product or service, and enhancing trust.

This method of influence is made up of a series of mental reflexes, known as "heuristics." These mental shortcuts shape perception by producing a conditioned response, enabling the brain to form a judgment quickly without actively contemplating the issue or situation at hand.[4] The brain is an incredibly efficient organ and it instinctively creates heuristics—rules of thumb—that allow it to make fast decisions so it can conserve mental energy.

Though it may seem odd or dismaying that your decisions are influenced without thinking them through, your brain performs these mental shortcuts out of sheer necessity. If it did not, you would be paralyzed by the staggering amount of decisions you make every day!

Even though heuristics drive our behavior, most people are unaware of them and, as a result, they do not suspect their impact. As Nobel Prize-winning cognitive psychologist Daniel Kahneman confirms, heuristics require "little or no effort and no sense of voluntary control."[5] Harvard Business School's Amy Cuddy agrees that they are instinctive and occur naturally through "very unconscious and implicit processes."[6]

There is one more very important thing you need to know about heuristics. They are not always rational. Because these mental constructs operate below the level of consciousness, they are not analyzed in the same way a thought or belief may be. As University of Chicago professor and behavioral economist Richard Thaler explains, "heuristics causes people to make predictable errors."[7]

One famous example of this is found in an experiment that asked international travelers how much they would pay for $100,000 of life insurance for their upcoming flight.[8] Some travelers were told that the policy would pay out if they died for any reason, while others were told that it would only pay out if they died in a terrorist attack. Shockingly, people were willing to pay more for the policy that only paid out if they died in a terrorist attack than the one that would pay out for any reason. (The fear that people associated with a terrorist attack provoked such a strong emotional response that it caused them to assign more value to the policy that directly addressed this threat.)

This behavior makes no logical sense, because, well, neither do heuristics. They are why our brains often don't make logical decisions. Yet what makes heuristics so powerful—even though they aren't logical—is that they are predictable. As Thaler mentioned, they cause "predictable errors." Another well-known behavioral economist, Dan Ariely, has even coined the term "predictably irrational" to describe this phenomenon. He states that human behaviors "are neither random nor senseless. They are systematic, and since we repeat them again and again, predictable."[9]

Herein lies the power of heuristics; they are the *rules of influence*. Once you know what they are and you begin to sell in accordance with them, your ability to influence others will be enhanced. Why? Because you are behaving in ways that are aligned with how the brain constructs choices.

The following are four potent yet practical heuristics that you can use to improve your ability to help potential customers perceive you and your message in favorable ways:

HEURISTIC #1: SINGLE-OPTION AVERSION

Does the number of product options presented impact whether or not a purchase will be made? This was the question that behavioral scientist Daniel Mochon sought to answer. His research, which was published in the *Journal of Consumer Research*, determined that the number of product options did heavily influence buying behaviors.[10]

In one of his experiments, consumers were asked to purchase a DVD player. When a single DVD player was shown, only 10 percent purchased. However, when two different brands were shown sales skyrocketed, as an impressive 34 percent agreed to purchase the original DVD player, while 32 percent agreed to purchase the second DVD player. In total, a whopping 66 percent of shoppers agreed to purchase at least one of the DVD players when two options were shown.

When buyers are presented with only a single product or service, they rarely feel confident enough to make a positive buying decision and will want to look at alternatives. The reason is because of *single-option aversion*. This heuristic causes the brain to assign more risk to a decision when there is only one option in a choice set. Without something similar to compare a product or service to, the brain struggles to identify value and the decision-making process will often stall.

On the other hand, when the brain is shown competing alternatives, it will automatically assess each and select the best. This evaluation drastically reduces the perception of risk and the fear of making a poor decision.

> When presenting your products or services, always give buyers a few options. Doing so will make it easier for their brains to arrive at a decision.

HEURISTIC #2:
ASYMMETRIC DOMINANCE EFFECT

When comparing vastly *different* product or service options, buyers will frequently struggle to make a decision. This is because it can be very challenging for the brain to analyze selections that are not alike. In fact, many describe this as trying to compare apples to oranges.

Just think about it. If you were hungry and were given a choice of either an apple or an orange and you had no inclination for one over the other, how would you choose? Most likely, your brain would have trouble comparing these options. This difficulty would impede the decision process.

This is what it can feel like for potential customers when they are trying to decide between dissimilar yet competing options. In these situations, a surprising yet extremely effective way to help the brain decide is to introduce a third option that is inferior to one of the others. The lesser alternative makes the option that it is dominated by look more appealing.

In this case, when a substandard apple is presented, the brain unconsciously judges the two apples and selects the better one. This victory over the inferior apple will cause the brain to find the good apple even more attractive, which increases the probability that it will be chosen over the orange.

The notion that offering a decoy will make it easier for the brain to arrive at a decision is a phenomenon referred to as *asymmetric dominance effect*. It was first put forth in 1982 by three behavioral scientists.[11] Since then it has been researched and confirmed in numerous studies.[12]

One of the most fascinating of these studies was led by Dan Ariely, who demonstrated how the asymmetric dominance effect shifts perception and can even cause the average sale price to rise. In one of his experiments, Ariely asked MIT's Sloan School of Management students to evaluate subscription options for the *Economist* magazine.[13]

Experiment #1: Students are presented with two annual subscription options:

> **Option 1:** $59 for online access
> **Option 2:** $125 for print and online access

In this experiment, 68 percent of the students chose the print and online option, while only 32 percent chose online only.

Experiment #2: Students are presented with three annual subscription options:

> **Option 1:** $59 for online access
> **Option 2:** $125 for print only (new option)
> **Option 3:** $125 for print and online access

The addition of the decoy—Option 2—caused the average sale to jump, as 84 percent of the students chose the print and online option, while only 16 percent chose online only. No one chose the print-only selection.

Buyers will often get overwhelmed when evaluating radically different options. This will prompt them to become frustrated, since they are unable to reach a decision. It is here that you can deploy the asymmetric dominance effect to relieve the pressure by making the task of comparing the options less cognitively demanding.

For example, I have a client who, when customizing their product with buyers, would frequently encounter stalls when those buyers could not make up their minds between two competing options. I showed my client numerous science-based strategies to remedy this dilemma; one of those was the asymmetric dominance effect. Here's what they would do. When potential customers were agonizing between two choices, the salesperson would introduce another option that was similar but inferior to one of the selections. The buyers would quickly say that the new option was not right for them and then more often than not choose in favor of the one it was dominated by. Why? For the brain to discard the new option it would compare it to the one that it was most similar to. This win made the option seem like a safer choice than its alternative and, as a result, significantly increased the likelihood that it would be chosen overall.

HEURISTIC #3: LIKABILITY BIAS

Think of someone you are almost indifferent to—you neither like nor dislike her. Now imagine that a close friend told you she said something extremely positive about you. Did your view of her change? Most likely, without any conscious effort, you began to look more favorably on her. The reason is because of a heuristic that I refer to as the *likability bias*.

You're not the only person with this heuristic; your buyers have it too. Likability matters a lot in selling because it impacts how potential customers view you and everything you do. One study by behavioral scientists Jonathan Frenzen and Harry Davis identified that likability shapes buying behaviors almost as much as the product or service.[14] What's more, a vast amount of scientific research has shown that likability also enhances one's ability to positively influence another person.[15] Freud profoundly described this reality when he wrote, "One cannot explain things to unfriendly people."[16]

The importance of the likability bias is clearly seen in one scientific study that analyzed the response two rival political leaders received from constituents when they matched their opponent's views, even using the exact words.[17] The research found that those who were supporters of a politician's political party were far more likely to agree with his position than they were when the opposing politician said the same thing.

Selling is relational and thus being liked is not a luxury, it is a prerequisite for survival. When buyers do not like salespeople, their focus will be on getting away from them, not on productively collaborating together to work toward a common goal.

A study published in the *Harvard Business Review* offers one very convincing piece of evidence that illuminates the positive outcomes likability has on relationships.[18] The study analyzed the traits of 51,836 leaders and determined that only a meager 27 of the leaders were rated in both the bottom for likability and the top for leadership effectiveness. This means that the probability of a leader being fiercely disliked and still being a productive leader is about 1 in 2,000.

Now that you know that likability matters and why, let's talk about how to be likeable. What you should not engage in are any shallow, disingenuous, or manipulative techniques. These tricks don't work; they erode your integrity and will make you come off as phony.

A direct and scientifically validated way to boost your likability is to show your buyers that you like them. Just like we saw in the example I shared earlier, when you find out that someone likes you, it is almost impossible not to like them back. Numerous scientific studies have confirmed that when a person finds out that someone likes him, he instinctively begins to look more favorably upon that person.[19]

One example of this I often share in my seminars involves my great-aunt, Aunt Ann. She was loathed by almost everyone in my family, and for good reason. She was argumentative, stubborn, and miserly. Aunt Ann never had any children; in fact, she did not enjoy being around children—with one exception, me. When I was a baby, just a few days old, Aunt Ann held me and formed a bond with me. From that moment on, she would go out of her way to demonstrate to everyone that she was fond of me. That may sound sweet, but I am not an only child. When my family visited her, she was not shy in showing that she liked me more than my siblings.

Aunt Ann passed away when I was twelve years old. Only a few people came to her funeral; most didn't care. Nevertheless, one person did miss her—me. As I reflect on why I liked Aunt Ann so much, I have to admit it was because she liked me so much. As I said, it is almost impossible not to like someone who really likes you.

A straightforward way to show buyers that you genuinely like them is to identify something about them that you sincerely appreciate. This could be anything from attire, business acumen, work performance, ideas, or character qualities. Once you have put your finger on something that you honestly admire, focus on it and then communicate it to that person. People can tell when you like them, and when they do they will instinctively respond in kind. Furthermore, by viewing your prospective customers in this way, you will naturally treat them in a more responsive manner, which will further increase your likability.

HEURISTIC #4: SOCIAL PROOF

Imagine that you are in a new city and you need to find a place to eat. You notice two diners next to one another. Neither are familiar to you, but you quickly notice that there is one big difference. One is jam-packed with people, while the other has no customers. Which restaurant would you choose?

If you are like most people I have posed that question to, an answer immediately comes to mind. You intuitively know that the busy diner is the better option. Yet why is eating at a full restaurant superior to dining at an empty one?

The reason your brain was able to quickly evaluate both restaurants and make a confident decision is because of a heuristic called *social proof*. In fact, social proof is one of the most powerful heuristics, because it connects the persuasiveness of an idea or behavior to how others are responding to it. Additionally, when many other people are engaging in something, it triggers the brain to reduce the perception of risk associated with an idea or activity. It is the reason we are all drawn to best-selling books, blockbuster movies, crowded restaurants, and businesses that have many satisfied customers.

Social proof also creates strong social norms, which are expected standards of behavior. It is very hard for most people to go against these behavioral expectations. One of my favorite examples of this is a standing ovation. How many times have you been in an audience when a few people give the performers a standing ovation, then more audience members quickly follow? Soon it seems that everyone around you is standing up and applauding. In spite of the fact that you had not planned on doing so, you find yourself rising to your feet and joining in. Why? What force caused you to stand and why does it feel so odd to resist the urge? By now you know that the answer is social proof.

There is a lot of research on social proof, more than a hundred years' worth,[20] although one of the most significant research studies ever conducted on social proof was led by renowned behavioral scientist Solomon Asch in the 1950s.[21] His study consisted of groups of seven to nine people being shown one straight line and then three additional lines that varied in size. The participants were asked to publicly share which of the three lines they believed was most similar in size to the first line shown (see example below). Almost every participant reported that the exercise was uncomplicated and they exhibited a 99 percent accuracy rate.

Standard Line

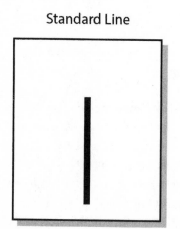

Comparison Lines

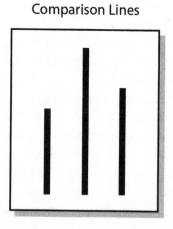

However, this study has an unexpected twist. Everyone in each of the groups—except one person—was collaborating with Asch. The goal of the experiment was not to test the participant's ability to estimate the length of the lines, but to see if he or she could defy the pressure that social proof stimulates.

After a few rounds of everyone answering identically, the accomplices would begin to intentionally select an incorrect answer. As the experiment continued and those working with the researchers kept choosing the wrong lines, the various test subjects began to show signs of extreme anguish. They became worried, awkward, embarrassed, and hesitant to select the answer they knew to be right and defy the choice of the rest of the group.[22]

The conclusion of the experiments was that most of the true participants could not withstand the pull of social proof. A shocking 75 percent later confessed that they deliberately chose the wrong answer because of the pressure they felt to conform to the group. (This experiment has been repeated many times, each time with similar results.)[23]

As fascinating as Asch's experiments were, even more revealing is research that was done in response to them. Neuroscientist Gregory Berns and his colleagues wanted to delve deeper into the effect that social proof has upon the human brain. To do this they conducted Asch's line study while participants' brain activity was measured by functional magnetic resonance imaging (fMRI).[24] The fMRI revealed that when the participants were judging the size of the lines, the posterior area of the brain, which is dedicated to perception, lit up.

However, when participants realized that the line they believed was the right size was different than the line that all the others in their group chose, the amygdala, which is the part of the brain responsible for intense emotions, was activated. As the amygdala was stimulated, Berns and his colleagues also noticed that the participants were experiencing visible emotional anxiety. In short, defying what others said elicited forceful emotional reactions within the brain that caused such feelings of discomfort that, more often than not, participants would disregard what they knew to be right.

How to Use Social Proof

When you utilize social proof successfully, you convey to potential customers that buying your product or service is the safe thing to do. Doing this is central to the success of the sale because, like the participants in Asch's and Berns's studies, people are risk averse. The higher the perceived risk associated with purchasing a product or service, the less likely it is that the buyer will make a positive buying decision.

Many businesses are already using social proof to increase their audience's desire for their product or service. For example, Ford Motor Company gave away Ford Focus cars to some key influencers so they would be seen driving the car. Hebrew National also sought to activate social proof when it hired "mom squads" to host hot dog get-togethers for friends.[25] Even the marketing firm that promotes Red Bull attempted to market the energy drink by filling up popular sidewalk trash cans with empty Red Bull cans.[26] The impact that social proof has on changing consumer behaviors is so significant that researcher Steve Martin said, "Organizations are getting good results from these techniques; in fact, some have begun realizing billions, not just millions, in added revenues and efficiencies."[27] Social proof is not just for big businesses; you can also use it to boost desire for your products or services. One study found that when salespeople described their products as "the most popular" or "selling faster than we can bring them in," potential customers' desire for the products and their assessments of their value surged.[28]

Another way to apply social proof is to tell buyers about your customer success stories. These types of stories demonstrate the widespread acceptance of your product or service. (How to create and share captivating stories will be covered in Chapter 9.)

When a lot of people are enjoying something you also want to try it, and when you do, because your expectation is positive, you are more likely to enjoy it as well. One fascinating example of how social proof can enhance perception can be seen in numerous studies that found that television comedies that have canned audience laughter generate more laughs from viewers and are rated as funnier than when they are aired without the laughter.[29] In the same way when you share how your customers are benefiting from your products or services, you will motivate others to purchase and experience the benefits for themselves.

When it comes to harnessing the positive power of social proof, remember that similarity matters. A significant amount of research has disclosed that the impact of social proof is amplified when people from one's own peer group have embraced the idea or behavior.[30] So if you show buyers how others similar to them have purchased your product or service and experienced positive results, they are much more likely to buy it as well.

> To activate social proof, you can reference your past customers by using phrases such as "so many people . . . ," "most businesses in your situation," or by offering customers' names or organizations.

THE SHORTFALL OF THE PERIPHERAL ROUTE

It is evident that the heuristics of the peripheral route of influence are potent motivators of human behavior and vital parts of the buying process. However, this method of influence does have a serious deficit. It's short-lived.[31]

When buyers are persuaded to purchase a product or service primarily through the peripheral route, their confidence in their decision will diminish over time, especially if the decision is challenged. This is problematic, because if a buyer does purchase, the decision is weak, since it was made not because of the salesperson's message (the central route), but because of factors outside of the message (the peripheral route). Moreover, in today's extremely complex and competitive marketplace, the peripheral route of influence is rarely enough to guide potential customers through the buying process. This is because the brain needs to process both routes of influence in order to create strong, confident buying decisions.

Yet, in my experience, most salespeople mainly focus on selling through the peripheral route. (The reason, as you will see later in this chapter, is because many of them are unsure how to sell via the central route.)

For instance, over the years I have asked countless salespeople what they attribute their success in selling to; by far the most common answer is that they believe they are good at building rapport. A prime example of this approach is commonly referred to as "relationship selling." This is when a salesperson focuses on persuading buyers to purchase because of the good relationship they've established.

As I confirmed earlier in this chapter, a lot of research has proven that likability improves influence and the likelihood of the sale. But if it is the main method of influence you use, remember that it exerts a strong but temporary sway on your buyers. Once the memory of their interaction with you fades, so will their commitment to you, your company, and the product or service. As a result, these customers are highly susceptible to being stolen by competitors or to canceling their orders. It is not that they are disloyal; they just made a purchasing decision predominantly based only on the peripheral route of influence.

Think of using only one route of influence as trying to fly on a plane with only one wing. You would never board that plane, because you know it needs two wings to get off the ground successfully. Likewise, you should sell via both routes of influence because they are what the brain uses to construct a positive buying decision. So let's learn about this second method of influence, the central route, because once you begin intentionally selling with both routes simultaneously, your sales influence will go to an all-time high.

THE CENTRAL ROUTE OF INFLUENCE

Through dozens of experiments, Petty and Cacioppo identified the second way influence occurs, which they called the central route.[32] This is the message of the persuader. As a salesperson, the central route of influence is mission critical to the success of every sale, because only after buyers contemplate and commit to the salesperson's message will they be able to confidently make a buying decision. In fact, your ability to convey and gain commitments to the key components of the central route will be the number one factor that will determine your level of sales success.

> The goal of every sales process should be to guide buyers to commit to the salesperson's message (the central route) while using heuristics (the peripheral route) to effectively convey that message.

Let's take a moment to make sure we're clear on the difference between the central route and the peripheral route. The best example of both of these means of influence noticeably on display is at a political debate. As politicians volley back and forth during the debate, viewers are being persuaded by both routes of influence. The message of the politician, which is how he or she will deal with various issues, is the central route of influence. This is what produces strong loyalty. It is also why in every political season many vote for a certain political party regardless of the candidate; they believe in what the party stands for—its message—more than they care about the candidate.

However, the peripheral route also persuades voters. Many, especially those who are undecided or not devoted to one side of a political issue, judge the candidates based on how they conduct themselves during the debate. These peripheral cues include the candidate's charisma, likability, dress, word usage, and so on. Though these peripheral signals are very persuasive, as we've seen, they fade quickly. When a politician displays mannerisms that convey him in a negative light, those who are not loyal to his message (the central route) may switch sides or find their positive feelings waning, which explains why minor political gaffes can often derail or even end a politician's career.

Just as voters are often intensely loyal to a political message, when buyers are persuaded by the central route they become deeply loyal to their decision to purchase. As potential customers reflect on and agree with the salesperson's message (the central route), their perception of risk is reduced. Also, unlike the peripheral route, the effects of being influenced via the central route last.[33] As behavioral scientists Robert Gass and John Seiter explain, "Persuasion that takes place via central processing also tends to be more resistant to counterinfluence attempts than persuasion via peripheral processing. This also makes sense: If you have thought through your position, you're less likely to 'waffle.'"[34] When you guide your customers in arriving at a purchasing decision through the central route, they will be significantly less likely to be swayed by the wooing of competitors. Because this method of influence grounds them with an understanding of why they purchased, they are more committed to their decision. Also, armed with this conviction, buyers are able to coherently explain why purchasing was the right decision. This has been proven to increase customer loyalty, which translates into heightened levels of customer referrals and retention.

What Is the Salesperson's Message?

What should your message (the central route) be when selling? When salespeople, managers, or trainers are asked this pivotal question, they often have no idea how to answer. At best they usually reference something about their company, products, or services. Yet a salesperson's ability to sell via the central route is linked with successful selling and is far too important to be based on mere guesswork. In addition, until you know what your message should contain, you cannot know which activities and behaviors you should use when selling because you don't know what you are trying to accomplish. Don't worry, there is a clear answer regarding what a salesperson's message should be.

LEVERAGE THE CENTRAL ROUTE: SELLING THE WAY THE BRAIN BUYS

We now know exactly how salespeople can apply the central route of influence, as the next chapter reveals. What the research shows is that a salesperson's message should mirror the way that buyers' brains formulate buying decisions. The more that sales messaging is aligned with the mental steps the brain goes through when creating a buying decision, the more effective it will be. As I shared in the last chapter, the more sales strategies are focused on how people buy, the more beneficial they are for everyone involved.

Until recently, how the brain arrives at a buying decision was unknown. Though previous scientific discoveries had uncovered the peripheral factors that influence buying decisions, the actual mental process that buyers go through when deciding whether or not to buy a product or service was considered a mystery. However, this is no longer the case!

Building on the existing knowledge of the central route of influence, I led an extensive research study that focused on deciphering the internal decision-making process. The revolutionary finding of this research showed how to apply the central route in the context of selling. It defined what most believed was unknowable: the steps the brain goes through when constructing a buying decision.

This innovation is a substantial breakthrough in the field of sales, because equipped with this knowledge you will be able to judge the effectiveness of any sales process by analyzing how it guides buyers through their mental journey and into a positive buying decision. This will eliminate the need to try out a sales process to see if it works. From now on you will know if it will help you sell more—prior to engaging in it—since you will have an objective, evidence-based standard to compare it to. But now it is time to learn how to sell via the central route by learning the mental steps that comprise a positive buying decision.

CHAPTER 3

How to Sell the Way People Buy

What enables one salesperson to outsell another? Why does one sales process produce superior results, while others do not? The good news is there's a clear, science-based answer to these questions. Today we know that heightened levels of sales performance are a result of how closely aligned sales behaviors are with how the brain creates a buying decision. In other words, the more your way of selling mirrors your buyers' decision-making process, the more effective it will be.

> The more your selling efforts are aligned with how the brain naturally formulates buying decisions, the more successful you will be.

However, the opposite is also true. If you sell in ways that are antagonistic to how the brain makes choices, you will impede the sale and diminish the likelihood that buyers will say yes.

For instance, at the beginning of Chapter 1 I shared a study published in the *Harvard Business Review* showing that an astonishing 63 percent of salespeople consistently behave in ways that hinder their performance. So what makes a sales behavior unproductive? When it conflicts with how the brain is wired to be influenced and construct buying decisions.

Now to be clear, the salespeople in that study were not trying to lose sales. To the contrary, they believed they were helping their prospective clients buy. And herein lies the problem: salespeople often don't know if how they sell is obstructing the decision-making process or is aligned with it. Let me explain why.

Imagine you are in your local grocery store pushing your cart down the cereal aisle. Out of the corner of your eye you see a new type of cereal and instantly recognize it as the one you saw advertised on TV a few days earlier. You pick up the cereal and notice the logo of a well-known cereal manufacturer. After scanning the list of ingredients, you check the price and then drop the box into your cart and continue shopping. You stroll down a few more aisles and then proceed to the checkout counter, pay for your groceries, and leave the store.

What ultimately triggered your decision to purchase the cereal? Was it the television commercial? The cereal's manufacturer, ingredients, or price? Your lack of interest in the other cereals in the aisle? Or some other factor entirely?

When I ask this question in my sales training workshops, there are a few common responses. Some contend it's the commercial that prompted the purchase. Others assert that the cereal's ingredients were the deciding factor. Some declare the price did it, while still others insist that brand loyalty made the difference. A few even say that it was some mysterious combination of all of the above. Finally, there is always a small group who will suggest it's impossible to determine the answer to that question.

What is always consistent about the responses I receive is that they are all guesses. If pressed to prove or explain why they picked their particular answers, most workshop participants simply shrug their shoulders. Now to be fair, this is a challenging exercise, but if anyone should be able to answer the question of how someone's choice to purchase a product or service is made, it should be professional salespeople. Why? Because guiding people through the decision-making process is the very reason salespeople exist.

Yet when I ask sales professionals to describe how the brain makes a buying decision, they either give me blank stares or offer some variation of the following vague process:

1. Recognition: Buyers must first realize they have a need.
2. Identification: Buyers identify possible solutions to meet their need.

3. Assessment: Buyers will assess each potential solution.
4. Decision: Buyers decide which solution is best.
5. Purchase: Buyers exchange funds for the solution.
6. Evaluation: Buyers evaluate, postsale, the chosen solution.

This simplistic model fails to provide any meaningful insights into the decision-making process. What's alarming is that both this and the cereal exercise highlight the great lack of awareness regarding how buyers make purchasing choices. And the grim reality is, if you don't understand how a positive buying decision occurs, how can you guide potential customers into making one for the product or service you're selling?

In this chapter, I'm going to show you the science that reveals how the brain forms buying decisions and how you can guide buyers through this process and into the purchase.

IDENTIFYING THE DECISION-MAKING PROCESS

Once I realized that basing sales behaviors on how the brain formulates buying decisions would vastly increase sales success, I set out to find accurate, research-backed information about this process. It was clear that until it was identified and broken down into manageable steps that could be incorporated into a sales approach, selling would never truly be focused on buyers.

For the foundation of my research in this area, I turned to the science of influence (which I discussed in the introduction), as researchers had already uncovered the factors that shape human decisions. Continually applying this science to the buying process also helped me validate each step of my own research and kept my biases from misleading me.

Armed with this knowledge, I began studying sales calls across a variety of industries and selling environments. Some were over the phone, while others were conducted face-to-face. The buyers ranged from consumers and small and midsized businesses to Fortune 500 companies. The size of the sale also varied; some were straightforward with short sales cycles, while others were large and complex. As I reviewed them, I began analyzing what specifically had to happen in each situation for the sale to occur.

In addition to that, I contrasted the successful sales calls with those that resulted in lost sales. On the calls in which the sale died, I paid special attention to the final objections buyers gave, figuring that if I could understand the causes of their objections, it might help me identify where the breakdown occurred in the decision-making process. This was an important deduction, because I found that objections fell into specific categories. When I began testing each category, I was surprised to find that when these objection groups were neutralized, the sale almost always happened, but if even one of the objections remained, the sale never occurred.

This also brought something surprising to my attention: there are certain commitments that enable and even create positive purchasing choices. Discovering these gave me clues about how buying decisions are made. But there was still one component of the buying process that I was perplexed by: emotions. I had evidence, both scientific and from the sales calls, that buyers' emotions sway the trajectory of the sale, but it took me years of additional research to fully understand and define their role in a purchase.

Once I was able to account for emotions (which will be discussed in Chapter 4), I had the pieces of the buying puzzle. As I continued to test my findings in the real world of selling, the results grew more and more promising. I was getting closer and closer. And then it finally happened. I found what I had been looking for—the missing link in selling. I had identified how people make buying decisions.

HOW BUYING DECISIONS ARE MADE

What had started out as an endeavor to find out how we make decisions to buy or not to buy wound up becoming an intensive six-year research project. But the effort was well worth it. In the end, my research revealed that buyers go through certain repeatable and predictable mental steps when arriving at buying decisions. These steps determine whether or not they will choose to purchase a product or service. In fact, this internal process is so ingrained in how we humans formulate buying decisions that we rarely notice we're engaged in it.

Two quick notes before going further: One of the findings that surprised me most was how the brain's decision-making process did not change regardless of the size or complexity of the sale. I had been expecting the evidence to show that the way the brain creates a decision varied depending on whether the sale was small or large, complex or simple, high- or low-risk. Rather, the research revealed that in larger, sophisticated sales, buyers were more likely to vigorously contemplate each component of the decision, but the buying progression remained unchanged.

This is because the internal decision-making process is derived solely from how the brain makes a purchasing choice, not the scope or intricacy of the sale.

The other important insight my research revealed was that the buyer's decision to purchase is not made in response to the salesperson's message after he has completed it, but rather *throughout* the salesperson's message. Think about it like this: During the sale, potential customers are committing to or rejecting your ideas, statements of value, and recommendations. Then at the end of the sale, the results of this mental process are unveiled by whether they decide to purchase or not. In other words, though the buying decision may be revealed at the conclusion of the sale, it's being cultivated throughout the entire sale.

This disproves the old model of selling that assumes the end of the sale, commonly referred to as the close, is when salespeople should guide potential customers in making the commitment to purchase. Instead, the evidence overwhelmingly confirms that when a positive buying decision is made, it is comprised of a series of small commitments I call the Six Whys®. These strategic commitments are what guide buyers through a natural progression of consent and into the final decision to purchase. They are the building blocks of the entire buying process, because if prospective purchasers do not make each of these minor commitments, they won't be able to agree to the sale. The process looks like this:

SCIENCE-BASED SELLING METHODOLOGY

(Strategic Commitments Throughout the Sales Process)

Greeting » Why 1 » Why 2 » Why 3 » Why 4 » Why 5 » Why 6 » Sale

But before we delve into the Six Whys®, I need to share with you the rest of what makes up the decision-making process. Then I'll explain each of the Six Whys® and show you how to answer them within the sale.

THE SALES EQUATION

What is the mental process that every buyer goes through when making a buying decision?

To accurately convey this in a simple manner I created the sales equation. This straightforward formula deconstructs how the brain arrives at a choice by showing the information a buyer must commit to in order to be able to make a positive buying decision. It also demonstrates, in a quantifiable way, the core components that should comprise your sales message (the central route of influence) and the role of emotions in the buying process.

$$BD = f(SW, ES)$$

The sales equation states that a buying decision (BD) is a function (f) of the Six Whys® (SW) (which we'll get to in a minute) and the buyer's emotional state (ES). This means that if you are selling to a qualified buyer who has the financial means and authority to purchase your product or service, and you guide that buyer into committing to each of the Six Whys®, and the buyer has a positive emotional state (the collection of emotions he is experiencing at a given time), you will always be able to earn the deal. Here's another way of saying this.

COMMITMENTS TO THE SIX WHYS® + POSITIVE EMOTIONAL STATE = POSITIVE BUYING DECISION (OR SALE)

If salespeople can consistently execute the components of the sales equation, they will be extremely successful. If they can't fulfill them, they will always struggle.

THE SIX WHYS®

The Six Whys® are six specific questions, each (unsurprisingly) beginning with the word "Why," that represent the mental steps all potential customers go through when making a purchasing choice. When salespeople structure their sales processes to answer and gain commitment to each of the Six Whys®, they are guiding potential customers through the buying process and into a positive decision.

My research confirmed that if a buyer rejects one or more of the Six Whys®, it will cause her decision-making process to break down, which will in turn halt the advancement of the sale. This breakdown, I learned, will reveal itself in the form of an objection. That is to say, the root of every objection is found in one of the Six Whys®. So when an objection occurs, it is because one or more of the Six Whys® has been rejected by the buyer.

Breakdown Causes an Objection and Halts the Decision Process

In sales training workshops, I've had salespeople from different industries list the common and not so common objections they receive. In every case, I can demonstrate that the source of each objection is found in a lack of commitment to one of the Six Whys®. Consequently, if you can preemptively inspire your buyers to commit to each of the Six Whys®, you will neutralize all possible objections.

The Six Whys® are important because they help you identify the source of a buyer's objection. This will enable you to accurately answer the objection and also to improve the likelihood you'll overcome it. (In Chapter 7, I'll go into the process you should follow when overcoming objections once they've been verbalized by buyers.)

The Six Whys® will also empower you to continually improve. Now when you do lose sales, you can pinpoint which of the Whys the buyers rejected and work on strengthening that part of your sales process.

So let's get started. The first step is to acquire an understanding of the

Six Whys®. Though they will be disclosed in a numerical order, answering and gaining commitments to each will occur at various times, with some overlap, during the actual sale. For now, focus on learning each of them and later on, in Chapter 8, you'll discover exactly how to gain commitments to each.

WHY #1: WHY CHANGE?

Is there a meeting that you attend on a regular basis? Perhaps it's a church, networking club, or weekly sales meeting. When you are at this gathering, where do you sit? Is that the seat you always choose? Most people confess that where they sit the first time they attend a group is the place they will sit every time. What's more, if someone else sits in their seat and they are forced to sit somewhere else, it feels odd. Why?

There is a powerful heuristic (mental shortcut) that explains this behavior: the status quo bias, which is the strong tendency to remain in one's current situation.[1] This is no ordinary heuristic; it is a controlling force over human behavior. In his book *Misbehaving: The Making of Behavioral Economics,* Richard Thaler describes it this way: "In physics, an object in a state of rest stays that way, unless something happens. People act the same way: they stick with what they have unless there is some good reason to switch."[2]

This is what makes the status quo bias so alluring: people have a natural aversion to change. The brain is wired to associate a high level of risk with accepting a new idea or purchasing a product or service. Not only that, but research published in *Scientific American* demonstrated that people feel greater regret for a decision they made that resulted in a negative outcome than if that same outcome was caused by their indecision.[3]

This is where the first of the Six Whys® comes into play: Why Change? Answering this question lays the foundation for the entire sale; it equips you to defuse any bias your buyers may have toward keeping things in line with the status quo. Ultimately, if you don't give potential customers a compelling reason to change, they won't. This is why the status quo bias is your most formidable competitor. Think about the sales you have lost in the past. The reality is that you have lost more sales to nothing than to someone. For this reason, this Why should be addressed as early in the sales process as possible.

The best way to answer and gain commitment to Why Change? is to help buyers fully understand the problems that make change a necessity. The buyers' problems are a central part of the sale and are one of their primary buying motivators, a term I've created to define the conditions that cause them to desire your product or service and that must be met for the sale to occur. (Primary buying motivators will be discussed in detail in Chapter 6.)

Showing potential customers they have a problem that must be solved is not always an easy task. They frequently don't recognize their own issues because they're part of the system or process that is causing or at very least sustaining the problems. So they will often see no reason to make a change.

Yet until they realize they have an issue that demands they adjust or modify something in their business, they will view you and your product or service as unnecessary, or worse, irrelevant. However, once they are aware of their problem and desire to solve it, they will view change as an imperative.

The following straightforward, sequential strategies will help you guide buyers into acquiring an accurate understanding of their problems and committing to making a change that will solve them.

1. Find Problems

In the past, salespeople were taught to be problem solvers. In our modern business climate, if you only solve concerns you will struggle to sell. To stand out from your competition you must now be skilled at problem finding and at problem solving.

Finding problems is a hallmark of successful people in any profession, especially sales. Behavioral scientist Jacob Getzels contends that it is the discovery of problems, more than any other special skill, that enables heightened levels of achievement.[4]

When you uncover concerns and bring them to your potential customer's attention, it gets you in front of your competition and allows you to show how you can provide solutions to the issues you found. This creates a significant advantage in today's market, where the average salesperson typically does not enter into the buying process until potential customers have already pinpointed both their problems and numerous potential solution providers.

One way to find problems is to challenge the status quo with insights that compel your buyers to think about how they can improve themselves or their business. This can be as simple as saying something like, "Many of our clients originally came to us because they were dealing with two particular issues . . ." You can then disclose the issues and ask questions that will allow you and potential buyers to discover if they are struggling with these same issues.

> To identify buyers' problems, challenge the status quo with insights that compel your buyers to think about how they can improve themselves or their business.

As you can imagine, once you have brought to light a significant concern, buyers will reciprocate with increased levels of trust and loyalty. You have also earned the right to solve the problem, since you are the one who found it.

Even if you're working with prospective clients who know they have an issue they need help with, do they truly understand it? Often, the issue potential customers think they have is only part of the larger problem. Do you take their word regarding what they think their problem is or are you adding value by asking diagnostic questions to find what is really going on?

Over the years, I have found that the primary reason that salespeople don't find more problems is because they simply aren't looking for them. In the coming chapters you will be given the insights to do this, but for now let's examine the next strategy that will help you answer and earn a commitment to Why Change?

2. Understand Problems

After a problem has been found, you must now assist your buyer in acquiring an accurate awareness of its cause (why is it happening) and scope (who and what is being affected). Look at it from your potential customers' perspective; until they fully know what their problems look like, they will not be able to know what a solution looks like.

You also need to understand why these issues are happening and how they are impacting your buyers and their businesses. Most often, the problems you initially find are just the symptoms, not the cause. You need to identify what is causing the problems, then you can connect the dots between the cause and your solution. Do this, and you will inspire in your buyers the confidence that you can eliminate their difficulties.

The scope of the problem is a second aspect you will need to be aware of. Who and what is the issue affecting? Is it minor, or is there a high cost to allowing this problem to remain unchecked? Asking probing questions that illuminate the scope will help you and your buyers more fully comprehend the issue, which will create urgency.

Yet this is an area that, unfortunately, salespeople struggle with. A recent Forrester Research study found that a shocking 88 percent of the buyers surveyed believed that salespeople do not understand their problems enough to be able to help solve them.[5] If potential customers don't believe you can help them solve a significant concern, why would they be receptive to you? This is one of the reasons why salespeople struggle to get an audience with potential customers. Moreover, this lack of understanding will hinder your ability to present how your product or service will help your buyer. Let me illustrate this.

Feature dumps: I dislike them and so do buyers, but without an ample grasp of the problems your buyers face you will fall into this inept selling practice. Feature dumping is when salespeople blindly list the various features and benefits of their product or service in the hope that one may pique their potential customer's curiosity. This does more harm than good, because even if one feature or benefit does kindle interest, the salesperson has also given the buyer numerous other reasons why his product or service is not a good fit.

Even more concerning, because feature dumps are not focused on what potential customers care about, they are perceived as boring. This is detrimental to the sale, as neuroscientist John Medina confirms that when the brain deems something uninteresting, it will disengage from it.[6] In short, bored people don't buy.

3. Make Problems Hurt

Here's the reality of this situation. Your buyers have problems. So what. Everyone has a lot of problems. I have problems, so do you. Often, these are things we have dealt with for years. So how do we break through this inertia and prompt change? The answer is pain. Only when problems begin to hurt, really hurt, will we do something to solve them.

Your potential customers are the same way. This is why making their problems hurt is the best thing for them and the success of the sale. I'm not saying *literally* hurt. But rather, it's crucial to make buyers feel the negative impact their issues are producing. The more pain potential customers associate with their issues, the more urgency there will be to solve them, which is where you can help. Ask buyers questions that guide them into disclosing the detrimental outcomes their problems are generating. (I'll show you how to do this when I reveal a science-backed way of asking questions in Chapter 5.) Because until they feel pain, they will procrastinate, causing the sale to stall and eventually die.

For example, there are certain moments in life that you never forget. Two of those for me were when my son and daughter were born, roughly two years apart. When my wife was pregnant with our daughter, she went into labor suddenly and began having intense pain. We quickly got in the car and raced to the hospital. Because of the discomfort she was in, I ignored all speed limits and red lights. A mere twenty minutes after arriving at the hospital, I was a father.

In contrast, when it was time for my son to be born, we preemptively went to the hospital before the labor pains began. This time we drove within the speed limit and red lights prompted me to stop the car.

The main difference between those two rides to the hospital was the pain my wife was experiencing. With our daughter, we felt a strong sense of urgency to get to the hospital. With our son, she was not uncomfortable, and so we did not have the urgency that only pain can provide.

As a general rule, how much pain you are experiencing will determine how fast you drive to the hospital. Likewise, how much a buyer's problem hurts will determine how urgently he wants to resolve it.

Cultivating your buyers' understanding of the cause and scope of their problems is what will guide them in committing to making a change and advancing deeper into the sale. Why Change? is only the first of the Six Whys®, but the entire sale is built on it. Accordingly, your ability to answer and gain commitments to Why Change? will determine your level of professional success and impact the quality of your life. It demands your attention.

3 STEPS FOR ANSWERING "WHY CHANGE?"

Step 1: Find problems by conveying challenging insights and asking leading questions.

Step 2: Identify the cause and scope of the problems.

Step 3: Ask deeper questions that help buyers feel the painful outcomes of allowing those problems to continue.

HOW TO USE THE STATUS QUO BIAS IN YOUR FAVOR

As detrimental as the status quo bias is to influence, there is one proven way to use it in your favor: change the default option. Normally, buyers are given a choice to opt in to something, but what if you change this choice and instead let them opt out? There is a large and growing amount of research that indicates that people are far more likely to embrace an idea or behavior if the default is yes, and they are given the option of saying no.

In one study, researchers Brigitte Madrian and Dennis Shea found that participation in retirement plans is much higher under automatic enrollment.[7] Similarly, a groundbreaking study led by behavioral scientists Eric Johnson and Daniel Goldstein examined why in some countries nearly every citizen is an organ donor, while in neighboring countries only a small percentage of the populace are organ donors.[8] The reason was not because of religion, culture, wealth, or views on organ donation. Instead, it was due to the way people were asked to become organ donors. Those countries with low rates of organ donors asked their citizens to opt in by checking a box if they *want* to become an organ donor. In contrast, those countries with extremely high rates of organ donation asked citizens to opt out by checking a box if they *do not want* to be an organ donor.

One of my clients used this concept to grow their average sale. Here's what they did. Instead of allowing buyers to choose the product options they wanted, they set up standard product packages and allowed buyers to customize (remove) the options they did *not* want. This simple change increased revenue and helped the company provide solutions that better met the needs of their customers.

WHY #2: WHY NOW?

Once buyers make the commitment to change, you will need to guide them in understanding and committing to why change must occur *now*. Why can't they wait? What's the hurry? I refer to this as *sales time*, because regardless of the type of sale, the more time it takes to obtain a purchasing decision the lower the probability that it will happen. Situations morph, new priorities surface, funding changes, and a host of other unanticipated issues can negatively impact the sale.

So how do you keep time on your side? You help potential customers realize that embracing change now rather than later is in their best interest. Buyers only put off those decisions they lack the confidence to make, so help them gain the certainty they need to commit right then and there.

I'm not saying you should become an overbearing hustler. No one likes that kind of person, and that approach often backfires. Besides, there are numerous scientifically proven ways to ethically create urgency throughout the sale, many of which I'll teach throughout the book. However, first you must become aware of the primary psychological barrier to creating urgency: *reactance*.

Reactance is our intrinsic desire to push back or resist when we perceive that our ability to freely choose is being restricted by another person. A vast amount of scientific evidence confirms that when people feel they are being forced to adopt behaviors or beliefs, they will rebel, even if what is being imposed on them is in their best interests.[9]

For instance, when you walk past a sign that says, "DON'T TOUCH. WET PAINT," what do you want to do? Of course, you want to touch the wet paint. Why is this? Why does a sign that tells you not to do something actually cause you to desire to do it? The answer is reactance. This is also why signs that state, NO LITTERING or DON'T LITTER actually increase littering in comparison to more empowering and inviting messages like, PLEASE PITCH IN.[10]

To be successful in selling, you must be able to build urgency, but not cause buyers to feel that *you* are pressuring them to buy. In fact, countless sales have been lost when salespeople try to create urgency, but instead trigger reactance. The reason reactance is so lethal in selling situations is that buyers will be blinded by the intense feelings of aversion it creates and, in an attempt to alleviate those feelings, will reject both you and your message.

The good news is that just as scientific studies have been conducted on what stimulates reactance, so too there is research on how to diminish it. Behavioral scientists Nicolas Guéguen and Alexandre Pascual studied how to counteract reactance when making a persuasive appeal.[11] They had collaborators, disguised as panhandlers, ask shoppers for money at a busy mall. They then calculated the percentage of positive responses in comparison to the total number of requests. When the scientists had their accomplices end their request with a phrase that conveyed that the passersby were "free to accept or to refuse," feelings of reactance lessened, which increased the number of donations by nearly 400 percent!

As the panhandler scenario suggests, when making financial decisions, people want to feel that they are in control. They don't want to feel pressured to act one way instead of another. Yet they often need a nudge in the right direction. So how can you do this? You can frame the nudge with statements that minimize reactance, such as "Of course, it's up to you," or "This is a great offer that you can participate in if you choose to do so," at the conclusion of your requests. This will reduce reactance and make them feel that they're still in control of their choices.

Here's how one of my clients used this strategy to speed up their sales cycles and increase closing rates. When I began working with them, it was clear that the sales techniques they had been using to create urgency were thwarting their attempts to advance the sale because they induced high levels of reactance. I implemented strategies to boost urgency and concurrently reduce reactance—for example, at the end of the sale, they would use an incentive to compel prospective customers to move forward now rather than delay. But after introducing this motivator and explaining its benefit to buyers, they would say, "You can just let me know if you want to use it." Now, don't mistake this for letting the buyer off the hook. By this point, the potential customer had already committed to the rest of the Six Whys®, so they were ready to buy. This final inducement worked because it gave them a valid reason to move forward with the sale without making them feel that the salesperson was pressuring them to do so.

> For our brains to make a positive buying decision, we must commit to acting now. If we don't, our brains will naturally procrastinate.

Those who become adept at answering Why Now?, showing buyers why moving forward without delay is essential while simultaneously reducing reactance so buyers feel it is their decision to do so, will see their sales and success skyrocket.

WHY #3: WHY YOUR INDUSTRY SOLUTION?

Imagine you are a salesperson selling classroom training for computer software. You have secured commitment from your buyer regarding her organization's need to be trained in the software. You must now show your potential customer why your industry solution will best meet that need. For instance, rather than use your industry solution of formal classroom training, couldn't your buyer just buy a book and teach her employees the software? Or couldn't she simply appoint someone on her staff to learn the software and then train the rest of the company's employees? Why should the buyer use your industry rather than the other available options?

In my research, I came to realize that this Why was a silent sales assassin. Many salespeople never saw it coming. Nevertheless, if your potential customers can subvert your entire industry and craft a solution on their own, this is a Why you must answer and gain commitment to in your sales process.

To be truly successful in answering this Why, you may need to rethink your definition of a competitor. Many salespeople consider a competitor to be an organization that provides a similar product or service. However, such a shortsighted view leaves these salespeople vulnerable to competitors outside of their industry, which are often the most challenging and difficult to compete with because they fly under the radar.

Let me explain: I once conducted training and consulting for a large company that was a dominant provider in their field. The organization had a competitor they lost more business to than all their other competitors combined. This competitor was not another provider: it was buyers simply bypassing my client's entire industry and designing a solution themselves. To counteract this, I injected into the company's sales process some scientifically proven strategies that persuasively answered and gained commitment to why their industry solution was superior to buyers creating their own solution. The results: by candidly yet professionally neutralizing their chief competitor, the company's sales grew by more than 30 percent in one year.

What about you? How can you compellingly answer this Why? There are two strategies that will help you do this:

1. **Demonstrate how you provide superior results in comparison to those outside of your industry:** What special knowledge and skills do you have that clearly reveal that you offer a better solution than those

beyond your industry? What results do those who purchase your product or service experience and why can't those outside of your industry match them? Clearly answering these questions when you present your company, product, or service will equip buyers with the knowledge they need to see the value in your industry solution.

2. **Convey the problems that may occur if buyers choose a solution outside of your industry:** In the software training scenario, the salesperson could share some of the common problems that others, similar to the buyer, have encountered when they have not had a professional development firm conduct the training. She could then ask the buyer about the negative impact these potential issues could have on their business. Finally, the salesperson should communicate why these concerns won't arise if the prospective customer uses a professional provider.

> ## HOW TO ANSWER "WHY YOUR INDUSTRY SOLUTION?"
>
> Let's stop and apply what we just learned to make sure you are demolishing competitors outside of your industry. What are some of the positive results your company, product, or service delivers that those outside of your industry cannot match? What are some of the problems that potential customers have experienced when they have chosen a solution outside of your industry? Once you have some evidence-based answers to the above questions, contemplate where you can incorporate these insights into your sales process.

Bottom line: a competitor is anything or anyone competing for the buyer's business. Potential customers are constantly thinking through their options, and once they have committed to making a change, be assured that they are weighing the pros and cons of *all* potential solutions.

If you can answer the question of why a buyer should go with your industry solution above all others, you'll help their brains move one step closer to buying from you.

WHY #4: WHY YOU AND YOUR COMPANY?

In 2001, the Nobel Prize in Economic Sciences was awarded to George Akerlof for his piece in the *Quarterly Journal of Economics*.[12] Akerlof famously asserted that there is "an asymmetry in available information" between buyers and sellers.[13] The core of what he meant was that though sellers know the true nature of their products or services, potential customers will not find it out until after purchasing it, which escalates the risk associated with making a purchase.

His research also revealed that the best way to reduce a buyer's perception of risk is through trust. The more a buyer trusts you and the company you represent, the more receptive they will be and the less risk they will associate with acquiring your product or service.[14] That is what trust does: it makes a decision feel safe. The opposite is also true. Without trust, a buying decision will feel hazardous.

It is helpful to think of trust and risk as opposite ends of a seesaw. When trust goes up, the perception of risk is reduced. When the estimation of risk is high, then trust is always lacking.

Trust also inspires open and honest communication. Behavioral scientists Lee Ross and Andrew Ward found that when people trust someone, they are more likely to communicate their concerns and needs.[15] And trust does more than just encourage buyers to disclose information; it also moves them to listen to your ideas.[16]

My research showed that the brain automatically connects the perception of the salesperson and the company. So if buyers trust the salesperson, that trust will be transferred to the company. But if a salesperson fails to stimulate trust, the company will usually suffer a similar fate.

Sometimes this may be unfair, other times it is justified, but regardless, it is something we all do. Think back to the last time you were frustrated with a salesperson or customer service representative. You don't just blame that person; you also blame the company. In fact, nearly every consumer has refused to do business with an organization because of an employee who poorly represented it.

This Why is important and must be attended to in the sale because without a commitment to you and your company, potential customers will not buy from you. Although there are many ways you can generate trust in buyers, here are two science-based strategies:

1. Demonstrate Expertise

A meta-analysis that analyzed fifty years of research found that expertise is a primary component of trust.[17] Cognitive psychologist R. Glen Hass maintains that when the brain recognizes that someone is an expert, it is far more likely to comply with that person's suggestions.[18]

If you are like most salespeople, you have worked hard to become an expert in what you sell. You have the ability to truly help your customers improve their lives and businesses. The question is: How can you most effectively convey this expertise?

One strategy you can use to position yourself as an expert is to share meaningful insights. This can take the form of a new idea, strategy, or research report that delivers value to buyers. When you impart these significant ideas to potential customers, you become more than a salesperson; you are now a valued resource. This will demonstrate your expertise, which will deepen your relationships with buyers and inspire trust.

Another way to communicate expertise is to briefly showcase your experience. People naturally associate experience with expertise. So if you or your company has a documented history of success, share it. Divulge success stories or credibility statements that exhibit your experience. Since stories will be reviewed in detail in Chapter 9, for now I'll share some examples of credibility statements. These are easy to construct and will go something like this: "Our company has been providing solutions just like this for more than forty years," or "I've been in this industry for twelve years and what you've just described is not unusual. In fact . . ." Though these simple statements may seem minor, they can have a big impact on how buyers perceive you and the organization you represent.

CREDIBILITY STATEMENT EXERCISE

Take a moment to think of one credibility statement you can incorporate into your sales approach. Make sure it clearly and convincingly communicates how you or your company is an expert in an area that will provide meaningful value to your potential customers. Once you create it, begin to use it when selling and you'll see how the statement will increase buyer receptiveness.

2. Communicate Confidence

A study conducted by Carnegie Mellon University identified that displaying confidence plays a vital part in establishing trust.[19] It's not enough to believe in yourself, your product or service, or your company. You must exhibit that confidence. The brain has a hard time placing confidence in someone who does not display it.

What's more, acting confident can even have a positive impact on your performance. The research suggests that confidence has a calming effect on the brain and, as a result, improves your capacity to think on your feet. It's very difficult for the brain to perform at optimal levels when you are overly anxious and tense.

You may be saying to yourself that acting confident is easier said than done. Confidence is not something you can control—or is it? An interesting fact we learn from the science of confidence is that even if you don't feel it, merely displaying confidence has a positive impact on your behavior. And the research shows us exactly how to do this.

A growing number of scientific studies have confirmed that self-affirmations increase confidence.[20] Now, before you roll your eyes at the idea of self-affirmations, let's be clear about what the research means by them. It is not claiming that hollow declarations you know are untrue will help you feel more confident. Saying inaccurate phrases like "I am full of energy" when you are tired is not a self-affirmation. Rather, self-affirmations are reminders of one's own competence—reminders of what you already believe.

Here is how you can create these self-affirmations. First, focus your mind on a past success. Then verbally proclaim how that past success is evidence that you will perform well in a similar, upcoming endeavor. This will prime your mind to behave in ways that are consistent with the affirmation.

Perhaps you are already doing a version of this. I can recall how, after one of my seminars, a participant who was a business owner told me that he realized that he had used a self-affirmation when he was nervous about promoting his business on one of the local television morning shows. He shared how on his second visit to the show he was tense, but then he recalled that he had performed well on the previous program and that it was evidence that he would do well again. This self-affirmation calmed his nerves and helped him project confidence.

A second scientifically proven strategy that will enable you to communicate with confidence is power movements. Science has verified that these body movements or poses can alter body chemistry and even boost performance.

For instance, behavioral scientists Dana Carney, Amy Cuddy, and Andy Yap's research confirmed that holding "high power" poses, such as placing one's hands on one's hips, will trigger an increase in testosterone.[21] This naturally amplifies feelings of confidence.

Constructing power movements is simple. Some, such as placing your hands on your hips, have already been identified through scientific inquiry. Others are best described as nonverbal behaviors that signify power. An executive who puts his arm over the empty chair next to him is claiming space, which both denotes power and makes him feel more confident.

Another way to create power movements is to observe how you naturally move when you are feeling extremely confident. You will notice that there are certain gestures or poses that you instinctively adopt. Power movements are simply the intentional use of those movements and poses. They vary from individual to individual. Two that I do on a regular basis are bouncing on the balls of my feet and slapping the back of my right hand on the palm of my left. These simple movements increase my energy, focus, and confidence. Those are mine; you may have similar ones, or yours could be very different. I encourage you to discover how you move when feeling assertive and then force yourself to move in the same way when you need to project confidence. You will quickly find that you will appear sure of yourself and then you will begin to feel what your body is representing.

WHY #5: WHY YOUR PRODUCT OR SERVICE?

How can you position your products or services so they are chosen by potential customers? This is a critical question, because in almost every industry there are more sellers than ever before. Not only that, but as we've seen, buyers have become accustomed to evaluating numerous potential products or services before deciding which to purchase. To earn your buyer's business, you must have clear, compelling reasons why they should choose your product or service over what your competitors offer.

The answer to Why Your Product or Service? is found in knowing the competitive advantage your product or service offers. That's how you will demonstrate to and gain commitment from your potential customers that your product or service is the best one for them.

The leading researcher on the topic of competitive advantage is Michael Porter, a professor at Harvard Business School. Porter's study of how companies compete has led him to the conclusion that there are two primary types of competitive advantages:[22]

1. Cost Leadership

Cost leadership is when an organization delivers a similar product or service as its competitors, but can do so at a lower cost to the buyer. A good example of this is Walmart. The majority of the products sold by Walmart can be found at other stores. Nevertheless, the reason so many people shop there is because they believe that it has the lowest prices. Walmart even touts their competitive advantage in their slogan "Save Money. Live Better."

Walmart has leveraged cost leadership with great success. But it is the exception. The vast majority of organizations that proclaim they are the low-cost provider find that this advantage is short-lived. There can only be one cost leader in a marketplace. Those salespeople who claim this as their competitive advantage will soon find that as competitors match or beat their price, their market position deteriorates. If you are like most of the salespeople I have trained, you don't sell the lowest priced solution, so this competitive advantage is usually used against you by competitors. Don't worry, because there is another competitive advantage that is even more influential than cost.

2. Differentiation

Most salespeople must use the competitive advantage of differentiation, which is how their product, service, or company is better than competitors'.

The challenge that many salespeople have when attempting to communicate how they are different is that to potential customers, they sound similar to their competition. Salespeople are often surprised to learn that their competitors are stating the same value propositions. For example, when I was recently making a large purchase for my firm, all the potential solution providers I spoke with gave the identical reason why they were a better choice than their competitors. Though this may seem humorous, it is frustrating for buyers and treacherous to the sale. When potential customers are evaluating numerous product or service options from providers who all appear to be roughly the same, how will those buyers make a decision? In those cases, price is the only competitive advantage left to consider.

So what can you do to differentiate in a way that will help your potential customers see that your product or service is right for them? My research identified that the most productive way to communicate differentiation is through what I call *distinct value*.

What is distinct value? It's the unique value that a buyer desires and will receive from your company, product, or service. It is what will determine whether they view your competitive advantage as unimpressive or captivating.

To determine distinct value the following two rules must be true:

RULE #1: DISTINCT VALUE MUST MATTER TO BUYERS

For a competitive strategy to be effective it must link the value that a company, product, or service provides with what's important to the buyer. A common mistake salespeople often make when forming their competitive advantage is basing it on what they think is important about their company, product, or service. However, what you think potential customers should care about, they will often consider irrelevant. Distinct value is only persuasive if it is centered on what matters to that buyer. What is important to one potential customer may not be for another. Because each buyer is different, distinct value is malleable and should change depending on the buyer's needs and desires.

RULE #2: DISTINCT VALUE MUST BE UNIQUE

Distinct value is something that a competitor cannot replicate. This is so compelling because it's built on the heuristic (mental shortcut) of scarcity. There is a wealth of research confirming that the brain assigns more value to something when it is less attainable.

For instance, a series of studies conducted by behavioral scientist Michael Lynn identified that, as a general rule, the harder something is to obtain, the greater its perceived value and the more people are willing to pay for it.[23] Additional research conducted by social psychologists Stephen Worchel, Jerry Lee, and Akanbi Adewole demonstrated that when something is in scarce supply, the desire for it significantly increases.[24] It does not matter if it is a painting, antique, limited-time offer, or even a toy, when something is valued and rare, demand always spikes. Because of this, scarcity is a driving force in economic decisions.

Likewise, when you convey that your product, service, or company offers buyers something your competitors cannot, it will increase desire and boost the perception of value.

APPLYING DISTINCT VALUE

These two rules will guide you in determining what the distinct value is for every potential customer, transforming your competitive advantage from an unconvincing list of general strengths to meaningful, buyer-centric reasons that your product or service is superior to that of your competitors. The more distinct value you can identify and communicate, the stronger your competitive advantage will be and the more likely buyers will be convinced that your product or service is right for them.

To leverage distinct value when presenting your product or service, you must already have acquired a detailed understanding of your potential clients and their situations. (I'll share with you how to do this in Chapter 6.) Then, when you identify something about your product or service that matters to your buyer, something that your competitors cannot match, disclose it.

As you articulate the distinct value of what you're selling, you'll want to help potential customers think through how they will benefit from it. So what does this all look like in a real sales call? Here's an example of what communicating distinct value should look like: "What is unique about our machines is their durability. Because the components we use are of the highest quality, each machine only requires preventative maintenance once per year, instead of the industry standard of every six months. How would reducing the need for maintenance by fifty percent improve your production efficiency?" (Notice how after the distinct value is disclosed, a question is asked that prompts the buyer to mentally digest the assertion of value.)

Once you have an accurate and in-depth understanding of your buyer, finding distinct value is clear-cut. But just in case you still have some questions, here's a reminder of how to apply it.

3 STEPS FOR APPLYING DISTINCT VALUE

Step 1: Understand what matters to your buyers.

Step 2: Identify something about your company, product, or service that competitors cannot match.

Step 3: Convey steps 1 and 2 to buyers and ask for their buy-in to the value you have presented.

WHY #6: WHY SPEND THE MONEY?

Imagine that you are a salesperson for a company that sells customer relationship management (CRM) software. You are on a sales call with an executive team, walking them through the business case for upgrading to your CRM platform. During your sales process, you have already guided them into committing to each of the previously mentioned Whys, and you're arriving at the sixth and final one: Why spend the money on your product or service?

As you discuss the price of implementing your software, they inform you that they aren't sure whether they are going to invest in your platform, or in a piece of machinery they also need to increase their production capabilities. They do not have enough funds to make both purchases, but they're quick to tell you that this is the only thing holding them back from agreeing to purchase from you. How would you respond?

It is obvious that the root of the objection you are facing is Why Spend the Money? It's important to realize that, regardless of the type of sale, any time you ask buyers to purchase your product or service you are also asking them *not* to do something else. Whether making a purchase for themselves or on behalf of their employer, buyers have access to a limited amount of funds.

The most effective way to guide potential customers in formulating an answer to why they should purchase your product or service is found in another of their primary buying motivators, known as *dominant buying motives*. Dominant buying motives are the emotional reasons buyers will purchase. They're how potential customers prioritize the decision to obtain your product or service. Dominant buying motives are highly influential on purchasing decisions because they are comprised of two scientifically validated triggers of human behavior.

1. Desire for Gain

The desire for gain is the positive outcome buyers will receive after they purchase a product or service. This can include benefits for the organization they represent, such as generating more revenue, improving productivity, or reducing waste. However, there can also be personal gains, such as job security, an increase in compensation, or peace of mind.

When assessing a potential client's desire for gain, take care not to make assumptions, as it's easy to jump to incorrect conclusions. Instead, focus on identifying the emotionally driven reasons why a buyer wants the results your product or service will produce. (In Chapter 5, I'll show you how to ask questions that will help you discover these reasons.)

The more you can understand what buyers want to gain from the purchase, the more you will be able to compellingly show them why purchasing your product or service is more advantageous than making another type of purchase. (We'll explore a sales tactic that will help you convey this in Chapter 7.)

2.   Fear of Loss

In 2002, the Nobel Prize in Economic Sciences was bestowed on cognitive psychologist Daniel Kahneman "for having integrated insights from psychological research into economic science, especially concerning human judgment and decision-making under uncertainty."[25]

His research challenged conventional wisdom and proved that people regularly make decisions that are irrational. The value inherent in Kahneman's research was the evidence that human decisions are not ruled by logic, but by "psychological principles that govern the perception of decision problems and the evaluation of options."[26]

He identified one of the "psychological principles" that heavily impacted decisions as loss aversion.[27]

For example, in one experiment, Kahneman and a colleague presented the following scenario to participants: Imagine the United States was going to experience an outbreak of a deadly disease that would kill 600 people and there were only two options for combating it:[28]

Option 1: This option guarantees that 200 of the 600 people will live.

Option 2: This option provides a ⅓ probability that all 600 people will live, but it also comes with a ⅔ probability that no one will live.

Kahneman found that the majority of the participants choose Option 1.

However, he then presented the same situation to other participants, but reworded the options. A minor shift in wording considerably changed the choices that were made.

The new participants, after learning about the same deadly disease that would kill 600 people, were given the following two options:

Option 1: This option guarantees that 400 people would die.

Option 2: This option provides a ⅓ probability that no one would die and a ⅔ probability that 600 people would die.

This time most of the participants choose Option 2.

In both scenarios the options are identical. Though the mathematical probabilities did not change, what was modified was how the options were framed. The options that emphasized loss were rejected.

Science has proven that fear of loss is such a powerful motivator that it is just too important to ignore. A recent meta-analysis led by seven behavioral scientists scrutinized the findings of 127 different research studies and found that fear-based appeals are a highly effective and predictable way to significantly influence behaviors.[29]

Neuroscientists have even studied how fear of loss affects the human brain. The results of one study that was published in *Cognitive Brain Research* identified that loss aversion is such a potent motivator that "typically, losses have at least twice the impact of equivalent gains so that people would require a 50 percent chance of gaining at least $200 to make up for a 50 percent of losing $100."[30]

For example, one telecom company lowered its cancellation rates by focusing customers' attention on what they would lose if they canceled their plans.[31] Formerly, when customers would call to cancel, company representatives would offer them a credit of a hundred calls if they remained with the company (desire for gain). Cancellations dropped when the representatives began informing customers that they had already issued them a credit for a hundred calls, but if they cancelled they would lose the calls (fear of loss). Customers assigned more value to the calls when they could be lost compared to when they would be gained.

Generating fear of loss alone is not enough to change behavior. Professor of psychology Howard Leventhal has analyzed why some messages that emphasize fear of loss fail to persuade.[32] He found that fear-based communication ceased to be compelling when the one being exposed to it was not shown how to alleviate it. Without a clear way to relieve the emotional stress that is created by fear of loss, people become frustrated and may ignore the message that caused the fear.

As a result, when you evoke the fear of loss, you must always reveal how buyers can escape that fear through the benefits they will receive from your company, product, or service.

How to Use Dominant Buying Motives to Earn More Sales

Once you know what your buyers' dominant buying motives are, you can use them to sway the buying decision in your favor. Here's what to do: when potential customers are struggling between buying from you and purchasing an unrelated product, help them think through what they will gain by moving forward with your product or service and what they will lose if they do not. This will bring the mental clarity needed for them to prioritize and justify the buying decision.

You can accomplish this by asking questions such as, "If you were to move forward and invest in this technology now, what do you think the primary advantages [desire for gain] would be?" or "If you were to wait to invest in this equipment, how could that negatively affect [fear of loss] your production capabilities?" After you guide buyers in disclosing this information, you can then build on it by stating, "That being the case, wouldn't you agree that it would make more sense to invest in this equipment now for the reasons you mentioned?" Remember: never tell buyers their dominant buying motive. Instead, guide *them* into stating their reasons (desire for gain or fear of loss) for purchasing and then use their reasons to help nudge them into a positive buying decision.

Focusing your buyers on their dominant buying motives also serves them well. As you know, making a buying decision involves a lot of complex mental calculations, which can overwhelm the brain. You are helping your prospective customers cut through this mental clutter by focusing their attention on the core reasons why they want to purchase (desire for gain and fear of loss), and thus assisting them in deciding to buy something that will truly benefit them.

THE NEW REALITY OF THE SIX WHYS®

Now, the way buyers formulate buying decisions has been decoded. The more adept you become at answering and obtaining commitments to the Six Whys®, the more success you will experience in sales. In later chapters, I'll show you more science-based sales strategies and tactics that will help you answer and gain commitments to each of these, but first we need to look at the second half of the sales equation: the emotional state and how it affects the decision-making process.

CHAPTER 4

Selling to Your Buyers' Emotions

There's an old sales adage that goes, "People buy on emotions and justify with logic." I recall hearing this saying often when I was first starting out in sales, and many times throughout my career since then. Yet is it actually true? Do emotions really impact a person's decision to buy something? And since the job of a salesperson is to guide prospective customers into making a purchase, how should emotions be addressed throughout that process, if they are indeed an important part of it?

Until recently, there was no way to know the answers to these questions. Sure, people had opinions, but no one had any demonstrable proof, because getting proof would require looking inside the brain and isolating emotions so that you could test how decisions would be affected if they were devoid of emotion. Which was impossible . . . until now.

Recent scientific findings have changed all that, and we now know more about emotions than ever before, and, most important, it is not based on speculation, but is grounded in hard evidence. These research findings disclose the role of emotions in the buying decision and reveal what you can do to help your buyers emotionally connect with you and your message. To fully understand how emotions affect the buying process, I will first introduce you to a group of people who have lost their capacity to use them.

THE ROLE OF EMOTIONS IN DECISION MAKING

The influence emotions have on decisions can best be explained through the work of neuroscientist Antonio Damasio. His groundbreaking studies have focused on individuals who have experienced trauma to certain parts of their brains, which has left them unable to fully process their emotions. These individuals contemplate every situation in an unemotional, exceedingly rational manner. Would this inability to exercise emotions impact their decisions? Tragically, the answer is yes.

Damasio tells of a particularly revealing encounter that occurred when one patient, who had limited access to emotions, agonized over when to schedule a follow-up appointment. Here's how he describes his experience with this patient:

> I suggested two alternative dates, both in the coming month and just a few days apart from each other. The patient pulled out his appointment book and began consulting the calendar. The behavior that ensued, which was witnessed by several investigators, was remarkable. For the better part of a half-hour, the patient enumerated reasons for and against each of the two dates: previous engagements, proximity to other engagement, possible meteorological conditions, virtually anything that one could reasonably think about concerning a simple date . . . He was now walking us through a tiresome cost-benefit analysis, an endless outlining and fruitless comparison of options and possible consequences. It took enormous discipline to listen to all of this without pounding on the table and telling him to stop, but we finally did tell him, quietly, that he should come on the second of the alternative dates. His response was equally calm and prompt. He simply said, "That's fine." Back the appointment book went into his pocket, and then he was off. This behavior is a good example of the limits of pure reason.[1]

Sadly, this patient and the others Damasio evaluated were almost pathologically indecisive and struggled to make even basic choices. To understand the reason why emotions matter so much in decision making, I'll need to share with you one of his most significant experiments.

Damasio had individuals with normal brain function and individuals who, due to brain injury, had lost their capability to access their emotions, look at a series of pictures while hooked up to a polygraph machine.[2] Though most of the pictures were bland nature scenes or abstract patterns, a few were graphic, highly disturbing images. When participants with normal brain function viewed the unsettling images, the measurements on the polygraph jumped, as expected. However, when those with brain injuries viewed the disturbing images, there was almost no movement on the polygraph. These individuals could not feel their emotional judgments of the images and that lack of emotion rendered them unable to respond.

This experiment allows us to peer into the brain and gain an understanding of how emotions influence decisions. The brain uses emotions to assign value and mark something as good or bad. It's how the brain distinguishes between what matters and what is irrelevant. Since they are how the brain evaluates options and determines preferences, these emotional assessments are the basis of the decision-making process. Neuroscientist Joseph LeDoux humorously illustrates this by stating that the rational part of your brain is what allows you to recognize the face of your cousin, but it is your emotions that remind you that you don't like her.[3]

> The brain uses emotions to assign value and mark something as good or bad. It's how the brain distinguishes between what matters and what is irrelevant.

In much the same way, buyers use their emotions to determine the persuasiveness of your ideas and the significance of your product or service. This emotional connection with your product or service will cause prospective customers to desire it. Social psychologists Chip Heath and Dan Heath affirm, "That's what emotion does for an idea—it makes people care. It makes people feel something."[4]

EMOTIONS SHAPE PERCEPTION

Though emotions are how your brain determines value and preferences, this is only part of a much bigger picture. The brain also uses emotions as the grid through which it perceives everything it encounters. In fact, a compelling amount of research shows that the collection of emotions a person is experiencing at a given time, known as the *emotional state,* pervades one's thoughts and heavily impacts how the brain processes choices. Nowhere is this more relevant than when you are trying to influence another person.

There are a slew of scientific studies showing that experiencing positive emotions boosts comprehension, enhances the mental capacity to make decisions, and increases receptiveness to persuasive requests.[5] Professor of psychology at Cornell University Alice Isen explains that when people are in a positive emotional state it's as if they see the world through rose-colored glasses.[6] This means that when your buyers are feeling these uplifting emotions, their viewpoints will be more optimistic because their brains are considering your message through the lens of those emotions. Research has also found that these positive feelings heighten the impact of the peripheral route of influence (discussed in Chapter 2) and allow heuristics (mental shortcuts) to take on added importance.[7] What's more, these upbeat emotions predispose buyers to be more likely to take your call, agree to a meeting, affirm your value propositions, or even purchase your product or service.

For example, when one large retailer focused on creating customer interactions that improved the emotional state of its shoppers, same-store sales growth tripled.[8] Similarly, after a major financial institution created a strategy that inspired positive emotional connections among a certain customer segment, new account sales within that user group increased by 40 percent.

Positive emotional states can even raise your average sale price. That is what an experiment led by social psychologists Karen O'Quin and Joel Aronoff found when they had sellers joke, "I will throw in my pet frog," when disclosing the price of a piece of art.[9] The amusing quip disrupted the tension and injected buyers with positive emotions, which caused them to agree to a higher price for the art than those who had not heard the remark.

What about negative emotions? How do they influence decision making? Behavioral scientists Michael Ross and Garth Fletcher found—bearing out Isen's research—that when people are in a negative emotional state it will cause their perceptions to be more cynical.[10] Moreover, if the brain is being overridden by negative emotions, it will struggle to perceive value, which will often prompt the rejection of ideas or decisions that are in the person's best interests. This is no small matter, because many sales stall or even die for no other reason than that buyers were in a negative emotional state during the sales call and this clouded their judgments and inhibited them from seeing the value a salesperson was presenting.

To fully grasp the clout that emotional states have on the decision process, let's look at a place where they should have no impact: judicial rulings. Three behavioral scientists published research in the *Proceedings of the National Academy of Sciences* that arrived at the conclusion that judges "can be swayed by extraneous variables that should have no bearing on legal decisions."[11] The scientists found that when judges were in a positive emotional state, they granted parole 65 percent of the time. Nothing too suspiring here, but what happens when the judges were in a negative emotional state, when they were tired, hungry, or just ready to go home at the end of a long day? In those instances, the probability of the judges granting parole was nearly zero. That's right, the emotional state did not merely effect how the judges ruled, it practically determined it! Well-known social psychologist David Myers summarized the power emotional states have on decision making when he acknowledged, "Our moods infuse our judgments. We are not cool computing machines; we are emotional creatures."[12]

If judicial rulings are not safe from the sway of emotions, neither are buying decisions. Though some prospective customers may believe they are able to rise above their emotions and make decisions based solely on logic, the evidence overwhelmingly confirms that emotions play an integral part in how the brain processes decisions, including business decisions. Leadership expert Jay Conger wrote about this in a *Harvard Business Review* article, in which he suggests, "In the business world, we like to think that our colleagues use reason to make decisions, yet if we scratch below the surface we will always find emotions at play."[13]

Dan Ariely and fellow behavioral economist Eduardo B. Andrade affirm that because emotional states operate below consciousness, people rarely attribute their positive outlook to their emotional state.[14] Instead, they actually believe the world has changed.[15] To use Isen's metaphor, they are looking at the world through rose-colored glasses, but they don't realize they are wearing them. Everything just seems, well, rosy.

For instance, do you think that eating peanuts and drinking Pepsi would make you more likely to agree with a sales message? Most people would balk at the idea that they could be so easily bought, but that is exactly what research conducted by behavioral scientist Irving Janis found. When participants listened to a persuasive appeal, some were given peanuts and Pepsi to snack on. Those who received the food and drink were notably more convinced by the message.[16] Why? Because the good feelings associated with eating and drinking naturally enriched their emotional states, which primed them to be more receptive to the message.

So what does your potential customers' lack of awareness of their emotional state mean for you? When they are stuck in a negative emotional state it will skew their view of every idea you present. In my research analyzing sales calls, I saw how this significantly undermined the effectiveness of salespeople; buyers who were normally receptive became indifferent, which impeded the advancement of the sale. This lack of interest had nothing to do with the salesperson or even the buyer's need for the product or service; it was caused by the buyer's emotional states. Until the salesperson addresses the emotional state, the sales call would be unproductive and could even halt the progress of the entire sale. Even more concerning, it was rare for prospective customers, who were experiencing strong negative emotions, to make a positive buying decision. It was as if these emotions inhibited their brains from arriving at a favorable decision, similar to what the study on judicial rulings found.

However, let me reiterate that while this was happening, potential customers did not realize it. Never once did buyers blame their distorted view on their negative emotional states. Instead, they blamed the salesperson, product, service, or company. From their perspective, because they could not discern high levels of value, they believed there were none.

By now it should be clear that emotional states dictate how buyers will respond to you and whether or not they will choose one direction or another. The role of emotions is so ingrained in buying decisions that it cannot be ignored. This is why I included them in the sales equation, which was discussed in Chapter 3. (As a quick reminder, the sales equation affirms that a buying decision is a result of commitments to each of the Six Whys® and the buyer being in a positive emotional state.)

I want to share one more crucial piece of information about emotional states—and it's good news. In fact, perhaps the most important scientific finding about them is that they can be altered. Your potential customers do not have to be held captive by their current emotional state; you can change it. Once you learn how to do that, you will enhance your ability to guide purchasers through their buying journey, which will also improve your influence and sales results.

However, before I share some strategies on how you can shift potential clients' emotional states, we must first review how to identify them.

IDENTIFYING BUYERS' EMOTIONAL STATES

Dr. John Gottman is a renowned marriage counselor who has forty years of experience studying what makes healthy marriages.[17] He has identified numerous marriage discord detectors that, according to research published in the *Journal of Family Psychology*, allow him to predict with 93.6 percent accuracy whether a couple will get a divorce.[18] Though this may seem startling, unbelievable, or even downright frightening to some, the way he pulls off this seemingly miraculous feat is surprisingly simple: he knows what early emotional signals to look for.

In much the same way, once you know what to look for, you will be able to quickly and accurately identify the emotional state of your buyer. Continually monitoring the emotional state of someone you are attempting to influence is vital, because before you can shift an emotional state, you must recognize it.

The key to discerning your prospective customers' emotional states is to focus on their nonverbal behaviors. But before we go any further, let's briefly define nonverbal communication. It's communication without words, and that includes gestures, tone of voice, rate of speech, body posture, body movement, facial expression, spatial distance, touch, and eye contact.

Concentrating on potential clients' nonverbal cues will help you discover their emotional state. The most common mistake I've witnessed salespeople make when attempting to gain an awareness of their buyers' emotional states is focusing *only* on their buyers' words and ignoring their nonverbal signals. This was evident during the first day of a multiday sales training workshop I conducted a number of years ago. In the afternoon, the salespeople were shown my science-based questioning model, which you will learn in Chapter 5. They then dispersed into groups to practice executing it. In one of the practice groups, a salesperson asked another, who was playing the part of the customer, a series of potent questions about his past experience with suppliers. When answering one particular question, the "customer" displayed noticeable emotions in both his voice inflection and gestures. The salesperson who posed the question did not notice the significance of what had just occurred and immediately jumped to another line of questioning. I stopped the practice session to help the group understand the magnitude of what had been missed. Why did the question shift the customer's emotional state? When I had the salesperson ask some revealing follow-up questions to uncover the reason for the flash of emotions, some very meaningful insights were shared that, had this been a real sales call, would have impacted the trajectory of the sale.

This is not an isolated incident. I have been on sales calls where buyers unveil nonverbal signs that stand out like neon lights, alerting everyone around them of their emotional state. If you are looking for them, you will see them. But if you are not watching for them, you will often miss the clues.

There are two reasons why nonverbal signals are such telling indicators of one's emotional state. Here's a look at both:

1. The Majority of Communication Is Nonverbal

One of the most famous and frequently cited studies on nonverbal communication was conducted by UCLA professor Albert Mehrabian.[19] He and a colleague studied the impact of facial expressions, tone of voice, and spoken words in communication. His experiments found that the words used accounted for only 7 percent of the message communicated, tone of voice was responsible for 38 percent of the message, and facial expressions composed 55 percent.

The importance of Mehrabian's study is not in providing the exact formula that is used when communicating. Instead, the value of his research is that it reveals that nonverbal cues play a significant role in the communication process. Mehrabian deduced from this and additional experiments that the bulk of what is communicated to another person is communicated nonverbally. He is not alone in his conclusion. Study after study has verified that the majority of communication is nonverbal.[20]

2. Nonverbal Communication Is Unfiltered

Mindless—that's what renowned behavioral scientist Ellen Langer calls the nonverbal signals people send.[21] She and many other researchers have found that unlike verbal communication, which is closely monitored, nonverbal communication is rarely filtered. From childhood all of us have been taught to pay attention to what we say, but our nonverbal communication does not undergo the same scrutiny.

When your buyers are conversing with you, they may be carefully guarding their words, but rarely are they restraining their nonverbal signals. As a result, their emotions will seep through their behaviors and alert you to their true feelings.

Learning how to observe nonverbal behaviors is not an arduous task; you already have the ability. All you must do is nurture it.

Even children know how to discern the emotional states of their parents. For example, if they need to share a failing grade with a parent, they will attempt to wait till the perfect moment, when mom or dad is in an upbeat emotional state. Why? Because they know that their parent is far more likely to be understanding if he or she is looking at the situation through the lens of positive emotions.

The key to identifying your buyers' emotional states is to train your mind to be attuned to the emotions they are presenting. Once you begin evaluating this, you'll be amazed at what you will notice.

For instance, could you predict how a teacher will be evaluated by students after observing only two seconds of his or her nonverbal behavior? If you said no, you're probably wrong. Behavioral scientists Nalini Ambady and Robert Rosenthal showed participants video clips ranging in length from 2 to 30 seconds of teachers' nonverbal behaviors.[22] By merely observing the teachers, most viewers were able to predict with surprising accuracy how they would be evaluated over the course of a semester by students and supervisors. This and other studies have found that the brain can make quick, alarmingly correct judgments about others, a phenomenon known as *thin slicing*.

Likewise, once you begin intentionally assessing the nonverbal behaviors of others, you will see their emotional states leaking out.

Below is an exercise that will train your mind to be aware of and better interpret the emotional states of others. Under each emotional state, jot down the nonverbal behaviors you have seen others display that reveal those emotions. Then on your next sales call begin looking for these nonverbal displays. You will find that this will help you discern the emotional states of your buyers.

EMOTIONAL STATE EXERCISE

POSITIVE EMOTIONAL STATE   **NEGATIVE EMOTIONAL STATE**

_____   _____
_____   _____
_____   _____
_____   _____
_____   _____
_____   _____

Note: I encourage you to not skip this exercise. Studies show that thinking a strategy through and then writing it down will cement it in your mind and increase your capacity to use it when influencing others.

HOW TO CHANGE YOUR BUYERS' EMOTIONAL STATES

If you're a salesperson, you know the feeling: that strange mix of excitement, fear, and anticipation that comes when you sense buyers are going to make a positive buying decision. This was what a salesperson (we'll call him Jim) felt as he met with a group of buyers who, he believed, were finally ready to purchase. The meeting went according to plan, and by the end of it, he was confident that all that stood between him and his large commission check was some paperwork. But to his amazement, the buyers refused to move forward, and when asked what their concerns were they confessed there were none, except that it "didn't feel right." Jim was unsure how to respond. He desperately searched for an objection to overcome, but there were none. I was introduced to Jim a while after this event, but time had not lessened the blow of the lost sale; it still bothered him. As he relayed the details to me, I quickly realized what had occurred. The prospective customers were in negative emotional states, which created the cynical viewpoints that made the decision feel wrong.

What would you do if you were in Jim's situation? The good news is that one's emotional state can be changed, but this is not always an easy task. Human beings are complex and their emotions are influenced by many factors. That being said, there are numerous scientifically proven strategies you can employ to shift someone's emotional state. But before we go into those, I want to call your attention to an important point my research identified: executing only one strategy is rarely enough. You will often need to utilize several of these strategies back-to-back to break someone from the shackles of negative emotions.

Here are four strategies that you can use to directly engage and change buyers' emotional states for the better:

STRATEGY #1: UTILIZE EMOTIONAL COGNITION

Have you ever been standing in line at the grocery store, grudgingly waiting for your turn to check out when the clerk greets you enthusiastically and begins talking in an upbeat manner? Without any conscious effort, you start to perk up and feel a little happier. After you banter back and forth for a few minutes, you walk away smiling, feeling significantly better than you did before the encounter. What happened? You just experienced what behavioral scientist Elaine Hatfield refers to as *emotional cognition*, the notion that "people tend to 'catch' others' emotions."[23] She has strong scientific evidence proving that when people encounter someone showing a strong emotion, like happiness or sadness, it evokes that same emotion in them.

Psychologist Daniel Goleman describes this in his book *Social Intelligence* as "the emotional equivalent of a cold."[24] He explains "when someone dumps their toxic feelings on us—explodes in anger or threats, shows disgust or contempt—they activate in us circuitry for those very same distressing emotions. Their act has potent neurological consequences: emotions are contagious."[25]

For instance, when behavioral scientist Peter Totterdell and colleagues conducted research experiments across a variety of professions, they found that those who work together infect each other with emotions to such an extent that they actually begin to share the same emotional state.[26] This is true regardless of whether that emotional state is positive or negative.

There is also a substantial amount of research showing that people are rarely aware that they adopt the emotions of others.[27] For example, if you have a coworker who is very negative, you may find that when you are around her you begin to unconsciously adopt a more pessimistic outlook. Likewise, if you are speaking with someone who is passionate and optimistic, you begin to feel inspired.

So how can you spread positive emotions to your customers and not allow others to infect you with their negative emotions? The answer to this important question was revealed in a fascinating experiment, published in the *Journal of Nonverbal Behavior*.[28] When three strangers sat silently in a circle for two minutes, the one who was the most emotionally expressive transferred his or her emotional state to the others. So when attempting to shift your buyers' emotional states, remember to project your positive emotions more intensely than they are conveying their negative ones. This will naturally cause their emotions to mirror yours.

There are many behaviors you can utilize when attempting to activate emotional cognition in your favor. Here are two straightforward, easy to execute, scientifically validated behaviors that will assist you in shifting the emotional states of others:

1. Use Productive Voice Inflections

Your voice inflections are one of the primary ways that the emotional frequency of your words is transferred. An amazing research study published in *Biological Psychology* verified that the brain gives more precedence to nonverbal speech sounds that express emotion than to words that express the same emotion.[29] As a result, when you utilize voice inflections you are both influencing listeners on an emotional level and aiding them in mentally processing what you are sharing.[30]

A scientific study that illustrates this was led by social psychologists Roland Neumann and Fritz Strack.[31] One of their experiments consisted of participants listening to a speech. Some of the participants heard the speaker present with an upbeat voice inflection, while others listened to the same speaker deliver the speech in a monotone voice. The researchers then asked both groups of participants to rate their own mood. Those who listened to the speaker who communicated in a positive manner felt much more optimistic than those who heard the speaker who talked with no inflection.

More importantly, voice inflections have even been shown to arouse emotions that impact future behavior. Nalini Ambady and colleagues led a study that analyzed how a surgeon's tone of voice influenced whether or not the surgeon would be sued by patients.[32] The research showed that surgeons who spoke in a warm, caring tone of voice were much less likely to be sued than those who used a harsh tone of voice.

As a sales trainer, I have witnessed countless sales presentations. One of the main initial indicators of a salesperson's presentation skills is their use of voice inflections. Those who use strong inflections are always able to hold buyers' attention better than those who use weak inflections, even when saying the exact same words. Voice inflections convey your passion and make you seem more interesting and engaging. Moreover, they also produce in others the emotions you are conveying.

A straightforward way to alter your buyers' emotional states is by using strong voice inflections. This will also boost your ability to capture and retain buyers' attention.

Finally, a word of caution: make sure you exercise wisdom when attempting to convey emotion through voice inflections. Though they are an effective way to transfer emotion, don't misuse them. I have seen salespeople who, in an effort to express positive emotions, behave in ways that appear exaggerated and abnormal. Remember, the productive transference of positive emotions will never distract from your credibility, it will enhance it. When attempting to apply new nonverbal behaviors, do so within the context of your personality. It should still sound like you, just an improved version.

2. Verbally Convey Strong Beliefs

Over the last few decades, social scientists have studied one subject more than almost any other—education. One of the foundational principles that has emerged from this research is that people, regardless of age, learn to the extent that they are motivated. An unmotivated person will rarely absorb or apply what he is being taught. So the question is: How can the motivation to learn be fostered?

What is surprising about the evidence on this topic is that it shows that learning is as dependent on the teacher as it is the student. Numerous scientific studies have found that when a teacher is knowledgeable, passionate, and conveys positive emotions about what he or she is teaching, those emotions infect the students and improve their capacity to understand and retain information.[33] As respected educational psychologist Raymond Wlodkowski states, "In educational research, enthusiasm has long been linked to increased learner motivation and achievement."[34]

Likewise, when you express positive feelings about some aspect of the sale, your buyers' feelings toward what you have shared intensifies. One of the simplest yet most persuasive ways to do this is to verbally disclose a strong belief you have about your company, product, or service. This should be expressed through emotional statements that are also meaningful to your buyers. For example, I believe that *selling is too important to be based on anything other than proven science.* This is not a trite motto. Rather, it undergirds everything I do and teach. It's why I am a sales trainer. This statement is packed with emotions that have meaningful implications for my clients.

Conveying beliefs that inspire positive emotions must always be a genuine, outward expression of what you actually believe. You can't fake it. People can tell when someone is feigning a belief.

Exhibiting positive emotions for your company, product, or service is an essential part of effective selling. Over the years, I have seen salespeople struggle with this, and they also struggle to inspire potential customers to care about what they are saying and selling.

Here are a few examples of what these emotionally charged statements look like:

- The reason I believe so strongly in our service contract is because it gives our customers the peace of mind that their equipment will be in working order. If there is ever an issue, it will be fixed promptly, so that your business is not disrupted.
- I am so confident that our company will exceed your expectations because over the eight years I have been here, I have seen our dedication to customer service, which is why we have a 98 percent approval rating from our customers.
- Can I share with you why I believe so much in this product? It's because of the lifetime warranty, which gives our customers peace of mind. It guarantees that if something does go wrong, it's not your problem, it's our problem.

One aspect of these statements is that they all have the word "because" in them. Behavioral scientist Ellen Langer conducted research that showed that adding the word "because" increases compliance.[35] It's not that the word is magical; it's true because (no pun intended!) numerous studies, including Langer's, have found that people are more likely to act on something if you provide a reason, any reason.[36]

In Langer's research experiment, an accomplice asked strangers who were waiting in line to use a photocopier, "Excuse me, I have five pages. May I use the Xerox machine?" This request prompted 60 percent of those asked to allow the accomplice to move ahead of them. However, when Langer had her collaborator say, "Excuse me, I have five pages. May I use the Xerox machine *because* I have to make copies?" an astounding 93 percent of people agreed to the request.

STRONG BELIEFS EXERCISE

Think through two beliefs that you have about your company, product, or service that have important implications for your buyers. Then jot down below two emotionally charged statements that convey these beliefs.

STRONG BELIEF STATEMENT #1

_____

_____

STRONG BELIEF STATEMENT #2

_____

_____

Now that you have created two statements that are fueled by your strong beliefs about your company, product, or service, and that are relevant for your customers, strategize where you will use them in your sales process. Once you memorize them and begin utilizing them, you will notice how they will help you better engage your buyers on an emotional level.

STRATEGY #2: LEVERAGE THE HAWTHORNE EFFECT

Would changing working conditions boost worker productivity? This was the question that Western Electric Company wanted to answer. The company conducted numerous experiments at their Hawthorne plant, which was located on the outskirts of Chicago. Managers set up a test room where conditions could be controlled and workers closely monitored. The first thing they investigated was if more lights would enhance production. However, when they compared the output of the employees in the test room with those who were working in normal lighting conditions, to the surprise of everyone, *both* groups had an increase in output.

If you are confused, you're not alone. So were those who were conducting this experiment. In fact, their bewilderment increased, because over the next five years they conducted a variety of experiments analyzing whether coffee breaks, financial incentives, shorter work days, different break times, free lunch, and a host of other aspects would enrich workers' productivity. The results showed that with each change, employee efficiency rose. At one point, the managers even reverted back to the original working conditions—and still production increased. What eventually became obvious was that the reason the productivity of the workers surged was not because of the changes in working conditions, but because they knew they were being watched.

The findings of the experiments were labeled the *Hawthorne effect*—that is, the change in behavior that occurs when a person realizes that he or she is being observed—and famously published in the book *Management and the Worker* in 1939.[37] Since then, this phenomenon has been studied and verified as a powerful influencer of human behavior.

When attempting to alter buyers' emotional states, you can leverage the Hawthorne effect by calling attention to their emotions. This is a powerful yet simple way to shake people free of the grip of negative emotions because, as you were shown earlier in this chapter, rarely are they cognitively aware of their emotional state. Yet by calling attention to these emotions, you will jolt prospective customers from their grasp and they will be able to see them objectively.

Some examples of how you can point out a negative emotional state in a professional, but caring manner are:

- John, you seem distracted today. Is everything okay?
- Sally, is something wrong? You seem upset.
- Bob, is now still a good time to discuss this? You seem like you have something else on your mind.

When you bring your buyers' negative emotions to their awareness, they will typically follow their natural human inclination to suppress them by saying something like, "No, I am fine," or "Yes, I was just thinking about something that happened earlier today, but please go on." This weakens the emotional state and prompts them to give you their full attention. Both outcomes will enable you to more easily guide the prospect into positive emotions.

One final point about the Hawthorne effect: it is important that it is implemented with a concerned tone. If you fail to exude compassion, the person may respond in a combative manner, which will direct her attention toward you and not her emotional state. Consequently, pay special attention to the way you convey the Hawthorne effect because when used correctly it is very effective.

STRATEGY #3: DISCUSS TOPICS THAT NATURALLY TRIGGER POSITIVE EMOTIONS

What should you do when you begin conversing with a buyer and you realize that he is in a negative emotional state? Though there are many strategies you can deploy, one of the easiest and most potent is to prompt him to think about and verbalize something that he connects with positive emotions.

Everyone has certain topics that naturally stimulate good feelings. Talking about things such as family, hobbies, or a vacation may cause positive emotions to flood the brain and instantly increase a buyer's receptiveness.

Although a buyer's emotional state is something you must pay attention to throughout the sale, it is especially crucial early in a sales call. If a buyer is in a negative emotional state, you should disrupt and refocus her mind on topics that are rich with positive emotions.

Research studies published in the journal *Group Dynamics* and elsewhere have confirmed that when negotiations and sales calls begin with casual chitchat, a favorable outcome is more likely to be achieved.[38] This type of informal conversation boosts rapport, and when focused on topics that are attached to upbeat emotions, the positive impact of the dialogue is further amplified because it improves the potential customer's emotional state.[39]

How can you identify these emotionally charged topics? Conduct pre-call planning on the buyer's hobbies, family, vacations, group memberships, associations, awards, and so on. For example, if you look up a potential client's social media accounts and find that he is an avid fisherman, has two young children, coaches high school sports, and is president of a local Toastmasters Club, you have numerous topics that are most likely bursting with positive emotions.

Still another way to identify subjects rich with uplifting emotions is to listen for references to things your potential customers are excited about, like upcoming trips, recent family outings, or sports teams. Also, when meeting face-to-face with buyers, look for visual clues (pictures, screen savers, plaques) that showcase potential topics to broach that will likely inspire good feelings. When you notice them, make a note so you can remember and reference them when planning for your next sales call with these customers.

Asking about these topics guides the conversation into an area that will enhance your prospect's emotional state and start the sales call off in an enjoyable, optimistic way. This simple strategy will produce big results, since buyers' emotional states linger and will impact their perception of the sales call.

STRATEGY #4: CHANGE NONVERBAL BEHAVIOR

Earlier, I showed you the evidence that nonverbal behaviors are very accurate portrayers of emotional states. However, that is only one side of the relationship. There is also substantial evidence suggesting that nonverbal behaviors can alter emotional states.

Numerous scientific studies have identified that behaviors such as clenching your fist magnifies feelings of anger, while slouching with your head down produces feelings of sadness.[40] Another scientific study published in the *Journal of Personality and Social Psychology* confirmed that when participants viewed their nonverbal behavior in a mirror, it intensified the emotions they were feeling.[41]

There is a large and growing amount of scientific evidence that shows if a person's nonverbal behavior shifts, so too will his emotional state. This is because the act of moving the body can interrupt the emotional pattern and guide one into a more receptive state. As the legendary psychologist William James, who was a pioneer in the psychological study of emotions, concluded, "Action seems to follow feeling, but really action and feeling go together; and by regulating the action, which is under the more direct control of the will, we can indirectly regulate the feeling, which is not."[42] James recorded how the grief that he experienced after his brother's death advanced into depression. Unable to find relief, James began to force himself to display nonverbal behaviors associated with happiness. Within a short time, he found that the nonverbal behaviors began to positively influence his feelings.

Salespeople are often amazed to find that if customers physically move, their level of emotional responsiveness will often shift as well. Standing up, walking, or leaning forward are simple movements, but potent ways to begin to shift negative emotions. So if your customer is leaning back in his chair with his arms crossed, you could say "Jeff, would you mind leaning forward so that I can show you this chart? This will answer the question you posed earlier." This modest shift in body posture will weaken his current emotional state and heighten his ability to experience more positive emotions.

There's also compelling scientific research proving that changes in one's facial expression can trigger changes in emotions.[43] Behavioral scientists refer to this phenomenon as the *facial feedback hypothesis*.[44] Social psychologists Saul Kassin, Steven Fein, and Hazel Rose Markus summarize the meaning of this well: "Facial feedback can evoke and magnify certain emotional states."[45]

One of the most influential movements in this context is smiling. Social scientists Simone Schnall and James Laird conducted numerous psychological experiments exploring how smiling impacts one's emotional state.[46] Their research concluded that when a person smiles it instinctively puts him or her in a more optimistic, energetic, and productive emotional state. They also found that these positive emotions linger, even after the act of smiling has ceased.

Smiling has even been shown to positively affect the human brain. Behavioral scientist Robert Zajonc's research disclosed that when facial muscles contort to produce a smile, blood flow to the brain increases, which lowers the brain's temperature.[47] This naturally produces feelings of pleasure and puts one in a more optimistic mood.

Inducing a smile can be accomplished with humor or even something as simple as smiling at the buyer. Research shows that smiling activates mirror neurons in the brain, which will often prompt the receiver to reciprocate the smile.

Monitoring, identifying, and changing your potential customers' emotional states is something that every salesperson must become proficient in. Here's how one salesperson put it after he learned how to sell to buyers' emotional states: "I used to struggle selling to those who were in a negative emotional state. I knew something was wrong, they knew something was wrong, but we all seemed powerless to do anything about it. If I could go back in time, I would be able to turn many of those situations around because now I know what was happening and how to resolve it."

Mastering the science of selling to buyers' emotions is a critical task because emotions make engagement occur and engaged buyers are the only ones who buy. This is why emotions must be addressed and at times altered throughout the sale. And now you know how to do this. What's more, I will share more strategies that are extremely effective in shifting emotional states in later chapters of this book.

So now that you have a basic understanding of how to appeal to a buyers' emotional state, let's turn our attention to one of the most important components of selling: questions. In the next chapter, I'll show you how to ask questions the way the brain is wired to disclose information.

PART TWO

———

THE
SALESPERSON'S TOOLKIT

CHAPTER 5

The Science of
Asking Powerful Questions

Can questions increase buying behaviors? If you answered yes, you're right. In fact, questions have such potency that behavioral scientists have found that just asking people about their future decisions significantly influences those decisions, a phenomenon known as the *mere measurement effect*.

For example, social scientists Vicki Morwitz, Eric Johnson, and David Schmittlein conducted a study with more than forty thousand participants that revealed that simply asking someone if they were going to purchase a new car within six months increased their purchase rates by 35 percent![1] It also turns out that according to a study published in the *Journal of Applied Psychology*, inquiring if citizens are going to vote in an upcoming election increases the likelihood they will by 25 percent.[2] The power of questions on future behavior is so compelling that four behavioral scientists wanted to see if it could even be used to trigger the prosocial activity of donating blood. It did. Their research, published in the journal *Health Psychology*, demonstrated that asking about one's intention to give blood raised donation rates by 8.6 percent.[3] Other studies have even found that such diverse things as computer sales, exercise frequency, and disease prevention behaviors can all be enhanced by asking about them.[4]

So why do questions have such influence on the decision-making process? First and foremost, they prompt the brain to contemplate a behavior, which research shows enhances the probability that it will be acted upon.[5] The mental digestion that questions inspire also help buyers discover, change, and solidify their thoughts. This highlights an essential point about questions and their role in the sales process: buyers need them. Questions enable potential customers to better understand their situation and to recognize how it can be improved. This is why they're such an integral part of selling. They guide prospective customers into realizing why they need your product or service.

But questions are not just for buyers. They can also help you be more successful at selling. How? Asking purposeful questions that help you acquire an in-depth understanding of potential customers enables you to effectively tailor your sales presentation to meet their needs and advance the sale. Without this awareness of your buyers, your ability to accurately and persuasively present your product or service will be diminished, which will hinder your ability to serve buyers and generate sales.

What's more, insightful questions reveal that you are mindful of your prospective clients' needs, and this will inspire them to have confidence in you. For instance, imagine that you were not feeling well and you went to the doctor. How would you respond if the doctor walked into the room and, without asking any questions or examining you, prescribed a medication? You probably wouldn't trust her conclusion or act on her recommendation since she didn't have enough information to accurately diagnose your illness. Likewise, buyers will only entrust you to solve their problems once they believe you understand them.

QUESTIONS DIRECT THE MIND

One of the most fascinating aspects of questions is that they focus the mind on a single idea. Here's a question to prove it:

What color is your house?

After reading that question, what were you thinking about? The obvious answer is the color of your house. Though this exercise may seem ordinary, it has profound implications. The question hijacked your thought process and focused it on your house or apartment. You did not consciously tell your brain to think about that; it just did so automatically. I refer to the mental reflex that questions trigger as *instinctive elaboration*, which occurs when a question is posed and it takes over the brain's thought process. This is what makes questions an indispensable selling strategy: the entire process of selling is dependent on potential customers contemplating and committing to certain foundational value propositions. Questions do just that—they guide buyers into thinking through the essential concepts that allow the sale to occur. However, what makes this phenomenon even more noteworthy is when your brain is thinking about the answer to a question, it cannot contemplate anything else.

Research in neuroscience has proven that the human brain can only think about one idea at a time. So when you ask buyers questions, you are focusing their minds on *only* your question. As Pierce Howard, director of research for the Center for Applied Cognitive Studies, describes, "Notwithstanding teenagers' claims that they can do homework in front of the television set, the brain cannot focus on more than one stimulus at a time."[6] Neuroscientist John Medina echoed this assertion: "Research shows that we can't multitask. We are biologically incapable of processing attention-rich inputs simultaneously."[7] Nobel Prize–winning economist Herbert Simon emphasized that human beings consciously "operate largely in serial fashion. The more demanding the task, the more we are single-minded."[8] Psychologist Edward Hallowell also aptly summarized the mental impossibility of multitasking by comparing it to playing tennis with numerous tennis balls at once.[9]

> Studies in neuroscience have shown that the human brain can only think about one idea at a time. So when you ask buyers a question, you are focusing their minds on *only* your question.

Scientists have identified that when the brain attempts to multitask it is actually diverting its focus from one task and giving it to another. Though your brain can maintain a basic awareness of its surroundings, it can only thoughtfully deliberate one notion at a time. Those who believe that they are skilled at multitasking simply have good memories that allow them to remember the thoughts they had before they jumped to another activity. As distinguished research scientist Mihaly Csikszentmihalyi explains, "Humans cannot really successfully multitask, but can rather move attention rapidly from one task to another in quick succession, which only makes us feel as if we were actually doing things simultaneously."[10] So as you read this book and ponder what it is espousing, your brain is unable to contemplate what you had for lunch yesterday. You can think about one or the other, but not both. (If you don't believe me, try to focus on both simultaneously—you'll see it's impossible to do.)

Because questions direct the mind, you can use them to guide the sale as well. Think about it this way: It is easy to assume that when two people are in a conversation, the one talking is in control. Yet is this really the case? When you are presenting to potential customers, do you know what they are thinking? They may be contemplating what you are saying or pondering something else entirely. In contrast, when you ask a question, you commandeer your buyer's thoughts and steer them toward the answer to the question.

Now, let's apply these insights to real-world selling situations. We'll look at how using questions to control the sale can improve sales effectiveness in two different common selling scenarios:

SCENARIO #1: HANDLING PRODUCT OR SERVICE QUESTIONS EARLY IN THE SALE

One dilemma that many salespeople regularly encounter early in the sale is buyers barraging them with questions about their product or service. Often, these questions cannot be answered properly, since at this stage, salespeople do not yet know enough about their potential clients' situations to accurately show how their product or service can help them in meaningful ways. Additionally, prematurely presenting your product or service will also steal from the persuasive clout of your sales presentation. So what should you do when dealing with stubborn buyers who keep showering you with questions you don't want to answer? Change the conversation by deploying a question to control the sale and move it forward in mutually beneficial ways. Here's what you do. First, succinctly answer the potential customer's question in one or two sentences. Then pose a question that will refocus his attention back to where you were in the sales process. You will find that this simple strategy will enable you to control the sale in a nonconfrontational, highly engaging, and productive manner.

SCENARIO #2: CONTINUING INITIAL CONVERSATIONS WITH BUYERS

When initially approaching buyers, they may attempt to prematurely shut down the conversation before you have a chance to qualify them or spark their interest. So what can you do? Deploy what I refer to as a *thought redirect*, which is using a question to interrupt their current thought process and redirect it to a topic that will grab their attention. Here's an example of what this might look like:

Salesperson:

> Do you currently have a social media strategy?

Buyer:

> I'm sorry, we are not interested in any social media help right now. We are already working with a firm that we are very happy with.

Salesperson:

> I understand, it sounds like you are happy with where you are at. How do your current social media efforts support your SEO and content marketing? *[Here the salesperson deployed a softening statement, followed by a question that redirected the buyer's attention.]*

Buyer:

> Um . . . I'm not sure. I don't think they do. How does your firm handle integrating social media with other online efforts?

ALL QUESTIONS ARE NOT CREATED EQUAL

Just asking a lot of questions will not make you more successful at selling. What matters is the quality of questions you ask. The better your inquiries, the more fruitful your potential clients' responses will be. When you ask mundane questions, buyers become bored and will perceive conversing with you as a waste of their time. Remember, prospective clients have a plethora of choices; if you cease to provide value, they will quickly look elsewhere. On the other hand, when you ask insightful questions, it produces something central to the success of the sale: trust.

Asking thought-provoking questions that provide meaningful insights will cause potential customers to reciprocate with increased levels of trust. Why? Because your questions prompt them to view you as a competent professional who is helping them think through complex and challenging issues. Competency is a core part of trust, as one meta-analysis that examined fifty years of research identified.[11] Additional studies have shown that trust will guide others in being more open to conversing with you and listening to your ideas.[12]

It is helpful to think of questions as investments you make in the success of the sale. You want your questions to generate a high rate of return. Yet how can you ask effective questions? To uncover this I will review the most common sales questioning model and show you why it inhibits you from constructing powerful questions. Then I will share the surprising brain science that reveals how to easily create *highly* influential questions.

THE PROBLEMS WITH TYPES OF QUESTIONS

The most common way that salespeople are taught to ask questions is by learning categories or types of questions. How many types of questions are there? It varies, depending on the industry and sales training methodology. For example, one popular training firm proposed that there are only three main kinds of questions, while others suggest there are four.[13] Yet, another sales trainer maintains that there are eight different categories of questions salespeople should use when selling.[14]

So that you have a basic awareness of what is meant by types of questions, the following are some of the most common ones cited by sales trainers:

- Open-ended questions
- Closed questions
- Situation questions
- About questions

- Barrier questions
- Framing questions
- Investigative questions
- Data questions
- Reflective questions
- Problem questions
- Implication questions
- Objective questions
- Amplification questions
- Internal Summary questions
- Solution questions
- Need-Payoff questions
- Outcome questions
- Probing questions

To ensure that you understand what these kinds of questions are, here are descriptions of five of them.

- **Amplification questions:** Questions that ask buyers to expound on a previous comment.
- **Probing questions:** Questions that focus on uncovering or clarifying the circumstances surrounding a potential client's problem.
- **Problem questions:** Questions that identify the problems buyers are experiencing.
- **Implication questions:** Questions that illuminate the consequence of a problem.
- **Barrier questions:** Questions that uncover what has kept buyers from resolving problems.

If distinguishing the types of questions seems confusing, that's because it is. In fact, even sales trainers who teach them often have a hard time telling them apart. For instance, one respected sales training firm that advocates using four kinds of questions confessed that they would argue internally about the difference between two of the types.[15] However, once you have figured out how to tell the questions apart, there is still a much bigger hurdle to overcome—using them.

The major stumbling block with types of questions is discerning which kind should be used to ask follow-up questions. Just think about the mental gymnastics required for you to listen to your buyer's response and then analyze which category of questions you should use to guide him in thinking through or disclosing more information. Here's what this would actually look like on a real sales call: you ask a situation question, followed by a framing question, and then you jump to an implication question, follow up with an open-ended question, navigate back to a framing question, and then pose an outcome question—all while intensely listening to and contemplating your prospective customer's answers. The dizzying amount of brainpower it would require to competently accomplish this is simply unrealistic.

What's more, remember the science that reveals that the brain cannot multitask and can only think about one idea at a time? This means that if you attempt to use types of questions when selling, your focus will be on what category of questions you should say next, which will undoubtedly cause you to miss some of the information your buyers are sharing. However, what is even more concerning about this method of questioning is who it is centered on.

The source of the problem with types of questions is that they are based on sellers' past behaviors, instead of how buyers disclose information. Allow me to explain. When those in the profession of sales study questions, they do so by analyzing the questions salespeople ask, and then categorize those questions into types. However, their focus is on the wrong group of people. They shouldn't be looking at salespeople; they should be looking at buyers—more specifically, on how buyers' brains naturally disclose information.

> The more a sales questioning method is based on how the brain naturally discloses information the more beneficial it will be.

THE SCIENCE OF QUESTIONS

How do people reveal information to one another? This is what Irwin Altman, a professor at the University of Utah, and Dalmas Taylor, a professor at the University of Texas, wanted to uncover.[16] Their research findings, which they labeled the *social penetration theory*, were first published in 1973 and are widely regarded as an important contribution to the study of how interpersonal relationships develop.

The social penetration theory describes how the human brain is hardwired to disclose information in layers. Altman and Taylor use the visually rich illustration of an onion to explain these layers. Much like the way peeling back a layer of an onion exposes another layer, so too when people unveil information they do so sequentially, one layer at a time. As each new level is accessed, more in-depth information is revealed.

Social scientists have utilized the social penetration theory as the basis for a variety of scientific research on human interaction. You can also benefit from the social penetration theory since it provides meaningful insights into how to ask questions: the most effective way to construct high-value questions is to mirror how the brain reveals information—not in types, but in levels.

THREE LEVELS OF QUESTIONS

I learned about the social penetration theory nearly twenty years ago, but it wasn't until I was struggling to identify a way of asking insightful questions that I realized its significance: science established that the brain imparts information in layers and, as a result, questions should reflect this.

Using this science, I created a system of questioning that was based not on categories, but on levels. When I began to test this concept with actual salespeople, there were three consistent outcomes.

First, they were able to gain more insight into their buyers, a lot more. Since their questions reflected how potential customers communicate, gaining access to deeper levels of information was not a complex endeavor, but a natural outcome. It was just as Altman and Taylor described it—like peeling back the layers of an onion.

Second, because the brain reveals information in layers, asking questions that mirror this process is almost intuitive. As a result, salespeople using this questioning model are able to create potent follow-up questions with ease. I even trained salespeople who were extremely poor at crafting questions and found that within a very brief period of time they were able to compose follow-up questions that were equal to those I would expect from highly experienced, accomplished salespeople. In short, I had cut down the learning time for becoming highly skilled at asking questions not by years, but in some cases by decades.

Third, this method of asking questions improved sales because it enhanced salespeople's capacity to help potential customers think through and impart information. And there are a host of studies that have proven that when you do this it will cause buyers to view you and your message more persuasively.[17]

There are three distinct "layers" or "levels" of questions you can ask. Each level is built on the previous one, and together will guide you in creating dynamic follow-up questions. Moreover, unlike the complexity inherent in types of questions, asking layered questions is a straightforward process. The rest of this chapter will be devoted to explaining each level and providing real examples of how they can be used in conjunction with one another.

FIRST-LEVEL QUESTIONS

First-level questions are preliminary questions that open up a topic by revealing thoughts, facts, behaviors, and situations. They are used to gain a basic understanding of a subject, so they're the best questions to use when beginning conversations with buyers. Furthermore, they are imperative to the success of a sale because they unveil the initial layer of a topic and allow you to dive deeper into it.

This brings up an important point about first-level questions: they are necessary, but not enough. They must be used in combination with the other levels of questions that allow you to identify the beliefs that sustain and direct a buyer's perspective or behaviors. Nevertheless, I have found that the majority of salespeople I meet predominantly ask first-level questions. Since these questions expose only rudimentary information, they do not give them a thorough understanding of their buyers, which will limit their ability to customize the sales process for those buyers. This will hinder sales, since anytime the sale ceases to be focused on the buyer, sales effectiveness will also wane.

Most likely you already have numerous first-level questions that you use when selling. But just in case, here are some examples:

- When will you migrate to the new software?
- What percentage of market share do you currently have?
- What are the requirements you have established for this project?
- What is your process for deciding which vendor you will choose?
- What is your budget for this project?
- How many other providers are you considering?
- What is your time frame for completing this project?
- What are your current assembly capabilities?
- When your organization considers an investment like this, who is involved in the decision process?

Once you ask a first-level question, how do you advance to the next layer of information? You ask *second-level questions*, of course. I discovered that these questions are what top salespeople ask more than any other. In fact, they are the key to asking powerful follow-up questions.

SECOND-LEVEL QUESTIONS

Second-level questions guide buyers in assessing and explaining first-level responses. These questions are vital because they prompt prospective customers to think through a thought, fact, behavior, or situation.

Interestingly enough, these powerful questions have been analyzed in a series of recent scientific studies. For instance, when researchers from Stanford University studied the effects of second-level questions, which they labeled *elaboration questions*, they found that the questions aided participants in understanding others' viewpoints.[18] Furthermore, the questions also prompted participants to be more receptive to someone else's ideas, even if those ideas were contrary to their own.

Other studies discovered that second-level questions help the brain process a persuasive message and even cause the presenter of the message to seem more influential.[19]

But perhaps the most intriguing research on second-level questions occurred at Harvard University, when researchers utilized functional magnetic resonance imaging (fMRI) to identify how disclosing information impacts the human brain.[20] The study revealed that answering second-level questions, which prompted participants to state their opinions, increased neural activity in the areas of the brain associated with reward and pleasure. These good feelings caused a change in the brain that naturally enhanced the participant's emotional state. In other words, potential customers enjoy answering second-level questions.

> Answering second-level questions, which prompt buyers to state their opinions, increases neural activity in the areas of the brain associated with reward and pleasure.

When you begin using second-level questions, you'll notice that the impact of your questions and the insights they generate are enhanced dramatically. This tier of questions is also linked with heightened levels of sales performance, because they guide you in obtaining an awareness of the perspectives and beliefs that are shaping buyers' behaviors.

Since these questions are based on how the brain naturally discloses information, formulating them will seem intuitive, and when you practice them, within a short time you will begin asking them with ease. For example, just ask customers to either assess or explain a first-level response. Here are some samples of second-level questions:

- Why did the board decide to go in that direction?
- Would you ever consider investing in a product that did not include this feature?

- May I ask why you chose that vendor?
- Is aggregating your data in this manner what you would like to do moving forward?
- That sounds like it is very important to you. May I ask why?
- If you could change one thing about the training your end users receive, what would it be?
- Based on what we have discussed, does it make sense why so many companies are choosing to use our consultants?
- Why is it important to solve this concern right away?
- Do you believe that this issue is causing the lack of production you described?

By now you should have a good understanding of second-level questions. So let's apply them to some real sales scenarios.

EXAMPLE #1

Salesperson (first-level question):

> Did you have a chance to review the data sheet I sent over?

Buyer:

> Yes, my team looked it over and everything seemed fine.

Salesperson (second-level question):

> This is an important decision. What feature did you and your team think was most significant?

Buyer:

> We were very impressed with the permissions management feature.

EXAMPLE #2

Salesperson (first-level question):

> How efficient is your current equipment?

Buyer:

> It's older equipment and not very efficient. In fact, I've been tasked with improving that, so any new equipment would need to make a difference in that area.

Salesperson (second-level question):

> If you were to invest in the new equipment we've discussed, how would that impact efficiency levels?

Buyer:

> Based on our conversation today, I would estimate that it should improve efficiency by around 6 percent.

As insightful as second-level questions are, there is still one more level that penetrates even deeper. It is the most consequential of all the levels of questions because it addresses buyers on an emotional level. And when it is leveraged, it will often reveal information that will transform the entire sale.

THIRD-LEVEL QUESTIONS

Third-level questions excavate the final layer of information by guiding potential customers in thinking through and verbally disclosing their dominant buying motives. As explained in Chapter 3, dominant buying motives are the emotional reasons why potential customers would purchase your product or service. They are comprised of two potent behavior stimulators: the desire for gain or the fear of loss.

Regardless of the type of sale, buyers only become willing to purchase a product or service when they believe that doing so will move them closer to what they desire or further from what they fear losing. This is why third-level questions are so powerful: they provide you with an understanding of how potential customers will benefit from investing in your product or service. Armed with this knowledge, you can then clearly show them how your product or service will satisfy their dominant buying motives.

However, that's not all third-level questions do. As buyers answer them, their feelings of trust toward you will increase. That is, the very process of disclosing their emotional responses will enhance their trust because they feel you understand them. This bond will separate you from your competitors because those buyers trust are also those they will buy from.

Creating third-level questions involves asking potential clients to reveal something they fear losing or desire to gain. Here are some examples of these potent questions:

- If we could reduce your costs as we have discussed, how would that positively affect your company's profitability?
- If the problem you have described is not resolved, how will it impact your organization's sales?
- This seems like a very important issue to you personally. May I ask what it would mean for you and those on your team if this issue is not resolved?
- If your end users were thoroughly trained and were using this platform effectively, how could that increase company productivity?

Now let's review the examples of second-level questions and add a third-level question to each:

EXAMPLE #1

Salesperson (first-level question):
> Did you have a chance to review the data sheet I sent over?

Buyer:
> Yes, my team looked it over and everything seemed fine.

Salesperson (second-level question):
> This is an important decision. What feature did you and your team think was most significant?

Buyer:
> We were very impressed with the permissions management feature.

Salesperson (third-level question):
> I hear that a lot from our clients. Our permissions management is very comprehensive and in-depth. What kind of impact will it have on your business if you're not able to effectively manage permissions?

Buyer:

> Our current system is not very good at limiting information, which has caused numerous problems. In fact, to be candid, several months ago I almost lost my job because someone was able to access some sensitive data. So your permission management feature is really a necessity.

EXAMPLE #2

Salesperson (first-level question):

> How efficient is your current equipment?

Buyer:

> It's older equipment and not very efficient. In fact, I've been tasked with improving that, so any new equipment would need to make a difference in that area.

Salesperson (second-level question):

> If you were to invest in the new equipment that we've discussed, how would that impact efficiency levels?

Buyer:

> Based on our conversation today I would estimate that it should improve efficiency by around 6 percent.

Salesperson (third-level question):

> May I ask, how would that positively affect the business if efficiencies improved by 6 percent?

Buyer:

> Well . . . it would be a big deal. It would increase our profitability and help us fund our new growth initiatives.

Whether you are trying to inspire someone to embrace your ideas or sell them a product or service, the insights derived from meaningful questions are an essential part of influence. By embracing the scientifically validated model of first-, second-, and third-level questions, you will be equipped to ask questions that are aligned with how the brain instinctively reveals information. This will guide you in obtaining a full and relevant understanding of your potential customers, which will enable you to adapt your sales presentation to address their needs. Salespeople who ask effective questions thrive, and likewise do the organizations they represent.

Here's a visual that illustrates the flow of the three levels of questions and how they will naturally guide you in creating impactful follow-up questions.

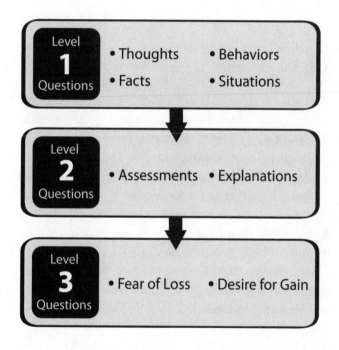

CHAPTER 6

Why People Buy

In a now legendary illustration, management consultant Mary Parker Follett tells of two sisters quarreling over an orange they both want.[1] After an intense argument, they decide to compromise by cutting the orange in half, so each would have an equal portion. One sister took her half, squeezed it, and drank the juice. The other sister peeled her half and used the peel in a cake she was baking. Yet had the sisters known what the other wanted, they could have both reaped the benefit of the whole orange. This anecdote serves as a reminder of how important it is to understand the perspective of those you desire to influence. And in no profession is this more essential than sales.

To sell in a persuasive and engaging way, there is compelling research that overwhelmingly confirms you must understand your buyers. For example, when the *Harvard Business Review* published an article entitled "What Makes a Good Salesman?" it concluded that one of the primary characteristics of top performers was their ability to see things from their customers' point of view.[2] Numerous research studies published in the *Journal of Personal Selling and Sales Management* also confirmed that salespeople who have an in-depth awareness of what matters to buyers are far better at establishing trust and achieve higher sales.[3]

Here's why this is the case. A study published in the *Journal of Marketing Theory and Practice* found that salespeople who are attuned with their potential customers' situations and perspectives are able to better customize their messages to meet the needs of those buyers, which improves sales results.[4]

This gets to the root of what enables effective selling: understanding and adapting to your potential customers. Every buyer is different. What is meaningful to one may be irrelevant to another. No longer will potential clients tolerate generic sales presentations. Today they expect value not only after purchasing your product or service, but through every stage of the sale. And this value is predicated on recognizing and addressing what matters to them.

But unfortunately, salespeople are struggling in this area. Forrester, the research and advisory firm, conducted a study that indicated that buyers believe only 25 percent of the salespeople with whom they meet have an adequate understanding of their business, responsibilities, and the issues they need help resolving.[5] What makes this even more disconcerting is that in the current competitive marketplace, buyers have a lot of options to choose from. If one seller does not meet their expectations, they will be discarded for another. (And this is exactly what is happening to salespeople at a shockingly high rate.) Forrester also reported that because buyers' expectations are going unfulfilled, 75 percent of initial sales calls fail to generate a second meeting. In other words, buyers disengage because, in their eyes, salespeople do not know enough about their circumstances to provide the value that would warrant the advancement of the sale.

What is causing this lack of awareness and what can you do to counteract it? To begin to answer these important questions, I'll share with you one of the most famous research experiments in recent decades, which offers a clue to the source of this obliviousness.

Behavioral scientists Daniel Simons and Christopher Chabris showed participants in their study a short video that featured two basketball teams, one wearing black jerseys and the other white jerseys, moving around a small space passing a basketball back and forth to others on their team.[6] Prior to watching the video, the researchers instructed viewers to count how many passes were made by the team wearing the white jerseys. After the video ended, the researchers recorded the number each participant counted and asked them if they had noticed anything unusual in the video. Half of the watchers said no, they hadn't. This stunned the researchers, because during the video a person dressed in a gorilla suit walked between the basketball players, turned, looked directly at the camera, thumped his chest, and then walked off. He was clearly visible for nearly 40 percent of the video—yet half of the participants *never saw him.*

This experiment has been repeated numerous times in various countries by different researchers with diverse audiences, and the findings are always the same.[7] Approximately 50 percent of the people don't see the gorilla. Why? The reason is a psychological phenomenon called *inattentional blindness*, which occurs when a person is focusing so hard on one thing that he does not notice something else happening simultaneously, however obvious or significant it may be.[8]

Inattentional blindness is not confined to psychological experiments—it occurs in the profession of selling every day. Salespeople frequently overlook essential pieces of information that are important to buyers. It's not that they don't care about their buyers or don't desire to understand where they're coming from. The problem is that many sales reps aren't sure what they should be focusing on. So, much like in Simons's and Chabris's gorilla experiment, they miss the obvious things that matter most to buyers.

THE KEY TO EFFECTIVE LISTENING

Few salespeople are surprised by the idea that listening will help them sell more. In fact, a multitude of studies have proven that effective listening increases sales success.[9] Yet too often when salespeople are trained in listening skills, they are simply given motivational speeches extolling the virtues of talking less and listening more. The problem with this approach is that it operates on the flawed assumption that they already know how to listen and only need to be reminded to do so.

> The key to effective listening is not to listen more, but to know what you should be listening for.

Salespeople lack listening skills not because they haven't been prompted to listen more, but because they do not know what to listen for. Within the context of the sale, a broad knowledge about buyers is not enough. The quantity of the information is not nearly as important as the quality of it. One of the most obvious examples of this I have ever encountered was a salesperson, who we'll call Mark. He had a deep desire to serve his buyers and would go out of his way to learn about them, even delving into many areas of their personal lives. But when I would ask him about the mission critical pieces of information that would impact the success of the sale, he was unnervingly silent. Though he knew a lot about his potential customers, he was not aware of the things the entire sale hinged on, which caused his sales to suffer.

In contrast, once salespeople learn the essential knowledge they must obtain for the sale to progress, they will begin to intensely listen to buyers in an effort to comprehend this information. What is this information? It's what I refer to as primary buying motivators.

WHY BUYERS CHOOSE TO BUY FROM YOU

"Why would buyers choose to purchase your product or service?"

When I ask salespeople this question they usually begin listing the features or benefits of their product or service that they feel are most important. More often than not, they end up telling me why *they* would purchase their product or service. Yet when salespeople impose their viewpoints on buyers and speculate about why their buyers would be motivated to obtain their product or service, they do a disservice to those buyers, since frequently their assumptions are inaccurate. (If you've ever been pitched a product or service and the salesperson fixated on features or benefits that you cared nothing about, you know what I mean.) Though there may be some similarities, the reasons for a buying decision will vary from buyer to buyer. Consequently, any guesses about why prospective clients will purchase your product or service before they disclose that information is dangerously premature and hazardous to the sale.

Truly understanding your potential customers' perspectives does not mean putting yourself in their place and asking, "What would I want?"

Instead, it is striving to recognize their primary buying motivators, which are the essential conditions that must be fulfilled in order for buyers to desire and be able to purchase your product or service. They are why potential customers will choose to buy from you.

Moreover, the process of identifying primary buying motivators will guide you in qualifying potential customers. For instance, if you find that your product or service is not designed to solve a certain buyer's unique problem—one of their primary buying motivators—then why would she purchase it? In this case, she wouldn't, nor would you want her to since it would not result in a happy customer. This is why it's recommended that you find these purchasing conditions as early in the sale as possible to ensure that you are investing your time in those who are actually able to become customers.

Every buyer has three primary buying motivators. I'll briefly recap the first two, since they were already discussed in Chapter 3, and explain the third in more detail, as it hasn't been covered yet. Then in the next chapter I will show you how to utilize each to improve engagement, build value, and close more deals.

PRIMARY BUYING MOTIVATOR #1: BUYER'S PROBLEMS

Though many things have changed in selling, one has not—the chief reason buyers choose to purchase a product or service is because they believe it will solve a meaningful problem. Before you can compellingly present your product or service, you must first unravel the problems your potential customers are struggling with. Only then will you be able to clearly connect the dots between their problems and your product or service.

Accomplishing this is a straightforward three-step process.

1. Identify the issues by providing insights and asking leading first-level questions that guide potential customers to reveal them.
2. Pose second-level questions that will enable you and your prospective clients to understand the cause and scope of those problems.

3. Deploy second- and third-level questions that help buyers become aware of the damage those issues are causing and the consequences of allowing them to fester instead of using your product or service to solve them.

How should you begin a conversation with buyers about their problems? If they are aware of their issues, you can ask first-level questions such as, "Is there anything about your distribution process that you would like to change?" or "How are you currently generating new business opportunities?" However, this approach only works if potential clients know they have a problem. Many will not. In these cases, you must pique their interest by sharing some problems that your other clients, who are similar to them, have resolved by purchasing your product or service. Then, after introducing these problems, ask some questions to find out if your prospective customers face the same obstacles or related issues. Here are a few examples of how this conversation might begin:

- **Salesperson:** Many of our clients come to us because they have two particular concerns: poor hires and the excessive amount of time and resources it takes to find the right person for an open position. Of the two, which has been the bigger issue for your organization?
- **Salesperson:** What alarms a lot of sales leaders like yourself is that research shows that 63 percent of salespeople regularly behave in ways that drive down performance and obstruct buying decisions. What has your organization done to ensure that your salespeople are behaving in ways that serve potential customers and enhance their ability to earn sales?
- **Salesperson:** Surveys show that between 15 and 35 percent of employees' time is spent searching for information. It's not that companies don't have the information employees need, it's that employees don't know where to find it. How is your organization addressing this concern?

DISCOVERING BUYERS' PROBLEMS EXERCISE

Let's create one example, like the ones I just shared, that you can use in your sales context to help buyers become more aware of their problems. To begin, think of one insight that you can share with prospective customers that will initiate a dialogue about the problems they may have. Now think of a transition question, such as, "How are you addressing this issue?" or "How much market penetration have you gotten in this area?" that you can use to apply that insight to your buyers' situations.

PRIMARY BUYING MOTIVATOR #2: DOMINANT BUYING MOTIVES

Why do your potential customers care about a buying decision? The answer to this question is found in your buyers' dominant buying motives, which, as I explained in Chapter 3, are the emotional reasons why they would purchase your product or service. Dominant buying motives are made up of two behavior triggers: the desire for gain and the fear of loss.

What is the main purpose of dominant buying motives? They are how buyers prioritize a purchase, how they know why investing in your product or service is a better decision than purchasing something else. Once you recognize your buyers' dominant buying motives, you can then show how buying your product or service will fulfill them. This is critical to the success of the sale, because if prospective clients do not see a clear link between your product or service and their dominant buying motives, they will lose interest and the sale will die.

So how do you find dominant buying motives? You ask third-level questions. These questions, which were described and demonstrated in Chapter 5, will help buyers think through and reveal what they desire to gain or what they fear to lose. Here are a few samples of these questions:

- If this issue is resolved and your division's production rates improve as we have discussed, how would that positively impact you and your team?
- If you did decide to move forward with us, what would be the advantage?
- If this issue is not corrected and the trend continues, how will it decrease your market share?
- If nothing is done to correct this issue and the loss to the company is as you have described, what would that mean for you and the other employees?

PRIMARY BUYING MOTIVATOR #3: BUYING REQUIREMENTS

The final primary buying motivator that you should pinpoint early in your sales process is a person's *buying requirements*. These are the specific factors that heavily influence the buying decision and reveal how you should position yourself and your message. This buying motivator unveils who is involved in the buying decision, how that decision will be made, and the specific criteria that will be used to judge your company, product, or service.

So how do you find out your potential customers' buying requirements? By learning the following two components of this powerful buying motivator:

COMPONENT #1: IDENTIFY THE DECISION PROCESS

Researchers Tom Atkinson and Ron Koprowski conducted a survey published in the *Harvard Business Review* that asked employees responsible for making purchases for some of the largest companies in North America what the biggest mistakes are that salespeople make.[10] The number one grievance against salespeople was that they do not follow the structured purchasing process that the buyers' companies have in place. What these buyers are referring to is the formal, predetermined process that many organizations have and that must be followed before a buying decision can be approved. If salespeople do not sell in accordance with it, they will frequently sabotage their chances of earning the sale. (This is different than the mental process buyers go through when making a buying decision, which was discussed in previous chapters.) Let me explain.

Many years ago I sold to a large organization that had a predetermined three-step procedure that everyone at the company strictly followed when settling on a large purchase. First, they would secure at least five different bids from potential vendors. Second, a group of individuals within the organization would narrow the list down to three. Finally, each of the remaining providers would be invited to meet with a committee and present how their service could meet the organization's needs. Only after all these phases were completed could a buying decision be made.

How would knowing the purchasing process an organization will follow help you earn more sales? Because it gives you the insights to better position yourself so that you can improve the odds of being the one chosen. To accomplish this, one of the first things you'll want to figure out is who is involved in the purchasing decision. To find these individuals, I'll introduce you to the two kinds of people you'll need to identify and then I'll show you how to pinpoint how their buy-in is achieved.

DECISION MAKERS: It is always a best practice to determine who the decision makers are in a sale as early as possible. Who's a decision maker? It's someone who can authorize the decision to purchase. Today, most sales involve multiple decision makers whose buy-in is necessary before a sale can be finalized.

How can you identify decision makers? Simply ask questions such as, "Who is involved in making this decision?" or "Who else from within your organization is part of this decision process?"

If possible, you should strive to meet with all decision makers so you can guide each of them through the buying process. However, in some sales environments, meeting with each decision maker is not possible. If this is the case, identify your internal advocate, the person in the organization who will represent you to the decision makers, and ask her questions about the decision makers' perspective on the primary buying motivators and the Six Whys®. Some examples of these questions are, "Can you walk me through what each of the people on the committee think about this issue?" or "What do those on the executive team think about why moving forward with this project now is imperative?" As you identify the decision makers' perspectives on the mission critical areas of the sale, you will be better able to equip your internal advocate with the specific information needed to win them over.

INFLUENCERS: A second group of people you should be aware of are influencers. These are the people in the company who have an effect on whether or not a purchase will be made. They do not make the buying decision itself, but rather offer opinions or feedback that can sway decision makers.

Recognizing influencers is relatively clear-cut. Ask questions like, "Will anyone else be helping with this decision?" or "Is there anyone else in your organization who will be offering insights on vendor selection?"

Once you identify influencers, bring them into the sale so that you can address their concerns and guide them through the buying process. Inexperienced salespeople often make the mistake of ignoring influencers, focusing solely on the decision makers. Nevertheless, I have been involved in many sales in which the suggestion of an influencer determined which vendor was chosen. This is why you should never downplay or ignore them. Always treat influencers with the same respect that you do a decision maker.

HOW BUY-IN IS ACHIEVED: Once you have identified who is involved in the decision, you now need to find how it will be made.

Is there a formal process, a series of meetings, or some other way entirely? If there is a predefined process the organization follows, you can strategize how to use it to your advantage. For instance, if the buying decision will be made at an executive committee meeting at the end of the month, ask if you can present to them or call in to answer their questions. Even though it may not be offered, ask for special privileges to meet with decision makers or influencers, because research suggests that more often than you expect, buyers will agree to it.

This is what behavioral scientists Francis Flynn and Vanessa Lake found when they conducted a series of experiments focused on expected rates of compliance. They identified that participants vastly underestimate the likelihood that others will agree to their requests, in some cases by as much as 50 percent.[11] So don't be afraid to ask for a meeting with decision makers, or inquire if you can make a special presentation. If you have offered insights that demonstrate high levels of value, you will often be surprised—much like those in the study—by how frequently others will comply with your requests.

> The brain underestimates the likelihood that people will agree with a request, in some cases by as much as 50 percent.

Discovering how an organization makes a buying decision is usually an uncomplicated endeavor that buyers will freely share if you ask. Here are a few ways to do so:

- How is a decision like this one made in your organization?
- After you gather all the information, what happens next?
- What are the steps your organization will go through as you evaluate potential suppliers?

- Would you mind laying out the process you'll go through when making this decision?

COMPONENT #2: ESTABLISH THE DECISION CRITERIA

How will buyers know if your product or service is right for them? By what standard will they judge if it's better than what your competitors offer? Sometimes prospective clients will have already pondered these questions and developed the criteria they will use to evaluate potential providers. Other times they are waiting for an aha moment that will prompt them to pull the trigger and make the sale happen. Regardless, you'll always want to identify how they will be evaluating your company, product, or service, and if possible, add insights that will shape the criteria in your favor. Here's how can you can do this.

Many buyers are not sure what they'll need in a potential solution and even those who have a vision of what it should be like will still be looking to you for guidance. This is a great opportunity for you to present useful ideas that will enable buyers to think through the specific criteria that any company, product, or service must fulfill for it to be a viable option. You can introduce these ideas with phrases such as, "What many of my clients just like you have found is that . . ." or "Have you considered . . ." Then, if your potential customers like your idea, you can say, "Is this something you would want in a potential solution?" or "I'll make note of this and later on I will show you our product's capabilities in this area. Sound good?" Once you have helped them establish the criteria they'll use to make a buying decision, you can position your product or service in a way that clearly demonstrates how it will fulfill the criteria.

For example, I have a client who does this on every sale. Early in the sales process, after they have acquired an awareness of their buyers' situations, they will present some valuable, thought-provoking ideas that most buyers have not considered. This demonstrates their expertise and also helps potential customers gain a fuller understanding of what they need in a potential solution. Then my client will guide potential customers in formalizing and committing to the criteria they'll use to discern which company and product is the right one for them. (I'll show you how to do this on the next few pages.) Because this strategy gives buyers confidence and certainty, they love it! Needless to say, this also provides my client with a massive advantage over competitors because it equips them with the knowledge to compellingly show how their company and products exceed the prospective clients' criteria, which enables them to obtain the strategic commitments necessary to earn the sale.

What is this decision criteria? I have found that it contains three essential parts. Here's a look at each:

1. DETERMINE PRODUCT OR SERVICE PARAMETERS: What are the specific parameters that your product or service must fulfill for it to be a viable solution for buyers? The best way to help buyers answer this question is to first find out what problems they want solved and what their dominant buying motives are. You can then focus on how to best satisfy these two aspects of their decision criteria.

When you seek their feedback about these specific parameters you can ask questions like, "When evaluating [state the specific product or service], how will you know if any option is right for you?" or "For any product to solve the problems we've discussed, what specifically would you want it to accomplish?" When buyers begin disclosing ideas, you can then offer insights and ask them if they would want to incorporate those into their criteria. This will allow you to guide the creation of the criteria so that it is comprehensive enough to truly meet their needs.

2. IDENTIFY A TIME FRAME: By time frame I mean the specific benchmarks that dictate when buyers need a product or service to be implemented, in part or in its entirety. Many prospective customers have strict time requirements that are driven by the severity of their problems or by trigger events. It is easy to overlook

them and to ask about them in the latter stages of the sale, after it's too late to make changes to accommodate them (if they don't work with your timeline). This is always a mistake, since timing requirements influence buying decisions. What's more, if you cannot meet buyers' time constraints, they will not purchase from you. And if you don't find this out until late in the sale, you'll have wasted their time and yours.

Identify a buyer's time frame by asking questions early on in the process, such as, "Is there a certain time you will need this installed by?" or "When are you looking to have this project completed by?"

3. FACE FINANCES: In our society, there is often a stigma that surrounds talking about money openly. Because of this, many salespeople are reluctant to discuss it. However, addressing finances early in the sale is crucial, as your buyers' financial situations will heavily influence their ability to agree to the sale. Determining whether potential customers have the means to purchase your product or service will also save you time and effort. Furthermore, knowing their financial limits will help you customize a solution that works for both of you, meeting their needs within their budget while allowing you to get the sale.

When dealing with the financial issues, try to focus on two key areas that influence the trajectory of the sale:

First, strive to understand whether potential customers are financially able to purchase your product or service. This entails discovering essential information such as:

- Is there a predetermined budget for this project? If so, what is it?
- Are there any limitations or restrictions on how the budget can be spent?

- Does the buyer need to have anyone approve spending the funds? If so, whose approval is needed and what is the process for obtaining it?
- Are there any time parameters, such as fiscal year, or specific allotments that will influence the availability of the funds?

Second, consider how buyers will acquire funding if they do not have a budget set aside. The following is what you'll want to look for:

- If buyers do not have the funds set aside to purchase your product or service, how will they obtain them?
- Are the funds available to use whenever required, or does the prospect need to go to a third party to secure the funds?
- Is there a process buyers must go through to secure the funds? If so, what is that process and who is involved?

Knowing the answers to these questions will enable you to provide buyers with the assistance and resources necessary for them to obtain the funds to purchase your product or service.

CONFIRM THE DECISION CRITERIA

After you've identified the decision criteria—product or service parameters, time frame, and finances—you should obtain buy-in. This will ensure that you accurately understood your buyers and will also demonstrate that you are listening. It is not uncommon for salespeople to misunderstand or misinterpret crucial information, which leads them to make incorrect decisions regarding potential customers' desires and needs. Confirming the criteria will prevent this from happening to you.

You can verify buyers' decision criteria through an *information confirmation statement*, a declaration that substantiates the essential insights that buyers share with you.

Numerous studies have proven that these powerful statements enhance the perception of trust and rapport.[12] For example, the power of an information confirmation statement was demonstrated by some psychological experiments led by behavioral scientist Rick van Baaren. The research analyzed the impact that repeating guests' food orders back to them had on the tips servers earned. When servers verbally confirmed what their guests had ordered, tips rose by 68 percent.[13] Why? Just think about the last time you ordered something at a restaurant. Perhaps it was a ham sandwich with no cheese, or steak, medium rare. Whatever your order, did you wonder if the server got it right? Imagine how those diners featured in the research felt when the servers repeated the order back and confirmed that they understood it correctly. This improved the perception of the server's competence and the enjoyment of the dining experience, which is why tips increased so dramatically.

How can you deploy an information confirmation statement? After buyers have identified their decision criteria you say, "Just so I understand, for anything to be a possible solution for you, you said that you wanted it to . . ." and then repeat back the core criteria that they agreed was important to them. Let's stop for a minute and briefly look at the statement I just shared. Do you notice anything odd about it? In that short statement the word "you" is used three times. The word is deliberately overemphasized for the purpose of guiding buyers in assuming mental ownership of the criteria. If they perceive it as theirs, that will inspire them to remain loyal to it throughout the sale.

After you've spoken the information confirmation statement, you should obtain a commitment to it. This will further assist potential customers in taking mental ownership of it. All that is required is for you to ask, "Is that correct?" Buyers will respond with "yes" or "no." If they say no, then pinpoint the misunderstanding and make corrections. If they say yes, then progress forward knowing that you have an accurate knowledge of your buyers' decision criteria.

I have seen over and over again how sales cycles shorten and effectiveness surges when salespeople identify, confirm, and gain commitment to the prospect's decision criteria. This pivotal activity is easy to overlook, yet when performed properly it sets salespeople up for success.

We've covered a lot of ground in this chapter. But before we move on, here's a visual summary of each of the primary buying motivators:

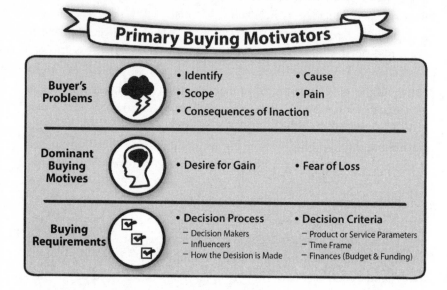

Now that you have a good understanding of each of the three primary buying motivators, let's look at how to leverage them in the sale. In the next chapter, I'll show you how to merge these buying motivators with some potent scientific principles to create high levels of value, shape perception, and even neutralize your biggest competitors.

CHAPTER 7

Creating Value, Neutralizing Competitors, and Overcoming Objections

Does what you are told about someone or something influence how you perceive and respond to that person or thing? This question was compellingly answered in a fascinating experiment conducted by behavioral scientists Myron Rothbart and Pamela Birrell.[1] The researchers showed University of Oregon students a picture of a man similar to the one below.

Though all the students viewed the same picture, their perceptions of the man were vastly different. Why? Because of the information they were told about him. Some of the students were told that he was a Nazi war criminal responsible for leading the most gruesome and heinous experiments ever performed on concentration camp victims. After learning that, they were asked to judge his facial characteristics. The students could sense from his picture that he was corrupt. They commented that his eyes were cold and his facial expression was cruel.

The rest of the students were told this man was a hero, responsible for an underground movement that enabled thousands of Jewish people to elude the Nazis, escaping almost certain death. These students gazed at the picture and perceived the man to be good. They remarked that his eyes were warm and his facial expression was kind.

This study and many others like it have proven that the way something is presented affects how people react to it. What's even more interesting is that scientists have identified the specific factors that influence how the brain perceives someone or something. This exciting, new knowledge can be applied to every area of life, including sales.

In this chapter I will show you how to use this science of influence to enhance how you create value, engage buyers, present your product or service, neutralize your biggest competitors, and overcome objections. Each of the science-based sales strategies I share will further equip you to guide your potential customers through the buying process and earn more sales.

THE SCIENCE OF VALUE CREATION

Why should buyers return your calls, answer your questions, or invest time developing a relationship with you? Imagine if you could peer inside your buyers' minds and acquire an in-depth understanding of how they assign value to relationships. This is what an insightful scientific model known as *social exchange theory* does.

Social exchange theory was put forth by social scientists John Thibaut and Harold Kelley in 1959.[2] Since that time, the relationship model has been exhaustively studied by behavioral scientists and has been supported by a substantial amount of empirical research.[3] Social exchange theory analyzes the social economics of human interactions. It affirms that engrained within human relationships is a desire to maximize value and minimize costs.[4] When the costs begin to exceed the value, the relationship will be cut off or minimized. And nowhere is this more evident than in the relationship between buyers and sellers.

Social exchange theory provides a scientific framework you can use to judge your sales behaviors to ensure you are providing potential customers with enough value to propel the relationship forward. It also reveals why some buyers ignore salespeople's calls, fail to return voice mails, cancel sales appointments, and refuse to advance further in the sales process. When potential customers behave in these ways it is because they believe that the cost of the interaction exceeds the benefits.

What is evident from the social exchange theory is that you must compellingly show potential clients why they should interact with you. If you speak about things they deem unimportant, the value they receive from the interaction goes down and so does the likelihood of the sale. Understanding this reveals the process of authentic value creation. Let me explain.

> Value is *always* defined by buyers. This is why value creation is not something you do *yourself*, but rather something that is done *with* your buyers.

Potential clients will only recognize something as valuable when it is noticeably focused on what matters to them. Make no mistake, potential customers will gladly interact with you—if you persuasively convey how you can help them in meaningful ways.

For instance, years ago I had a client who was struggling with buyers canceling their scheduled appointments with salespeople. This loss of potential customers was causing the organization's customer acquisition costs to skyrocket. The CEO of the company approached me and asked for help. After learning about the situation, I informed him that the high cancellation rate was a symptom of potential customers not perceiving enough value in keeping the appointment. I then explained how to fix this issue immediately. He was so surprised at how easily I diagnosed the problem, which had perplexed his sales leaders, that he asked me, "Are you sure?" I confidently responded that I was absolutely certain. He then had me show his sales team how to correct the cancellation problem. The company's rate of cancelled sales appointments instantly plummeted by more than 60 percent. (On the next page, I'll show you how I utilized the social exchange theory to produce this result for my client.)

The reason I was able to identify why the cancellations were occurring and how to reduce them was because I was *not* relying on my own opinion or prior experience, but on the social exchange theory. This scientific model is objectively true and when it is properly applied it will produce such positive results that those who are unaware of the science view it as almost magical.

As you saw in the previous chapter, what matters to buyers are their primary buying motivators. Once you've recognized these, you can build high levels of value by demonstrating how your company, product, or service will satisfy them. The following sales tactic will guide you in connecting the dots between the value you can provide and what matters to your prospective clients.

HOW TO DEMONSTRATE VALUE

In 1937, legendary sales trainer Elmer Wheeler authored a book titled *Tested Sentences That Sell.*[5] In the book, he shared five core principles that he promised would help salespeople be more successful. The most famous of them is "Don't sell the steak—Sell the sizzle!" In fact, the phrase has become so engrained in sales culture that few know that it was Wheeler who said it. He used the saying to remind salespeople that they should not merely emphasize the features of their product or service, but also stress the practical benefits that those features provide.

Despite the fact that the majority of salespeople agree with Wheeler's idea, many struggle to execute it. Why? Traditionally, salespeople have been taught to describe the value of their product or service through feature-benefit statements. These declarations link the features of a product or service to its assumed benefits. An example of this would be, "Our software has in-depth reporting [feature]; the advantage to you is that the reports will be very comprehensive [benefit]." However, in today's complex marketplace, feature-benefit statements have been proven to be highly ineffective!

The foundational flaw of the feature-benefit statement is that it assumes that every buyer will benefit the same way from a certain feature. Yet each prospective customer will benefit from your product or service in different ways. And this is what makes these one-size-fits-all assertions so detrimental to the success of the sale—they treat all potential customers the same, ignoring their unique perspectives and situations.

Let's be clear: buyers do not personally care about the features or benefits of your company, product, or service. What they do care about are their specific needs and how you can meet them. This is not an issue of semantics, but an important distinction that reveals how you can enhance your sales presentations. The bland, unpersuasive feature-benefit statement should be replaced with a buyer-centric way of sharing about your company, products, or services.

Many years ago I conducted some experiments in this area that led me to devise a sales tactic that will guide you in conveying your company, product, or service in a way the brain perceives value. This is also how I helped my client, who I mentioned earlier in this chapter, decrease their cancelled appointments by more than 60 percent! The sales tactic is called a Primary Buying Motivator Statement®. It reveals how one or more of the aspects of your company, product, or service fulfills at least one of the buyer's primary buying motivators. Think of this statement as a bridge that will enable you to clearly connect the dots between what your potential customers care about and the value your product or service will provide them.

You devise and execute a Primary Buying Motivator Statement® by following three straightforward steps:

1. **Identify how your company, product, or service meets your buyers' primary buying motivators.**

    As you pinpoint your potential customers' primary buying motivators—their problems, dominant buying motives, and buying requirements—you should make note of when in the sale you can convey how your product, service, or company meets them.

2. **Remind your buyers of their primary buying motivators.**

   It is recommended that you state the exact words your buyers used when describing their primary buying motivators. Mirroring their words will enhance the persuasiveness of the statement.[6] This will also grab their attention, since they will eagerly listen to every word you say when you are quoting them.

3. **Link the value that your company, product, or service delivers with buyers' primary buying motivators.**

   When you clearly and succinctly share how you can meet your prospective customers' buying motivators, it will guide them to acquire an understanding of the value they will receive from the purchase.

Here are two examples of a successful Primary Buying Motivator Statement®:

Example #1: "Sue and John, earlier you had both mentioned that for any system to be a solution for your organization it needed to have in-depth reporting. John, you specifically said that this was a top priority, and Sue, you agreed and said that detailed reporting was an absolute necessity. As I have just demonstrated, our reporting functionality is extensive and will allow you to easily generate the in-depth, detailed reports that you both need to effectively run your business."

Example #2: "Mark, a few minutes ago you mentioned that one of your primary concerns was making sure that any payroll service would file everything correctly and that if there were issues you would have support. As I mentioned, with our unique process that contains numerous checkpoints, we ensure that everything is filed correctly and if there is a question from the IRS, we'll be there with you to provide expert assistance."

IMPROVE BUYER RECEPTIVENESS
WITH RECIPROCITY

Reciprocity is a highly influential trigger of human behavior that every salesperson should utilize. In fact, decades of research have proven that it significantly increases receptiveness to persuasive requests.[7] What is reciprocity? It's a powerful social norm that affirms that you should repay others for what they have done for you. Sociologists have confirmed that reciprocity influences human behavior across virtually all cultures.[8] It has also been shown to impact how buyers respond to salespeople.

For example, one of the most famous scientific experiments on reciprocity was conducted by behavioral scientist Dennis Regan.[9] He found that if people were given an unsolicited bottle of Coca-Cola a few minutes before being asked to purchase raffle tickets, they purchased twice as many tickets as those who had been presented with the same invitation but without the gift.

What makes Regan's experiment even more intriguing is that at the conclusion of the study he asked the participants how much they liked the person who had given them the Coca-Cola. Remarkably, even those participants who did not like the seller purchased just as many raffle tickets as those who did once reciprocity was activated. In other words, reciprocity is such a strong motivator of behavior that it even trumps likability.

> Reciprocity is such a potent motivator of behavior that it even trumps likability.

Nonprofit organizations are using reciprocity to increase donations. For instance, the Disabled American Veterans organization reports that when they send out a mailer requesting donations, the median response rate is 18 percent. However, if the mailer includes a gift, such as address labels, the response rate nearly doubles to an impressive 35 percent.[10]

Even restaurant servers can use the influence of reciprocity to improve their tips. Research published in the *Journal of Applied Social Psychology* indicated that when servers gave guests a piece of candy with their check, tips rose an average of 3.3 percent.[11] The study also revealed that if the servers gave each guest two pieces of candy, the tip jumped 14.1 percent.

Reciprocity creates a debt that obligates the receiver to the giver, and instinctively causes the receiver to want to make good on the perceived debt. A prime example of how you can leverage this when selling is when hunting for new business. Regardless of the channels you use to identify potential customers (telephone, social media, networking events, or referrals), you must present enough value so that they want to develop a professional relationship with you. And this is where reciprocity can be a game changer.

To begin utilizing reciprocity when contacting potential customers, you'll need to document some insights that will provide value to them in ways that are meaningful and are aligned with what you're selling. So for example, if you sell a service that helps companies make better hiring decisions, you could offer potential customers a report that discloses three hiring strategies that are proven to reduce bad hires. This will establish your organization's expertise in this area and provide buyers with something that is useful to them, which will trigger reciprocity and demonstrate the value your service will deliver. The cost of documenting these ideas is minimal, whereas the payoff can be substantial.

Furthermore, to ensure that buyers assign high levels of value to the information, make sure that you state the monetary worth of what you are offering. This is important, because studies have verified that if something is viewed as merely a "free gift," its value is diminished in the eyes of the recipient.[12]

How can you include reciprocity in your value statements when initially communicating with buyers? To answer this question, I will show you an example of a regular value statement commonly used by salespeople, and one that includes reciprocity:

Traditional value statement: "We have helped a number of companies like yours reduce the time it takes to bring new employees up to speed. The reason for my call today is to learn more about your business and determine if we would be able to help you.

Would you be open to exploring how we might be able to reduce your hiring costs?" *(This statement sounds like everyone else's and asks the buyer to invest her valuable time in the hope of finding value.)*

Value statement with reciprocity: "We have helped a number of companies like yours reduce the time it takes to bring new employees up to speed. The reason for my call today is I wanted to share a research report our firm created that showcases three hiring strategies that are proven to reduce bad hires. We normally sell this report for $459, but I would like to give it to you at no cost, because rather than just tell you about how we can help improve your hiring process, I'd like to show you so you can see for yourself." *(Once the buyer accepts this report, he will be more likely to answer your questions because you have triggered reciprocity by providing him with something valuable.)*

Of the two value statements, which one do you think gets the most positive response? If you choose the one that leverages reciprocity, you are right. What's more, the results of using reciprocity when initially engaging buyers are often stunning. Salespeople find that using this scientific principle causes potential clients to be more receptive to entering into a dialogue with them. The reason is because they begin by offering value, and potential customers respond by giving of their time and providing the information necessary to propel the sale forward.

In short, reciprocity is just too potent to ignore. It grabs buyers' attention, shapes perception, and creates a psychological debt that intensifies customer loyalty. Use this tool of influence and you will enjoy the outcomes it produces.

BOOST YOUR INFLUENCE WITH LABELING

The process of buying requires the brain to decipher a lot of information and make a myriad of choices. Sometimes buyers can become mentally stuck and will need your help in making a decision. One way to nudge prospective customers to behave in ways that are beneficial for them is through labeling. This is when you assign a standard of behavior to a person or situation and then request conduct that is consistent with it.

Many research studies have confirmed that labeling increases the likelihood that people will comply with persuasive requests.[13] One study asked citizens about their past voting behaviors.[14] The researchers told a random sample of the participants that they were above-average citizens who were extremely likely to vote in the upcoming election. The rest were informed that there was only an average probability they would vote in future elections. When the scientists later analyzed whether the participants did vote in the upcoming election, they discovered that those who had been labeled "above average" and told they were very likely to vote actually voted at a much higher rate.

Another research study found that children who were told that they seemed like the kind of girl or boy who understood the importance of writing well were more likely to choose to work on improving their penmanship days later, in comparison to those not given the label.[15] (On a side note, be especially mindful about the labels you give children. There is considerable amount of research that shows—for better or worse—they can impact children's school performance, behavior, and self-esteem, even years later in life.)

Here are two labels you can utilize to boost compliance rates and more capably navigate the buying process:

1. Expectation Label

It is easy for the brain to get overwhelmed when deciding between products or services. This is perilous to the sale, because a confused brain will struggle to make a confident choice. It is here, when your buyers are at a mental standstill, that you can use an expectation label to prepare them to make the decision.

This sort of label is uncomplicated to construct because it is linked to an event. It essentially says that once x happens, you will know which option is the right one. This has been proven to create such a strong expectation that it sways future behavior.

Here is an example of an expectation label: "A lot of people in your situation have a hard time deciding between these two products, but what always works is when they can compare them side by side. Once they see a list of the features of both products right next to each other they always know which is the best option for them."

This label is highly influential because it first informs potential customers that their indecision is common among others who have been in a similar position. Then it replaces their current perspective that is causing the indecision with a new, optimistic standard of behavior. When salespeople learn how to create expectation labels, they find that they work profoundly well, even on the most stubborn buyers.

EXPECTATION LABEL EXERCISE

Create one expectation label that you can use in your sales context to help buyers get unstuck when evaluating numerous options.

2. Positive Label

Positive labels are built on the notion that the behavior you publicly praise will increase. These labels are extremely compelling because they are readily accepted (rarely will anyone argue with a positive label) and people feel a strong, instinctive desire to live up to them.

Consider how you would respond if a coworker told you that she thinks you are very generous and thanked you for the help you have given her in the past. Perhaps you would think to yourself, "She's right. I am a giving person who genuinely cares for others." Instantly this label becomes part of your self-concept. If a short time later that coworker asked you if she could borrow something, do you think you would be more or less likely to respond positively to her request? Research shows that the probability that you would comply with her request is extremely high, because you would be motivated to live up to the standard that she established and you embraced.

One way that you can use positive labels to sell more is to praise buyers for the past behaviors that you would like them to replicate, then make a request that corresponds with the label.

As I write about this, I remember William, the first salesperson I taught how to create positive labels. I was a vice president of sales and William reported to me. On one occasion, he came into my office frustrated by a particular buyer who was very slow in responding to him. As we talked about the situation, he assured me that the potential customer was interested and needed the product, but was just slow in replying to his calls and e-mails. These delays were stalling the sale, which was detrimental to everyone involved.

After we discussed the situation, I recommended that he use a positive label to compel the buyer to respond. I asked him if the potential client had ever responded quickly to him. He told me that there was one instance a few weeks ago when the buyer had uncharacteristically e-mailed him some information very promptly. Since we identified the behavior we wanted to duplicate, I asked William to reach out to him with a positive label focused on how quickly he had sent the information. Then I told him to make a request that would allow the potential customer to live out that label.

William excitedly went back to his desk to attempt this new strategy. Within a short time, he scurried back into my office grinning. Before I could even ask what happened, he blurted out, "You are not going to believe it. I did what you suggested and sent an e-mail with the positive label. I got a response back in less than five minutes!"

How can you use positive labels? There are many ways, but one of the most valuable is with influencers. As you may recall from Chapter 6, influencers do not make buying decisions, but offer feedback that can sway decision makers. Influencers are also important to the sale because they supply insights that will help you better meet the needs of your potential customers. When conversing with an influencer—attempting to identify decision makers, developing an internal advocate, or conducting research on a buyer or organization—you can deploy positive labels to increase compliance. Here are some examples:

- You really know a lot about this company and I really appreciate your help. Could I ask you for one last piece of information?

- I'm glad we connected. You seem to really understand this expansion and who is involved in it. Who would be in charge of purchasing printing equipment for the new location?
- It sounds like you know a lot about Mr. Wilson's schedule. When would be the best time to contact him?
- You were so helpful last time we spoke, I wonder if I could ask you for a favor.

> ## POSITIVE LABEL EXERCISE
>
> Create one positive label that you can leverage to prompt influencers to share information with you.

THE SCIENCE OF NEUTRALIZING YOUR COMPETITORS

As we saw earlier, at the conclusion of World War II and during the following decades, the U. S. government implored behavioral scientists to identify reliable methods for protecting its soldiers and citizens against enemy propaganda. In response to this request, social psychologist William McGuire published research in 1961 regarding how a persuasive message can be defended against.[16] McGuire asserted that one way to induce resistance to a persuasive appeal was through what he called the *inoculation theory*, because of its similarity to how disease inoculation works.[17] When a person is inoculated against a disease, a weakened form of the virus is injected into the healthy person. This helps the person's body to build up a resistance to the virus. Likewise, the inoculation theory is the idea that resistance to a persuasive argument can be enhanced by first exposing someone to a weak, easily defeated version of that argument.

A multitude of scientific studies have confirmed that the inoculation theory reduces the likelihood that an individual will be persuaded by a request.[18] It has been shown to keep youths from joining gangs, stop minors from smoking cigarettes, and prevent voters from being swayed by political attack ads directed at a candidate.[19] Trial lawyers also commonly utilize it in their opening statements when they declare a weak version of their opponent's case and then disclose its flaws. And you too can use the inoculation theory to neutralize your biggest competitors.

The inoculation theory is powerful because it guides buyers in preemptively developing and committing to arguments against a competing persuasive message. Then when a stronger version of the message is later presented, the person will automatically defer to the previously formed counterarguments.[20] Moreover, behavioral scientists Zakary Tormala and Richard Petty have found that once people defend themselves successfully against a persuasive appeal, they will have more confidence in their decision and be far less likely to change their mind.[21]

Does the inoculation theory impact sales? Yes! In fact, one of my clients first approached me when their sales team was struggling against a larger competitor. In the past, when they had gone head-to-head with this opponent, they won only 36 percent of the time. I devised a multipronged, science-based competitive strategy that transformed how their sales team positioned themselves against their rival. The outcome: the company's win rates jumped to 71 percent. Though there were numerous scientific principles that were used to neutralize this formidable competitor, one of the most impactful was the inoculation theory.

There are many ways you can apply the inoculation theory. The following are two situations when you can use it to knock out your competitors:

1. Immediately After Stating Distinct Value

One of the most useful times to deploy the inoculation theory is after you have shared distinct value, which, as I shared in Chapter 3, is the unique value that a buyer desires and will receive from your company, product, or service. How can you do this? After you present distinct value and obtain agreement that it is something your buyers desire, you can assert, "One thing that is unique about our company is that we are the only provider who offers [distinct value]. From what you have expressed, it sounds like a solution that did not include [distinct value] would not meet your needs, is that correct?" The prospective client will remain in agreement with what she has previously stated and respond affirmatively. You should follow up with a question such as, "If someone proposed a solution that did not include [distinct value], how would you respond?" This question will prompt the buyer to verbalize an argument against your competitors.

What just occurred in that brief interaction was extremely influential. When you conveyed the distinct value and then leveraged the inoculation theory, you inspired the prospective customer to eliminate any competitors from consideration. Perhaps most important of all, you never said anything about how your company, product, or service is better than your competitors—your buyer did.

2. After the Sale

Another time you can utilize the inoculation theory is after the sale is completed. Frequently, when you acquire new customers, competitors will continue to contact them and attempt to steal them away. The best defense against this attack is to use the inoculation theory to prepare your clients to resist your competitors.

After the sale is finalized, ask your customer, "Out of curiosity, what were the primary reasons why you chose to move forward with us?" Once he has verbalized the reason why he chose you over a competitor, you should then state, "You mentioned that you have been talking with [competitor]. It is likely that [competitor] will contact you in the next few days and try to get your business. What will you say if they contact you?" Your client is prepared to answer this question since he just informed you why he chooses you over the competitor.

Using the inoculation theory at the end of the sale will assist your buyers in thinking through and verbally committing to an argument against your competitors. This will strengthen their resolve and significantly reduce the influence of your competitors. Also, if for some reason they do waver and suggest that they may be tempted by your competitor, you can address the issue and solidify the sale.

HOW TO OVERCOME BUYERS' OBJECTIONS

When I began my second job in sales I was put through numerous weeks of new-hire training with a group of nearly thirty other salespeople. On the last day, a bunch of tables were set around the office and next to each stood one of the company's sales managers. On each table was a piece of paper with a topic written on it, which the manager would conduct deeper training on for twenty minutes. Though all the topics were intriguing, there was one table that more than 90 percent of the salespeople, myself included, chose to gather around. The reason so many flocked to the table was because the topic was important, yet inspired a strange mix of excitement and fear. What was written down on the table was one word: Objections.

These salespeople were not alone in their desire to master this significant component of selling. However, what should you do when you encounter an objection in the final stages of the sale? What I have learned over my years of selling is that the way you handle objections will determine how successful you are at overcoming them. Because of their importance, throughout the rest of this chapter I will share with you a proven way to resolve objections once they are verbalized by buyers. To begin with, I will draw your attention to three rules of effective objection handling:

RULE #1: IDENTIFY THE OBJECTION(S) QUICKLY

There is no doubt that the most unproductive place to handle objections is at the end of the sale. This is because although the objection may only have been revealed at the end of the sale, it has usually been festering for some time, corrupting the buyer's perspective. In fact, once price has been disclosed, if potential customers raise an objection, from their viewpoints they are saying no, and their objection is the reason why. This is why it is best to attempt to deliberately neutralize all objections before asking for the decision to purchase. And as I have shared in previous chapters, you can accomplish this through gaining commitments to each of the Six Whys®. However, in those instances when this is not done and an objection does arise at the final commitment of a positive buying decision, what should you do?

Addressing objections rapidly is paramount, because at this point in the sale time is not your friend. What I have found is that there is a direct correlation between the length of time it takes to close a deal and the closing rate. I refer to this concept as sales time, which was introduced in Chapter 3. Sales time affirms that regardless of the type of sale, the longer it takes for the sale to occur, the lower the probability that it will. So with every minute that goes by after price has been shown and you have asked for the sale, the likelihood of the sale decreases. This is why if an objection is presented after price, you must identify and overcome it as quickly as possible. In the ensuing pages I will show you an objection-handling process that will guide you in detecting objections quickly and easily.

RULE #2: MONITOR YOUR BUYERS' EMOTIONAL STATES

As I shared in Chapter 4, buyers' emotional states, which are the collection of emotions they are experiencing at a given time, shape perception and heavily influence buying decisions. It is common for them to fall into a negative emotional state when presenting an objection. This is because the objection focuses the mind on more pessimistic thoughts, which naturally breed negative emotions. When this occurs, you will need to shift their emotional state so that they are receptive to you and your ideas.

One quick way to do this is to refocus them on the benefits they will experience by acquiring your product or service. Asking questions that help them reevaluate and expound on these benefits will inject them with positive emotions and keep them in an upbeat, receptive emotional state as you advance the sale.

The following are some examples of how to introduce and ask these questions:

- From our conversation over the last few weeks, it seems like you are very interested in our technology. If you were to move forward, what do you feel are some of the biggest benefits you would experience?
- I appreciate your being so thoughtful and thinking this through. I know we have discussed some of your concerns, and I have answered them to your satisfaction. To be fair, we

should also look at the advantages of our inventory management system. From your perspective, if you had our system, what are some of the biggest benefits that you would experience?

- I want to make sure you are one hundred percent satisfied if you do move forward, so what benefits do you believe you would experience if we did become your supplier?

RULE #3: FOLLOW THE OBJECTION-HANDLING PROCESS

As a young salesperson, when I began following a process for overcoming objections my sales rose. Prior to that point, my objection handling was based on hope. I hoped that a profound response would pop into my mind at the right time. Sometimes it did. Other times it did not. By following a process, I became effective each time I faced an objection. Similarly, when you follow a process for overcoming objections you will become more consistent and your ability to quickly overcome an objection will be enhanced.

If you are wondering what objection process you should use, here is the one I have found is extremely effective at recognizing and resolving objections.

THE PROCESS FOR IDENTIFYING AND OVERCOMING OBJECTIONS

Step #1: Use a Softening Statement

A softening statement is a non-confrontational way of introducing a response to an objection or difference of opinion. Often, when prospective customers deliver an objection at the close, they are ready for a confrontation. Their amygdala, the part of the brain that triggers strong emotional responses, is stimulated. The aroused amygdala is ready to commandeer the brain and veer the conversation in a highly emotional, very defensive direction. A softening statement calms the amygdala down by validating the objection—not as correct, but as a thoughtful response that is legitimate and merits a reply. It conveys a respectful tone that prompts buyers to reciprocate by attentively listening to your response.

Here are some examples of softening statements:

- I understand. This is an important investment in your business.
- I can see how that could be a concern.
- That is understandable. This is an important decision.

Step #2: Isolate the Objection

Isolating is when you ask a question that guides potential customers to reveal whether they have any other objections. Frequently, buyers will only convey one objection, even though they may have many. It is imperative that you acquire an understanding of all their objections. This will ensure that you are able to quickly overcome each of them and advance the sale.

What's more, sometimes potential clients, in an effort to avoid conflict, will come up with an excuse not to complete the sale rather than outright object to it. An excuse is just a way to amicably end the sales call. What is dangerous about excuses is that they mask the real objection. Although objections block the sale, overcoming them causes the sale to advance. Asking isolation questions is the best way to identify whether a buyer's response is an excuse or a legitimate objection.

Here are some common ways to isolate an objection:

- Other than [objection], is there any other reason why you would not invest in this product?
- If [objection] were not a concern, would you like to move forward?
- In addition to [objection], is there anything else that concerns you?

Step #3: Identify the Root of the Objection

After making a softening statement and asking isolation questions, you should mentally identify which of the Six Whys® the objection is linked to. From there, you can address the objection at its source, which significantly increases the likelihood of overcoming it.

Sometimes, when an objection is uttered in an ambiguous manner, a clarifying question may be necessary to determine which of the Six Whys® it is linked to. In this scenario, you can simply ask the prospective customers for commitments to whichever of the Whys you have not previously obtained a commitment to. For instance, you can say, "Do you believe that because of the production issues we discussed, which are costing you around $1.5 million a year, that making a change now is imperative?" This question combined Why #1 and Why #2. This strategy will guide you in identifying which of the Six Whys® is behind the objection.

Step #4: Answer the Objection

After identifying which of the Six Whys® is causing the objection, you should respond to it. To prepare yourself for this, conduct an *objection anticipation exercise.* This will guide you in preemptively thinking through and documenting how you will respond to each of the root causes of an objection. The way you conduct this exercise is to list each of the Six Whys® and then write out responses to each. So for example, think of an objection that originates from a lack of commitment to Why Now?, and write out responses that address this concern. Then, when the objection arises in the sale, you simply remember your planned responses and customize them to the situation and buyer. This is a great exercise to do with a sales team or by yourself, because it allows you to create a collection of highly effective rebuttals to all the major objections you will encounter.

When creating the responses for each of the Six Whys®, you should focus on two particular areas:

1. Evidence: This is new information that will resolve a prospective customer's objection and allow them to make a new decision. Once an objection has been made and verbalized publicly, unless presented with new evidence or a way to save face, buyers will feel external and internal pressure to be consistent with their objection. This is why it is vital that the evidence you share be compelling enough for them to be able to remain consistent with their original decision, while at the same time making a new, different choice based on the additional information you have provided.

I recommend contrasting your evidence with the buyers' objections. This will allow you to persuasively frame the evidence in a way that both dwarfs the objection and is highly persuasive. For example, if the objection is the cost of your product or service, reframe cost with the monetary gain buyers will experience after purchasing.

2. Third-party Stories: These are true stories about a customer, similar to your buyers, who have used the product or service and experienced positive results. These stories allow you to address the buyers' objections in an entertaining way. I will show you how to create these highly persuasive stories in Chapter 9.

Step #5: Gain Commitment

After a salesperson has addressed the objection, she must ensure that it is overcome by asking for a commitment. The commitment should focus on whichever of the Six Whys® was prompting the objection. This will instantly reveal if the answer to the objection was persuasive enough to overcome it and advance the sale.

Here are some examples of how you can ask for commitment in this step:

- Based on what we have just discussed, would you agree that now is the best time to move forward with this investment?
- Do you believe that we are the firm that will best be able to meet the needs you expressed a few minutes ago?
- Since you agree that the ROI on this service would more than justify the investment, are you ready to move forward?

WHY USE THESE STRATEGIES AND INSIGHTS

The insights in this chapter will guide you in aligning your sales process with how the brain perceives and responds to information. As a result, these strategies should not be thought of as something you do to others, but something you do with and for them.

Now that you have a firm grasp on how to create value, engage potential customers, neutralize competitors, and overcome objections, let's turn our attention to one of the most celebrated parts of the sale: closing. In the next chapter, I'll show you a revolutionary, science-based way of closing that will improve your ability to generate more sales.

CHAPTER 8

Closing Redefined:
Obtaining Strategic Commitments

Imagine being led into a room where a large, heavy candle, a box of tacks, and a book of matches are lying on a table. You are informed that your task is to figure out a way to adhere the candle to the wall, using only the three items on the table, so that the wax does not drip on to the table. How would you solve this problem?

Many who have attempted to complete this exercise try to use the tacks to hold the candle to the wall. However, this doesn't work because the tacks are too small to secure the large candle. Others light a match and melt some wax on one side of the candle and try to use the melted wax to adhere the candle to the wall. Though it's a creative solution, it's also unsuccessful.

The only solution that works is to take the tacks from the box and use them to fasten the empty box to the wall, then place the candle in the box and light it.

This is known as the "candle problem," which was created by psychologist Karl Duncker and published in 1945.[1] Since then, it has been used by many behavioral scientists in a variety of research experiments to analyze problem-solving ability. One finding that has emerged from these studies is that regardless of age, socioeconomic status, or level of education, it usually takes participants between five and ten minutes to solve the puzzle.

The reason the brain initially struggles to identify the solution to this simple dilemma is because of what behavioral scientists refer to as *functional fixedness*. When participants look at the items on the table, they initially assume that each has only one function. This limits their ability to recognize the dual function of the box: initially to hold the tacks, and then the candle. It's only after they begin to think outside the box (pun intended) that they are able to summon the creativity necessary to identify the solution.

Many salespeople experience this same functional fixedness when it comes to closing sales. Traditionally, closing has been defined as the time during the sales process when a salesperson asks buyers to commit to purchasing the product or service she is selling. This commitment occurs at the conclusion of the sales message and closes the sale (hence the use of the word "closing"). However, is this way of closing the one you should use when you sell? The evidence would suggest that it's not.

To understand how we should close sales, we need to first reexamine how we view closing. The more that closing strategies mirror the mental steps the brain takes when buying, the more successful they will be. This is why the current method of closing is highly unproductive because it clashes with how the brain instinctively formulates a purchasing decision.

For too long, closing has focused *only* on the commitment at the end of the sale. This limited perspective (functional fixedness) has caused many to miss the key to effective closing: small commitments throughout the sale. A multitude of scientific studies have confirmed that the brain uses the commitments that it has already made as its reference points for constructing a much larger choice on a related matter. In other words, small commitments naturally lead to bigger ones. This is why the best way to lead someone into any sort of major decision, such as a buying decision, is to first guide him in making a series of small commitments that are consistent with the larger decision. Let's take a look at why this is the case.

> The best way to lead someone into making any sort of major decision, such as a buying decision, is to first guide him in making a series of small commitments that are consistent with the larger decision.

WHY SMALL COMMITMENTS ARE THE BUILDING BLOCKS OF THE SALE

In a now legendary social experiment, behavioral scientists Jonathan Freedman and Scott Fraser led a team that canvassed a California neighborhood asking residents, "Would you allow us to put a billboard in your front yard?" Posing as volunteer workers, the researchers showed each homeowner a picture that clearly portrayed how the large sign would obstruct the view of their house. Inscribed on the billboard was the recommendation DRIVE CAREFULLY. Only 17 percent agreed to the request; most residents refused to allow the billboard to be erected on their front lawn.

However, when the research team went to a nearby neighborhood and posed the same request to its residents, they were shocked by the response. A staggering 76 percent of the homeowners in the second California neighborhood agreed to allow the billboard to be placed in their front yard. After witnessing the stark contrast between the two neighborhoods, one of the research assistants commented, "I was simply stunned at how easy it was to convince some people and how impossible to convince others."[2]

The reason the second group of homeowners overwhelmingly agreed to the daunting appeal was because they had received a prior visit from the researchers. Two weeks earlier, the research team had asked them if they would be willing to display a small, three-inch sign that read BE A SAFE DRIVER in a front window of their house. This minor request was met with widespread acceptance. Freedman and Fraser concluded that this seemingly trivial commitment influenced the residents to such an extent that the vast majority complied with the larger request to allow a billboard promoting safe driving to be placed in their front yard soon after.

Freedman and Fraser's findings were published in the *Journal of Personality and Social Psychology* in 1966.[3] Since then, there have been many similar studies confirming that once a commitment is made, the brain will begin to act in a manner that is consistent with it.[4] For example, small commitments have been shown to boost charitable giving, increase show rates for blood drives, and even reduce smoking.[5]

Commitments, even seemingly minor ones, are highly influential and shape the outcome of the sale. Why? Because they change future behavior.

So now let's take what I've shared about the importance of small commitments and apply it to closing. Because when we do, the data reveals a very clear picture: closing is not one large commitment that occurs at the conclusion of the sale, but a series of small, strategic commitments that occur throughout the sale.

CLOSING WITH STRATEGIC COMMITMENTS

As I disclosed in Chapter 3, though a buying decision may be revealed at the end of the sale, it is being cultivated during the entire sale. For the brain to construct the decision to purchase a product or service it must make certain foundational commitments to the Six Whys®.

THE SIX WHYS®

1. Why Change?
2. Why Now?
3. Why Your Industry Solution?
4. Why You and Your Company?
5. Why Your Product or Service?
6. Why Spend the Money?

These small, strategic commitments are the building blocks of the sale, because they lead buyers through a natural progression of consent that enables the larger decision to purchase.

As a result, the final commitment to a buying decision that occurs at the end of the sale is intertwined and even dependent on the series of essential commitments to the Six Whys® that buyers have already made. Ignoring these necessary commitments during the sale and only focusing on the final one at its conclusion forces the brain to take an unnatural mental leap that produces negative feelings of pressure and anxiety. Yet this is exactly what traditional closing strategies have done.

So how should you approach closing? No longer can it be viewed as the event at the end of the sales process when salespeople obtain one isolated commitment, because that does not reflect what closing is supposed to do—guide potential customers through the decision-making process and into a positive buying decision. Because the brain constructs a decision to purchase incrementally, throughout the sale, closing should be thought of in a similar way.

As I shared in Chapter 3, here's a reminder of what this process looks like.

SCIENCE-BASED CLOSING METHODOLOGY

(Strategic Commitments Throughout the Sale)

By now I hope you are convinced that commitments are a central part of buying and, as a result, selling. But to acquire a full awareness of how to use commitments to enhance your influence and close more sales, I'll need to share with you the reasons why they are so influential. The research shows that commitments impact and even determine future decisions because they activate two powerful psychological motivators. Here's a quick look at both of them.

WHY BUYERS DESIRE TO BE CONSISTENT WITH THEIR COMMITMENTS

Why are some juries unable to reach a verdict? This was the question that social psychologists Norbert Kerr and Robert MacCoun sought to answer in a unique study that analyzed the factors that hinder juries from arriving at decisions. The conclusion of this research suggested that hung juries are far more likely when jurors express their views in the presence of others, instead of by anonymous ballot.[6] Why? Because once jury members had shared their viewpoint publicly they felt the need to be consistent and not abandon it.

Behaving in a manner that is in line with your words is something others expect you to do. When people act in ways that are inconsistent, they are often described as liars, hypocrites, untrustworthy, or worse. This strong social pressure is what causes the public commitments buyers make within the sale to be so influential.

But consistency is not just a social norm (we expect it of others); it's also an instinctive desire that each of us has. In fact, the urge to be consistent is so strong that it will often override a person's thinking. Numerous scientific studies published in the *Journal of Personality and Social Psychology* have found that when a person makes a public commitment, the intrinsic desire to be consistent with that commitment can be so intense that the person's belief in what he or she committed to is strengthened.[7] In other words, one way to bolster your potential customers' resolve to follow through on a commitment is to encourage them to state it publicly.

When acclaimed behavioral scientists Edwin Locke and Gary Latham conducted a meta-analysis of thirty-five years of research studies on goal attainment, they found that there was one piece of advice that prevails within this scholarly literature: You are significantly more likely to achieve your goals if you state them publicly. Locke and Latham explain, "Making a public commitment . . . makes one's actions a matter of integrity in one's own eyes and in those of others."[8]

This is one of the reasons why commitments are so powerful; people feel the need to be consistent with them. Consistency is the glue that holds commitments in place. It's what makes defying them feel wrong.

So how can you use the principle of consistency to close more sales? The key is to leverage it throughout the sale by asking for strategic commitments, like the Six Whys®, which will increase compliance and improve your sales effectiveness. For instance, you can use the principle of consistency to speed up your sales cycle. Here's how.

Imagine that you are going to meet with numerous decision makers from a company. Though you have requested they all be present and even informed them of the benefits of having all of them at the appointment, how do you know they will be there? Or at the conclusion of a sales call, when you and your prospective customers talk about next steps, what can you do to ensure that they actually follow through on what you have suggested? The answer to both scenarios is found in using the principle of consistency in your favor by not making requests or recommendations. Instead, ask for commitments. Here are some examples:

- If for any reason something does change and either you or
  your CIO or VP of sales will not be able to be present at the
  appointment, will you send me an e-mail or give me a call so
  we can reschedule?
- Will you talk to your production manager about these
  requirements before our next meeting at the end of the
  month?
- Will you send me over the revised agreement by Monday, so I
  can review it before our appointment on Tuesday?

All of these questions ask for small commitments that, once made, will spur buyers to be consistent with what they have promised. I have seen many businesses improve their sales results by effectively triggering the principle of consistency. For example, when one company I trained began asking for commitments that all decision makers be present at sales calls, productivity surged, which caused sales to grow by 12 percent.

But perhaps my favorite example of how the principle of consistency can transform a business comes from a piece in the *New York Times* titled, "In War Against No-Shows, Restaurants Get Tougher." The article featured a popular eatery in Chicago named Gordon that was losing $900,000 a year because of its 30 percent no-show rate.[9] Remarkably, the restaurant was able to reduce its no-shows to less than 10 percent by changing how they confirmed reservations. In the past, when taking a reservation a Gordon's employee would say, "Please call us if you change your plans." Even with this plea, three out of every ten reservations resulted in a no-show. However, once the statement was changed to a question that inspired a commitment—"Will you call us if you change your plans?"—no-shows plummeted.

The principle of consistency is just too powerful to not actively use it when selling. I encourage you to think through your sales process and identify where you are making suggestions and instead ask for small commitments. When you do, you will find compliance rates will rise and so will your sales.

HOW COMMITMENTS CHANGE
SELF-PERCEPTION

When you vote for a political candidate, are you more likely to believe your candidate will win after you vote or just before?

Dennis Regan and fellow behavioral scientist Martin Kilduff conducted experiments that analyzed this question.[10] On Election Day, the researchers visited numerous polling stations and asked voters before they placed their votes what they believed was the likelihood that the candidate they were going to vote for would win the election. A short time later, after the voters placed their votes, the scientists asked the same people the identical question. Regan and Kilduff reported, "The results showed that people were significantly more confident of their candidates' chances after voting than before."[11]

Another study, which was conducted at the unusual venue of a horse race, came to the same conclusions as Regan and Kilduff had. The psychologists leading the study approached participants, who were going to place a bet, and asked them how confident they were that the horse they were going to bet on would win the race.[12] Later, after those who had been surveyed made their bets, the researchers again approached them and asked them the same question. The study found that people were more confident their horse would win the race after betting than prior to it.

In both of these experiments, participants were more convinced of their decision after they committed to it than they were just before. Yet why would the act of voting or placing a bet boost one's confidence? The reason is because a change occurred after the commitment was made. The change did not occur in the candidates or on the racetrack. The change occurred in the people who made a commitment *because* of the commitment. Here's why.

In 1972, behavioral scientist Daryl Bem proposed a groundbreaking concept he called *self-perception theory*. He asserted that "Individuals come to 'know' their own attitudes, emotions, and other internal states partially by inferring them from observations of their own overt behavior."[13] Since then, the self-perception theory has been scrutinized and tested through many scientific studies and today is considered a well-established principle of behavioral science.[14] And this reveals another side of what commitments do: They change beliefs.

Think of it like this: as you saw in Chapter 4, your beliefs and emotions influence your behaviors. However, it is equally true that how you behave shapes your beliefs and emotions.

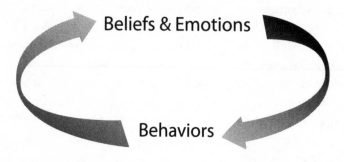

Beliefs & Emotions

Behaviors

As you observe your behaviors, your beliefs and emotions are affected and consequently so is your self-image. Saul Kassin, Steven Fein, and Hazel Rose Markus summarize this phenomenon: "When people are gently coaxed into saying or doing something, and when they are not otherwise certain about how they feel, they often come to view themselves in ways that are consistent with their public statements and behavior."[15] Behavioral scientists maintain that when people make commitments, those commitments impact their self-image, which shapes their future behavior.[16]

To explain this, let's go back to the Freedman and Fraser study from earlier in the chapter. They found that obtaining a small commitment from homeowners before a larger request caused compliance rates to skyrocket. The reason for this drastic increase was summarized by the researchers this way: "Once he has agreed to a request, his attitude may change. He may become, in his own eyes, the kind of person who does this sort of thing, who agrees to requests made by strangers, who takes action on things he believes in, who cooperates with good causes."[17] What these researchers are describing is the self-perception theory.

This is also why those in Daniel Howard's research experiments (explored in Chapter 1) were more likely to invite salespeople into their home after positively answering the question, "How are you feeling this evening?" Because the homeowners declared they were feeling good, they actually began to feel better and this predisposed them to comply with the request.

What the research shows is that after buyers make commitments they will begin to see themselves in light of those commitments.[18] This altered self-image will guide them into making more and even deeper commitments that are consistent with the previous ones they have made.

> After buyers make commitments they begin to see themselves in light of those commitments. This altered self-image guides them into making more and even deeper commitments that are consistent with the previous ones they have made.

For example, one of my clients sells in a very competitive industry. They are priced toward the top of the marketplace and yet they dominate competitors. Why? They win by focusing buyers on the quality of their products. However, it is interesting that when their future customers are asked, before meeting with a salesperson, the factors that will determine whether they purchase or not, price is always first and quality is far down on the list, almost a nonfactor.

So how does my client shift their buyers' focus in their favor? They help their prospective customers make small, strategic commitments to quality over cost. What happens is actually quite amazing. After agreeing to these commitments, the customers' beliefs actually change. They become the kind of people who believe in quality. What's particularly revealing, though, is that when my client sends out postsales surveys, customers report the number one reason they chose to purchase was quality, while price—the original factor they picked as the most important—is rarely even mentioned.

There is no doubt that commitments are a central part of buying and, thus, selling. But how do you obtain them? I have found that the best way to generate commitments is by using questions commonly referred to as *trial closes*. There are two classifications of trial closes: involvement and commitment. You should use both, since they have been proven to enrich your customers' view of you (peripheral route of influence) and enhance the persuasiveness of your message (central route of influence).

INVOLVEMENT TRIAL CLOSES

Involvement trial closes are an important sales tool that will enhance the effectiveness of every salesperson. These second-level questions (second-level questions were discussed in Chapter 5) should be used throughout the sale, because they guide buyers to actively participate in the sales process. What's more, they also help prospective customers think through and affirm the concepts of value that the Six Whys® are built on.

Involvement trial closes have two specific functions:

Function #1—Implying Ownership: Answering this sort of involvement trial close prompts prospective customers to envision what it would be like to own your product or service. This mental imagery has a surprisingly strong impact.

For example, imagine that you sip some lemon juice. What does it taste like? As you briefly think about lemon juice, notice the sensations occurring in your mouth. You'll find that something totally beyond your control occurred—you began to salivate more and you could almost taste the tartness of the lemon juice.[19] What happened? You just experienced the power of mental imagery.

You can use mental imagery to help your buyers imagine owning your product or service because when you do, it makes it more likely they will purchase. Why? There is a wealth of scientific research that has proven that visualizing a decision triggers the brain to create new synaptic connections that are associated with the action, which makes it easier to make the choice.[20]

Composing these trial closes is relatively easy. Below are some examples of involvement trial closes that imply ownership, and that are commonly used across a variety of sales environments:

- Would you want the installation to occur during normal business hours or would you need the software installed after business hours?
- If you were to invest in training, would you take advantage of our classroom training or utilize our online training?
- Of these three service options, which one would best meet your organization's needs?
- If you were to move forward and invest in this product, would you use our financing or put the down payment on a credit card?
- If you did have this product, how would you utilize it?

I recommend using involvement trial closes that imply ownership whenever it fits naturally into the conversation. The most common time in the sales process is when discussing features and functions of your product or service. And though the buyer is not committing to anything, she is imagining owning your product or service, which increases the likelihood that she eventually will.

Function #2—Confirming Value: These trial closes have been proven to amplify the persuasiveness of sales messages because they guide buyers in mentally digesting and verbally appraising an assertion of value.

Interestingly enough, these involvement trial closes have actually been analyzed in numerous scientific studies.[21] The behavioral scientists who conducted the research were unfamiliar with the sales terminology "involvement trial close" and, as a result, referred to them as *tag questions*. The researchers concluded that when credible presenters with strong messages use tag questions it amplifies the persuasiveness of their appeal. Moreover, behavioral scientists Robert Gass and John Seiter note that tag questions help people mentally assess a compelling message.[22]

These trial closes also help buyers develop a sense of ownership in discerning the value of your company, product, or service.

This matters because, as Harvard Business School's Thomas Steenburgh suggests, "A critical component . . . is that the prospect feels that they participated in defining the benefits that would be attained or, better still, that they defined them on their own. This leads to stronger commitment and a sense of urgency to complete the purchase. It also increases the prospect's willingness to 'sell' the product to others in the decision-making unit."[23]

The following are an array of common involvement trial closes that are focused on confirming value:

- Does this program meet all the requirements that your team laid out?
- What does the fact that we have an A+ rating with the Better Business Bureau say about our company?
- Is investing in a product that has a comprehensive warranty important to you?
- It sounds like having a service contract is essential. May I ask why that is?
- Does it make sense that so many people are choosing science-based sales training?
- Waiting to install this equipment will cost you more than $9,500 per week, won't it?

INVOLVEMENT TRIAL CLOSE EXERCISE

Create four involvement trial closes (two implying ownership and two confirming value). I recommend that you plan where in your sales process you will deploy each. Then practice them beforehand so that your delivery is engaging and persuasive. If you do, you'll find that it will help you create deeper levels of buyer engagement and obtain buy-in to the value that your company, product, or service provides.

COMMITMENT TRIAL CLOSES

Commitment trial closes are the key to successfully closing sales. Why? Because they ask buyers for active, verbal commitments that will predictably change their future behavior. These trial closes are vital to your sales success because they are what you will use to obtain the strategic commitments you need to naturally guide the sale on a progression of consent and into a positive buying decision.

What makes commitment trial closes different from involvement ones? Involvement trial closes guide potential customers in envisioning owning your product or service and acquiring buy-in to your statements of value. Commitment trial closes do just what their title suggests—they guide buyers in making commitments.

> Commitments demand action from buyers and predictably change their future behaviors.

When salespeople fail to obtain strategic commitments throughout the sales process, they will often mistake their buyers' comprehension of an idea with commitment to it. Now, there's no doubt that comprehension matters in selling; if people don't understand what you are communicating you will always struggle to influence them. However, comprehension is not enough. Even though prospective customers may mumble phrases like, "That makes sense," or nod their heads when shown some significant piece of information, this does not mean they will act on what you have presented.

I have witnessed salespeople on sales calls not ask for any commitments and just assume that buyers are in agreement with them. Then later, when these buyers say no to the sale or just refuse to return their calls, the salespeople have no idea why. Because they did not ask for commitments, they never understood their prospective customers' viewpoints enough to know why the sale died or what could have been done to save it.

The following are a sampling of commitment trial closes taken from a variety of sales situations:

- Based on what you have shared, this problem sounds like something you need to solve immediately, is that correct?
- Would you ever invest in software that did not include this feature?
- Knowing what you now know, would you ever attempt to create a solution internally?
- Is your organization committed to resolving the production issues that you disclosed?
- Considering what you have learned about our company, is there any reason why you would not choose us to be your provider?

Before we go further into creating commitment trial closes, I need to share with you a powerful scientific strategy that will significantly enhance your ability to obtain positive responses to them. Although it is important that you ask for commitments throughout the sale, what is equally important is *how* you ask for those commitments. Once you learn how to present commitment trial closes in the way that will cause the brain to perceive them in a positive light, your compliance rates will surge and so will your sales effectiveness.

HOW TO ASK FOR STRATEGIC COMMITMENTS

How can you improve the likelihood that you'll obtain the strategic commitments necessary to close more sales? To answer this question, I'll need to introduce you to a powerful scientific framework known as *choice architecture*. What is choice architecture? It's the science of how to structure choices in a way that is consistent with how the brain formulates decisions. Research has proven that the brain makes decisions contextually. As a result, the way a choice is presented shapes how it will be perceived and whether or not it will be acted on. Let me provide you with an example of this that is easy to spot and that you will instantly relate to: menu engineering.

When the principles of choice architecture are applied to restaurant menus, surveys show that sales go up by as much as 10 percent. Here are a few secrets of menu psychology:

- Placing an entrée in a box or putting a graphic next to it draws the eye and significantly improves the chance that it will be chosen.
- Customers will pay extra for an item that is labeled attractively. Restaurants can charge you much more for "Fresh-Squeezed Florida Orange Juice" than mere "Orange Juice."
- Menu items at the top or bottom of a list are twice as likely to be chosen than those in the middle.
- Dollar signs increase the perception of price and drive down average ticket size.
- Placing high-priced entrées at the top of a list creates an anchor and makes it much more likely that patrons will choose one of the more expensive entrees. In fact, one study found that this alone increased sales by 25 percent!

Just as the way menu items are presented affects whether or not they will be chosen, so too the way commitments are presented influences how buyers will respond to them.

When I originally studied the science of choice architecture searching for the best way to present a commitment trial close, I stumbled on the psychological principle of *priming*. This concept affirms that exposure to one idea shapes how you will respond to subsequent information. For example, think back to the last scary movie you watched. After watching the movie, you were keenly aware of any unusual noise in your home. Though you may have heard the same noise before, this time it caused you to jump. Why? The scary movie put your mind in a heightened state of awareness to strange sounds.

Priming has a profound effect on the brain. Even things that seem insignificant can prime the mind to act in very predictable ways. One fascinating example of this is found in an experiment conducted by behavioral scientists Charles Lee, Sally Linkenauger, and three colleagues.[24] The researchers randomly split forty-one amateur golfers into two groups. The first group was led, one at a time, to a putting mat. Each golfer was handed a putter and asked to estimate the diameter of the hole at the end of the mat. Then the golfer was allowed to attempt ten putts.

The second group of golfers had a similar experience as the first group, except for the fact that as each golfer was handed the putter he was told that it had once belonged to professional golfer Ben Curtis. Astonishingly, this seemingly insignificant piece of information had an astounding affect upon the golfers.

Though both groups were asked to answer the same question and used the identical putter, those golfers who believed that the putter belonged to Ben Curtis perceived that the diameter of the hole was 9 percent larger than the other group thought it was. Furthermore, these golfers also experienced an increase in performance as they sank 32 percent more putts than the golfers who had been told nothing of the putter's history.

As I applied this scientific insight and conducted research on how to create an environment within the sale that would nudge buyers to agree with a commitment trial close, one finding was proven over and over again: the best way to receive a positive response to a commitment trial close was to first ask an involvement trial close.

Involvement trial closes prepare the brain for future commitments by guiding it in affirming the value that the commitment is based on. This, I found, significantly increases the probability that the commitment will be agreed to. Here are three examples that demonstrate the impact of using both trial closes together:

EXAMPLE #1

Involvement trial close:
>   Waiting to install this equipment will cost you more than $9,500 per week, won't it?

Buyer's response:
>   Yes, I guess it would.

Commitment trial close:

> Knowing that, is there any reason why you would delay investing in this equipment?

Buyer's response:

> No, it would be foolish to wait.

EXAMPLE #2

Involvement trial close:

> Based on what you have shared, it seems like this feature is important to you. May I ask why?

Buyer's response:

> It will enable us to increase our efficiency.

Commitment trial close:

> Would you ever invest in software that did not include this feature?

Buyer's response:

> Definitely not.

EXAMPLE #3

Involvement trial close:

> Does it make sense that so many people are moving away from conjecture-based sales training?

Buyer's response:

> Sure, I understand the problems with it.

Commitment trial close:

> Is there any reason why you would invest in conjecture-based sales training ever again?

Buyer's response:

> No, I definitely want sales training that is based on science.

COMMITMENT TRIAL CLOSE EXERCISE

Use the two involvement trial closes confirming value that you created in the previous exercise, and now craft two commitment trial closes that are in line with the value those involvement trial closes affirmed. I encourage you to practice using them and you will notice that your ability to generate the strategic commitments necessary to close more sales will improve.

HOW TO HANDLE NONCOMMITTAL RESPONSES

By using the strategies and tactics I've shared in this chapter you will significantly increase the chances that you obtain strong commitments from your buyers. That being said, there will be times when buyers will answer your commitment trial closes with noncommittal responses. By noncommittal response, I am referring to any reaction that is not a strong commitment. Here's how to address the two most common forms of noncommittal replies:

1. **Objection:** When buyers refuse to make a commitment and instead utter an objection, you should seek to diagnose what is prompting the objection and then resolve it. This often means clearing up a misunderstanding, presenting new information, or reframing the situation. (Information on the process for overcoming objections is in Chapter 7.) Once you have received buy-in that the objection has been addressed, you can then confidently ask buyers to respond with a commitment.

If you cannot settle the objection that is preventing the commitment, make a mental note and revisit the commitment after presenting some new, relevant information later on in the sales process.

2. **Weak Responses:** Imagine you loaned a friend $500 and you asked him if he could repay you the full amount by the end of the month. If he responded, "Maybe . . . I will see if I can have it to you by then," how confident would you be that you'd get your $500 back

by then? I'd guess your answer would be "Not very." Just as your friend's lack of a concrete yes to your question likely indicates he won't be able to repay you by the end of the month, weak responses to strategic commitments often indicate a problem with the sale.

When dealing with an indecisive response it is important to realize that potential customers are not saying no. To the contrary, their reaction indicates that they are actually leaning in your direction, but they are not yet ready to say yes to the commitment. So how can you guide them into making the commitment? I have found that the most effective way to address a feeble response is to ask buyers to explain their response, but in your favor. You do this by asking potential customers second-level questions that help them contemplate and confirm the ideas that the commitment is built on.

Let's apply this strategy to the scenario that was shared in Example #2. You ask the commitment trial close, "Would you ever invest in software that did not include this feature?" The buyer answers, "I see your point, but I want to think about it more." You can answer this noncommittal response by saying, "I understand. It sounds like you are interested in this feature. If you did have software that included it, how would that benefit your organization?" Now he is prompted to think through and publicly state the value that would support a commitment. After this has occurred, you can ask, "That being said, is there any reason why you would ever consider software that did not include this feature?" Your buyer is now very likely to make the commitment.

Since correctly handling indecisive responses is such a central part of obtaining commitments, below is another example of what this looks like in the real-world sales dialogue shared in Example #1:

Involvement trial close:
> Waiting to install this equipment will cost you more than $9,500 per week, won't it?

Buyer's response:
> Yes, I guess it would.

Commitment trial close:

> Knowing that, is there any reason why you would delay investing in this equipment?

Buyer's indecisive response:

> I am not sure. I still need to think about it.

Shifting the buyer's perspective:

> It doesn't sound like you are excited about waiting to correct this issue. May I ask what your primary concerns are about waiting?

Buyer's response:

> Well . . . I guess not resolving this would be very expensive and it's definitely hurting our productivity.

Commitment trial close:

> That makes sense. Based on your concerns about how expensive this issue is and how it is hurting your productivity, do you really want to wait to purchase this equipment?

Buyer's response:

> No. When you put it like that, it does not make sense to wait.

WHEN TO ASK FOR THE SALE

How do you know when buyers are ready to purchase? Ironically, this is one of the questions that stump most salespeople, managers, and trainers. The answer to this important question used to be a mystery. However, when you align your selling process with how the brain constructs a buying decision, you know exactly when they are ready to purchase. The answer is after the sales equation (shared in Chapter 3) has been fulfilled. You'll recall that the sales equation is: $BD = f(SW, ES)$. The equation confirms that a buying decision (BD) is a function (f) of the Six Whys® (SW) and the buyer's emotional state (ES). In short, it means that if qualified buyers commit to each of the Six Whys® and adopt a positive emotional state, then they are ready to make the final commitment to a positive buying decision.

HOW TO ASK FOR THE SALE

Asking for the sale is simply asking the buyer for the final commitment to purchase. Provided you have already obtained all of your essential commitments, this is a straightforward process.

There are two recommended ways to obtain this last commitment. Both are field-tested and work in the real world of selling. You can decide which best matches the tone of the sales call and the personality of your potential customers.

1. **Use a closing statement:** This is a crisp, assumptive statement that leads potential customers into a positive buying decision. Some examples of these are:

   - The next step would be . . .

   - Here is the contract I need you to sign. It states . . .

   - To begin, I will need to have you sign an agreement . . .

   - The initial investment to begin this project is . . .

2. **Use a closing question:** This is a question that is posed to buyers and that when answered positively will result in a positive buying decision. Closing questions are succinct and very direct. There is no need to use any elaborate closing strategies at this point in the sale because if your potential clients have committed to each of the Six Whys® and are in a positive emotional state, it would be abnormal not to ask them to purchase, since that is the next logical step. Some examples of closing questions are:

   - Would you like to move forward?

   - Are you ready to give [your company] a try?

   - The next logical step would be to finalize the contract, wouldn't you agree?

   - When would you like us to schedule the installation?

PUTTING IT ALL INTO PRACTICE

When you begin to think about closing the sale as a series of strategic commitments, it brings clarity, focus, and intentionality to the sales process. Over the years, I have seen this perspective positively transform sales effectiveness. One of the salespeople I trained, who used strategic commitments to improve his closing rate by nearly 60 percent, summed up the reason for his improved results with the following statement: "Commitments unlock the sale. In fact, it's just so easy when you get your commitments."

I couldn't have said it any better.

CHAPTER 9

Five Science-Based
Sales Presentation Strategies

Throughout my career I have given sales presentations, thousands of them. Sometimes they were face-to-face with groups of buyers, other times on the phone with only a single decision maker. Over the years, one thing has become very apparent: sales presentations matter. In fact, there's a lot of evidence that they significantly impact the decision-making process. According to the research and advisory firm SiriusDecisions, buyers rank them as one of the most important factors in their buying process.[1] Hillary Chura addressed this in her *New York Times* article "Um, Uh, Like Call in the Speech Coach," in which she cites numerous examples of how sales presentations determine whether funding requests are met with acceptance or rejection.[2]

The reason sales presentations matter is because they are the primary way that a sales message (central route of influence) is conveyed. It's how buyers' knowledge requirements are satisfied, so that they are able to confidently commit to each of the Six Whys®.

Yet have you ever thought about what makes a sales presentation effective? Why does one increase the likelihood of the sale, while another reduces the probability of the purchase? There are many scientific studies that have decoded how the brain determines if a presentation is engaging and persuasive or confusing and uninspiring. Once you begin applying this science, you will be equipped to present in ways that will arouse buying behaviors.

Here are five science-backed sales strategies that will guide you in delivering sales presentations that will effectively convey your ideas and amplify buyer receptiveness:

STRATEGY #1: LESS REALLY IS MORE

Try to solve the following puzzle as quickly as possible:

> A bat and a ball cost $1.10 in total. The bat costs $1.00 more than the ball.
> How much does the ball cost?

What was your answer?

The majority of those who have encountered this classic problem instantly conclude the ball costs 10 cents. However, this is incorrect. If the ball costs 10 cents that would make the bat, being a dollar more, $1.10. This would bring the total for both to $1.20.

After reading that, you may have figured out that the right answer is that the ball costs 5 cents and the bat $1.05, which together equal $1.10. (If you got the answer wrong, don't feel bad, more than 80 percent of university students given the puzzle get it wrong too!)

Why does the brain automatically assume the ball costs 10 cents before doing the math that would make it clear that answer isn't correct? The reason has to do with how our brains are wired. In an effort to conserve mental energy, the brain makes assumptions that reduce the cognitive effort required to form a conclusion. This is why it is so easy to presume the ball costs 10 cents. Your brain, almost instinctively, supposes the answer without thinking through the puzzle. Here's why.

Our minds can perform incredible feats, but they also have limited cognitive resources. Research across a variety of scientific disciplines, such as neuroscience and cognitive psychology, have proven the brain can only process a small amount of information at any given time.[3] And once the brain's threshold is surpassed, its capacity to cognitively grasp information is severely diminished.

For instance, George Miller, the great cognitive psychologist, wrote about the brain's limited capacity to be attentive to and process information in his famous piece, "The Magical Number Seven, Plus or Minus Two: Some Limits of Our Capacity for Processing Information," which was published in *Psychological Review*.[4] Miller demonstrated that the brain can only grasp a small amount of information at one time. This is why phone numbers, excluding area codes, are only seven digits. Scientists maintain that if phone numbers were more than seven numerals they would be forgotten with far greater frequency.

When too many options are presented to the brain it has trouble making a buying decision, which drives down sales. Social scientists Sheena Iyengar and Mark Lepper demonstrated this in a well-known experiment they conducted at an upscale grocery store in Menlo Park, California.[5] The researchers set up a tasting booth that allowed consumers to sample an assortment of jams. The first week, twenty-four different jams were available for patrons to taste. Despite many people trying the jams, only 3 percent purchased any. The following week, the researchers went back to the store, but this time they offered only six jams for the shoppers to taste. Sales skyrocketed by 900 percent! The conclusion that this and other experiments reached is that limiting the amount of selections boosts buying behaviors.

Why is this the case? It does not take much at all for the brain to become overwhelmed when evaluating numerous products, even those as simple as jam. When the brain reaches its cognitive limits, it becomes stunned and confused.[6] This will cause buyers either to refuse to make a buying decision or, if they do purchase, to be plagued with doubt over whether they made the right decision.

For example, some enlightening research published in the *Journal of Personality and Social Psychology* analyzed what influenced the participation of nearly eight hundred thousand employees in their company sponsored 401(k) plans.[7] The study disclosed that when a company provided an abundance of investment options, an alarming amount of employees declined to participate in the 401(k) programs. One company that participated in the assessment only gave its employees two mutual funds to choose to invest in. In spite of offering so few options, an impressive 75 percent of its employees chose to participate. Another organization, which offered its employees fifty-nine different mutual funds to choose from, had a participation rate of only 60 percent. The analysis of the overall participation rate revealed that for every ten investment opportunities, employee participation declined by 2 percent.

Likewise, many salespeople frequently hinder the effectiveness of their sales presentations by engulfing buyers in a plethora of options. They mistakenly assume that more options will help buyers make better choices. But as we've seen, too much information obstructs the brain's capacity to make a decision.

This presents a magnificent opportunity to better serve your buyers. When you begin to make it less cognitively demanding for their brains to perceive and evaluate the worth of your product or service, it will give you an advantage over your competitors. So how do you do this? Only provide buyers with the information necessary for them to confidently make a positive buying decision. This has been shown to make such a difference in sales that even mass retailers are changing how they present products to consumers. Walmart eliminated two brands of peanut butter and their peanut butter sales rose. Procter & Gamble also reduced the range of skin-care products at some of their retail outlets and sales of the products still on the shelves increased.[8]

In fact, my favorite example of the difference this strategy can make is personified by a salesperson we'll call Katie. When we met, she had been selling for her employer for more than two years, and though she was passionate about serving customers, her sales were unremarkable. She insisted to me that what her customers loved most was how many options they could choose from to customize the product to their exact needs. I asked her to show me what she meant, and with a smile she pulled out her iPad and scrolled through pictures of more than one hundred different options that, to me, looked nearly identical. "Which do you show in your presentation?" I questioned. Beaming with pride, she said, "All of them, of course." I was speechless. I'd been dazed by what she had shown me for just a moment; I couldn't imagine how her customers felt having to choose from so many selections at the end of a long sales presentation. I gently explained to her that showing all of these choices was killing her sales and hindering her potential customers from choosing the best one. I then suggested that she identify the most popular options and show only four of them. If customers needed to see more, she could remove the ones they were not interested in and replace them with other options, but never show more than four at once. Reluctantly, she agreed and began to follow my suggestion. She later reported that customers were pleased with the choices she presented and rarely did anyone ever need to see more than the initial four. Most telling of all was her sales, which rose by nearly 30 percent.

If you are like many of the salespeople I have trained, over time more and more information may have crept into your sales presentation. I would encourage you to review your sales presentation and ask yourself, what can be removed? Do you share too much information? Think through what your buyers need to be able to confidently make a positive buying decision. Anything more than that—cut. Adopting this approach will increase the effectiveness of your presentation, because when it comes to the brain's ability to process information, less really will help you sell more.

STRATEGY #2: ANCHORING

The Tonight Show with Johnny Carson was a treasured part of the television landscape for thirty years. One of Carson's interviews has achieved almost mythical status within the sales and marketing community. It was with the Girl Scout who set the record for selling the most Girl Scout cookies. It went something like this:

Johnny Carson begins the interview by inquiring, "What is the secret of your success?" To the amazement of everyone, she replied, "I would ask people if they would give a $30,000 donation to the Girl Scouts." Carson chuckled. "What did people say when you asked that?" "No!" retorted the young girl. "But then I would ask them, 'Would you at least buy a box of Girl Scout cookies?'"

This humorous illustration reveals how once people compared the larger request for a $30,000 donation to the purchase of a box of cookies, few could resist. The reason this was so persuasive is because of a highly influential heuristic (mental shortcut) known as anchoring.

Anchors are reference points the brain intuitively creates to help it make rapid judgments.[9] Once an anchor is formed, it creates a bias that shapes how the brain perceives subsequent information. In other words, the brain uses the anchor as its starting point and contrasts new information with it.

> Once an anchor is formed, it creates a bias that shapes how the brain perceives subsequent information. In other words, the brain uses the anchor as its starting point and contrasts new information with it.

For instance, how do buyers know if the price of your product or service is fair or unfair, good or bad? They compare it to something else. Perhaps they contrast it with what they paid before, a competitor's price, their potential return on investment, or what they thought it would cost. All these are anchors they are using to evaluate your price.

What makes anchors so potent is that they occur automatically, without our awareness. As a result, people grossly underestimate the effect that anchors have on them. Even arbitrary anchors that contain obviously irrelevant information can create biases that have an alarming impact on perceptions of value. Consider the following research experiment led by three behavioral economists.[10]

The researchers asked participants to share the last two digits of their social security number. They then had them state how much they were willing to pay for numerous products, such as a keyboard, wine, chocolates, and a book. Amazingly, those with higher digits at the end of their social security numbers were willing to pay as much as 300 percent more than those with lower ones!

Another example of how unrelated anchors influence buying behaviors occurred at a supermarket that was running a promotion on Campbell's soup.[11] On some of the days during the sale a sign was displayed that stated, NO LIMIT PER PERSON. However, on other days the sign was changed to read LIMIT OF 12 PER PERSON. The restriction created an anchor that caused shoppers to purchase twice as many cans than on days when there was no limit.

In your sales presentations you should be very deliberate about the anchors you introduce. I have witnessed salespeople share stories or statements that convey low anchors that actually devalue their product or service and undermine the sale.

However, there is another side to anchoring that can transform the effectiveness of your sales presentations. Science has shown that if you introduce new anchors or change existing ones, you can shape how your potential customers perceive the value and price of your product or service. Let me explain how.

Anchoring Increases Sale Prices

Though anchoring may seem like a new concept, it is one that you have already experienced on a regular basis as a consumer. Many restaurants put exorbitantly priced wines on their wine list since they know it inspires patrons to purchase more expensive wines than they normally would. The inflated wines create an anchor that makes the lesser-priced (but still expensive) wines look like more favorable choices.[12] In another instance, a popular electronics manufacturer found that sales of their highest-priced headphones stalled until they created an even more expensive option.[13]

Even charities use anchors to increase giving. Many of them suggest the size of potential donations. If a charity offers you a range of options such as $75, $100, $300 or $500, you are more likely to give a much larger donation than if the options are $5, $20, $50, or $100.

How much sway do anchors have on donations? When researchers asked potential donors if they would make a contribution to save seabirds from offshore oil spills, the donors were given either a $5 anchor, a $400 anchor, or no anchor at all.[14] The difference the anchor made was staggering. The median contribution of those who were given the $5 anchor was $20, while those who were provided no anchor contributed an average of $64. The most impressive response was from those who were presented with the $400 anchor. That group gave an average of $143, more than 600 percent higher than the low-anchor group.

Because anchors are something the brain naturally creates, they affect everyone, even people you wouldn't expect to be vulnerable to them. An example is found in a thought-provoking experiment led by two behavioral scientists that analyzed the effect of anchors on seasoned real estate agents.[15] When agents were invited to a house and asked to evaluate it, some were shown a low price, while others were presented with a much higher price. As was predicted, those who were shown the low anchor appraised the house for much less than the agents who were given the high anchor.

What makes this research study even more intriguing is that when the agents were asked how they arrived at the home's value, all of them denied that they were influenced by the price they were shown before they did their appraisal. This underscores the fact that the impact anchors have on the decision-making process is rarely recognized, even among experts.

How to Anchor Price in Your Sales Presentations

By now it's clear that anchors impact the brain's perception of price. So how can you use them in your sales presentations? Here's how one of my clients used anchors to raise their prices *and* grow their sales.

This client is in an industry where potential customers often have very unrealistic price expectations. To counteract this, I had them inject anchors into their sales process. So, early in their sale presentations, they brought up the idea of price (a subject that buyers are all too eager to discuss) and then showed buyers two highly credible, independent sources that detailed the normal costs for the project they were considering. Then they explained why the project costs what it did. The result was that later on in the sale, when they showed their price, they encountered little resistance, since buyers compared it to the anchor that had already been established. This also improved their understanding of the value that was being offered, which caused sales to increase.

Anchors should also be used when you are negotiating with prospective clients. In fact, because of the psychological power of anchors, negotiation experts like Harvard Business School's Deepak Malhotra and Max Bazerman suggest that you always try to set the anchor.[16] If those you are negotiating with set an anchor first, it is recommended that you protect yourself by adamantly rejecting it and focusing your mind on a new anchor. So if you are beginning a negotiation on a deal and the other side begins with a low-ball offer, immediately shift the conversation to a more advantageous anchor such as the cost to the other side of not coming to an agreement.

Another way you can use anchors is just before you present price. It is here that you can recap the return on investment that the buyers will experience from your product or service or briefly state the price others have paid for larger, much more expensive projects. When anchors are used at this part of the sale they have been shown to boost closing rates.

This is what behavioral scientist Jerry Burger found when he led a research study that analyzed whether anchoring when price is revealed would increase sales.[17] In one of his experiments, he set up a cupcake stand. When the cupcakes were priced at 75 cents, compliance rates were 44 percent. However, when Burger changed the way price was presented by informing potential patrons that the cupcakes used to cost $1, but now were only 75 cents, sales skyrocketed as 73 percent of the people purchased.

APPLICATION EXERCISE: ADVICE FOR A FRIEND

Imagine that a friend who has just begun a career in sales asks you for advice. He tells you that he just got a job working in a men's store. A lot of his customers come in to purchase a suit, but they also need a dress shirt and tie. He is wondering in what order he should present them when a buyer comes into the store and needs all three items.

When I initially pose this question in sales workshops the feedback varies until they learn about anchors. Once you understand the anchoring effect the answer is clear: your friend should present the most expensive option (the suit) first. Someone who agrees to buy a $1,200 suit will perceive a $150 shirt and a $70 tie as much less of an expense than if they were shown the tie first and then the shirt and the suit. Why? Even though the prices do not change, the first item creates an anchor that alters how the subsequent items and prices are perceived. Failing to show the highest priced item first will trigger anchoring to work against you, which will reduce your sales.

STRATEGY #3: MIRRORING

In the introduction, I shared a career-altering discussion I had with a colleague named Bill. We were chatting about the merits of a certain sales strategy—mirroring. He thought it was an old sales gimmick, but I believed it was useful. At the time, I could not prove my point as I had only anecdotal evidence. It was only later, after studying the science of influence, that I found the vast amount of data proving that mirroring is a productive strategy that will improve your sales presentations.

What is mirroring? Think about it like this: If you notice someone yawning, why do you also feel the sudden urge to yawn? When you see a person take a nasty fall, why do you cringe? If you witness someone experiencing tremendous sadness, you literally feel their pain. Why? What makes the experiences of others evoke similar feelings in you?

The answer to all these questions is found in a powerful behavior called mirroring, in which one person emulates aspects of another person's verbal or nonverbal behavior.

An overwhelming amount of scientific evidence confirms that mirroring will increase one's ability to influence another. For example, two different studies published in *Psychological Science* concluded that mirroring boosts rapport, which, as you were shown in Chapter 2, increases receptivity to a persuasive message.[18]

That's not all. Other studies have found that when you mirror the behaviors of others, it induces feelings of sameness, which inspire trust and fosters likability.[19] Social psychologists Douglas Kenrick, Steven Neuberg, and Robert Cialdini summarize this aspect of mirroring when they write that "people like us more when we subtly imitate their nonverbal behaviors."[20]

A large body of research has concluded that mirroring naturally deepens your awareness of another person's perspective.[21] The process of mirroring doesn't just help you understand what others are thinking, according to neuroscientists Michael Gazzaniga, Richard Ivry, and George Mangun, it also improves the brain's ability to recognize the emotional states of others.[22]

The evidence is conclusive: mirroring will enhance your ability to persuasively present your ideas. This is what a team of behavioral scientists led by William Maddux found when they conducted numerous experiments to identify the effects mirroring has in business situations.[23] In one of their experiments, the scientists arranged for MBA students to participate in negotiation exercises. Some of the students were informed that during the negotiation they should subtly mimic the verbal and nonverbal behaviors of those they were negotiating with. What occurred next was astonishing. The students who did not engage in mirroring arrived at a negotiated settlement 12 percent of the time; in contrast, the students who had mirrored the behaviors of those they were in negotiations with were able to reach an agreement an impressive 67 percent of the time.

The findings of Maddux's research are not unique. Another illuminating study, which was published in the *Journal of Consumer Research*, analyzed the effect of mirroring on selling. The study found that when salespeople mirrored buyers' behaviors, buyers rated the salesperson and the product or service more favorably.[24]

The power of mirroring in sales situations was also profiled when the *Harvard Business Review* reported the conclusions of a psychological experiment in which researchers measured the closing rates of retail salespeople who were attempting to sell an electronic device.[25] Those buyers that were mirrored by the salesperson purchased 79 percent of the time. Whereas the buyers who had not been mirrored purchased at a rate of only 62 percent. Mirroring enhanced the closing rate of these salespeople by 17 percent!

Mirroring and the Human Brain

Why does mirroring work? Trust me, it's not magic. Rather, mirroring is influential because of how the human brain functions. Neuroscientists contend that the brain contains what are known as "mirror neurons," and that they are why people instinctively model the behavior of others. They are also why you feel the impulse to yawn when you watch somebody else yawn, why you wince when you observe someone fall, and why you feel sadness when you witness another person grieve.

Mirror neurons were first detected by a team of Italian researchers who were led by renowned neuroscientist Giacomo Rizzolatti. The scientists were conducting studies on monkeys when they noticed that the monkeys would routinely mimic the behavior they saw.[26] For instance, when the human handler stuck out his tongue, the monkey would as well. Rizzolatti and his team were fascinated by this and wondered what brain functions enabled the monkeys to emulate human behavior. Their experiments led them to the realization that monkeys have neurons in their brains that allow them to imitate the behavior they see. The researchers even determined that these mirror neurons in the monkey's brain would fire when the monkey grabbed an object and would also fire when the monkey watched a human grab the same object.[27]

Rizzolatti's breakthrough prompted a flurry of research in the field of neuroscience to discern whether the human brain also had mirror neurons. After years of analysis, neuroscientists concluded that there are within the human brain, particularly in the premotor cortex, certain types of neurons that mirror behavior.[28] The discovery that the human brain contained mirror neurons was significant; one neuroscientist even said it was one of "the most intriguing scientific discoveries of the past decades."[29] It also has numerous important implications in the understanding of human social interaction.

Mirror neurons are what allow the human brain to recognize the intention of another and to engage in observational learning. They also explain why people often unconsciously mirror the verbal and nonverbal behavior of others.[30] The human brain's innate aptitude for emulating behavior is evident in the research of social psychologists Tanya Chartrand and John Bargh.[31] In one of their most revealing experiments, they had a collaborator sit next to random people and sporadically touch his face or shake his foot. Incredibly, without conscious awareness, the people would copy the nonverbal behavior they witnessed. This mirroring reflex was referenced by Michael McCaskey in a *Harvard Business Review* article, "The Hidden Messages Managers Send," when he stated, "In moments of great rapport, a remarkable pattern of nonverbal communication can develop. Two people will mirror each other's movements—dropping a hand, shifting their body at exactly the same time."[32]

Another study published in *Social Psychology Quarterly* analyzed the posture of students in the classroom.[33] The research identified that the more similar students' postures were to their teacher's, the deeper their feelings of rapport and the higher their level of participation.

What's more, remarkably, when a person is in deep rapport with another, the mirror neurons in the brain automatically fire. This is an important insight—by mirroring others, you can trigger the mirror neurons in their brains to fire. This will intensify the feelings of rapport and receptiveness.

You may think that people must notice when others mirror them. However, what is strikingly consistent about the research on mirroring is that rarely are those whose behaviors are being mirrored aware of it. Mirroring is something that occurs naturally, it's literally wired into the brain. When it is being done, it does not feel odd enough to stand out. To the contrary, it just feels right.

Four Behaviors to Mirror

Mirroring is a powerful tool of persuasion that you can use to enhance your sales. Here are four behaviors that you can mirror to produce maximum impact in your sales presentation.

Behavior #1—Mirror your buyer's posture: If your buyer is leaning back in his chair, cautiously listening to your presentation, you should also lean back slightly and mirror his body language. This will aid you in aligning yourself with your potential customer by conveying a similar perspective.

Behavior #2—Mirror your buyer's gestures: Most buyers will favor certain gestures over others. As you notice their style of gesturing, you may want to exhibit similar gestures. This simple act will increase rapport and your capacity to compellingly communicate your ideas.

One of the most intriguing psychological experiments conducted on the persuasive potency of mirroring was overseen by psychologists Jeremy Bailenson and Nick Yee.[34] The researchers had college students enter a virtual environment one at a time, where they were seated across from a virtual, humanlike character. The character would deliver a persuasive speech saying that college students should be required to carry identification cards on them when on campus. In half of the sessions, the virtual character would mirror the head movements of the participants at a four-second delay. So if the student listening nodded her head, four seconds later the virtual character would as well. In the other half of the sessions, the virtual character would not mirror the student's head movements. At the conclusion of the experiment, each student was asked to rate the likability of the virtual person and the persuasiveness of the speech. In spite of the fact that all the students heard the exact same speech and encountered the same virtual character, those students whose head movements were mirrored indicated that they found the character more likeable and its message more persuasive.

Behavior #3—Mirror your buyer's rate of speech: Scientific studies have identified that people are more likely to comply with a request when the one making the request is matching their rate of speech.[35] This is due to the fact that people generally like to listen at the same speed at which they speak. If a prospective client speaks slowly, he may find it distracting to listen to a salesperson who speaks rapidly. By adjusting your rate of speech to match your buyer's, you will foster rapport and facilitate effective communication.

Behavior #4—Mirror your buyer's word usage: You will find that buyers favor certain phrases or words. You may even notice they will use the same word repeatedly when describing some aspect of their problem or desired solution. Mirroring their words heightens your ability to communicate in a way that potential customers will understand and relate to. When you mirror customers' words you are literally speaking their language.

One prime example of the power of mirroring another's words was demonstrated by Rick van Baaren. As we saw in his study on the monetary impact that verbal mirroring had on the size of tips servers earned, when servers repeated their guests' words, their tips rose by 68 percent.[36]

The debate is over: science has proven that mirroring is a useful sales strategy that is rooted in the workings of the human brain. It will boost rapport, increase influence, and guide you in getting and staying in sync with buyers. But perhaps most important, the very process of mirroring will help you keep your focus where it should be—on others.

STRATEGY #4: THE PICTURE SUPERIORITY EFFECT

When you think about New York, what comes to mind? A busy city street filled with taxis? The Statue of Liberty or the Empire State Building? Times Square? Or something else entirely? Your answer depends on your past experiences and what you associate with New York, but if you are like those I posed this question to, what came to your mind was not words, but a picture. Your brain pictured something that represented New York.

This provides an insight into the inner workings of our brains, namely that they don't think in words but in pictures. Neuroscientist John Medina explains: "To our cortex, unnervingly, there is no such thing as words."[37] When the human brain encounters a word, it links the word to its corresponding picture. This is so well established that scientists have a name for it: the *picture superiority effect*.

Because the brain thinks in terms of pictures, it is able to process and retain them more easily than words.[38] As a result, learning and retention can be improved by explaining a concept with pictures. This fact has been validated in numerous scientific studies.[39] One such study was conducted by educational psychologist Kirsten Butcher and was published in the *Journal of Educational Psychology*. It demonstrated that people learn complex data with less difficulty when words and visual illustrations are used, in comparison to only text.[40] Cognitive psychologists Richard Mayer and Roxana Moreno echo this notion when they state, "It is better to present an explanation in words and pictures than solely words."[41] Furthermore, John Medina concurs: "Text and oral presentation are not just less efficient than pictures for retaining certain types of information;

they are way less efficient. If information is presented orally, people remember about 10 percent, tested 72 hours after exposure. That figure goes up to 65 percent if you add a picture."[42]

How can you use the picture superiority effect to enhance your sales presentations? Make sure that your presentations are dominated by pictures. Don't just explain a concept verbally; instead show a picture that illustrates the concept, then explain the picture. This will improve your customer's ability to absorb and retain your ideas.

I can still recall one presentation I witnessed where the presenter used PowerPoint slides that contained nothing but text, a lot of text. He then proceeded to read the slides to the audience. Not only was he disengaged from the audience, but the presentation was boring and hard to follow. Even more alarming was the fact that he rendered himself unnecessary, since everyone in the room needed no help in reading the slides.

If you use slides in your sales presentations, I recommend having as little text as possible. Also, evaluate whether your presentations help buyers easily picture the concepts you are sharing. Do you use vivid word pictures and actual pictures to explain your ideas? How could you improve in this area? Thinking through these questions is vital, since the easier it is for the brain to picture what you are presenting, the more favorably buyers will respond to you and your message.

STRATEGY #5: USE STORIES

Everyone loves stories. Whether watching a movie, reading a novel, or hearing a friend talk about a situation at work, we all find stories interesting and highly persuasive. Throughout history, leaders have used stories to convey their ideas and rally people to their causes. But what is it about stories that makes them so compelling?

If you asked Walter Fisher, a behavioral scientist and emeritus professor at the University of Southern California, why stories are so impactful, he would share his research on what he refers to as the *narrative paradigm*.[43] This describes how the brain organizes information into stories. Fisher states that people interpret "experience and comprehend life as a series of ongoing narratives, as conflicts, characters, beginnings, middles, and ends."[44] Neuroscientists Louis Cozolino and Susan Sprokay agree, as their research has identified that the stories the brain creates are highly influential and determine how it responds to people and situations.[45] For instance, buyers instinctively form mental stories about you, your company, and the impact your product would have on them. In other words, people are not buying you, your company, or your product or service—they are buying the stories they believe about them.

Because the brain thinks in terms of stories, you have a choice: either you can present your buyers with narratives to embrace or you can hope they make up accurate and favorable ones. This is why every sales presentation can benefit from having well-constructed stories within it. Any salesperson who has capably used them will tell you that it helps them earn sales. In my own sales career, I have found that they are an extremely effective selling tool. In fact, many customers have even told me after they purchased that one of the primary reasons was because of a story I had told them. But before we go into how to create powerful stories, I need to share with you another piece of information: stories provoke strong emotional responses.

Stories stimulate emotions, sometimes intense emotions. Because of this, they are able to shift emotional states and inspire people to care. Leadership expert Jay Conger concurs: "Numbers do not make an emotional impact, but stories and vivid language do."[46] This is why they will often get results when nothing else can. They are sometimes the only thing that will penetrate the most thick-skinned, combative buyer.

What is remarkable about stories is that the brain processes them differently than facts or assertions of value. When you are presented with data, your brain analyzes its validity but stories do not undergo this same method of evaluation. They evoke emotions that cause the brain to interpret them less analytically and more emotionally. It is why you can have an emotional reaction to a movie while knowing that the characters are paid actors and the story is fictional. You don't analyze a movie the way you do the words on this page. Your brain processes it differently and that changes how you respond to it.

Stories are also sticky. Because they produce an emotional response that will often cause the brain to release dopamine, a chemical that improves memory, the retention rate of stories is elevated. One experiment conducted at Stanford University found that after listening to a series of speeches, 63 percent of the students remembered the stories the speaker used, but only 5 percent remembered any statistics from the same speech.[47]

Perhaps the most significant finding about stories is that the brain actually reconstructs them as they are being told.[48] Princeton researchers monitored brain activity in pairs of subjects, one who told a story and the other who was listening to the story.[49] The researchers noticed that the neural activity in both of the participants' brains was synchronous. When the speaker imagined the story while articulating it, the listener had the same brain activity while he was mentally recreating the story he was hearing. Neuroscientists refer to the formation of a mental image of a behavior, idea, or situation that a person hasn't witnessed in real life as "mental imagery."[50] As I shared in Chapter 8, mental imagery is a powerful element of persuasion, but only if you know how to use it properly. For example, research conducted over a forty-year period revealed that the simpler it is for a person to imagine doing something, the more likely she is to do it. But the opposite holds true as well. Studies have shown that the more challenging it is to imagine a behavior, the less likely it is that people will be persuaded to embrace it.[51]

> Research suggests that when you tell stories, your prospective customers are not just listening; they are recreating the story in their minds. The easier it is for buyers to picture a story, the more likely it is that they will be influenced by it.

This science discloses an important insight into successful storytelling—anything that hinders your buyers' ability to imagine the story will also hinder its influence. So how do you tell impactful stories that are easy for the brain to digest? Here are six essential components of highly effective stories:

1. Remove All Unnecessary or Distracting Details

One of the most common mistakes that I see salespeople make when sharing stories is cluttering them with unnecessary details that distract the brain from the point of the story.

One example of this occurred a number of years ago at a sales workshop I led. During the workshop, everyone was tasked with creating and delivering a story to the group. After each of the participants told their story, the group would offer suggestions for improvement. One of the participants, a salesperson, told a powerful story about a past customer. She did exceptionally well, but one phrase she used stood out like a blinking neon light. She referred to one of the buyers as being "tight as bark on a tree." As the other participants gave her feedback, everyone commented on how much they liked the phrase. One of the salespeople said that he had never heard that expression before, but it was something he would never forget. A sales manager mentioned that the saying grabbed his attention to such an extent that he began wondering whether all trees have bark. After the group was done giving feedback, it was my turn. After communicating the many things she had done well, I amazed everyone by telling her to remove the phrase from the story. The reason was because it overshadowed the narrative and caused everyone to think about the phrase rather than the actual point of the story.

I encourage you when creating stories to consider if there is anything that will divert attention away from the core message you are trying to convey. Keep them lean and be relentless in removing any details that may be distracting or unnecessary.

2. Use Stories with Characters Who Are Similar to Your Buyers

Similarity breeds trust. We are more likely to trust those who are like us. In the same way, studies conducted by several social psychologists have confirmed that the more alike the characters in a story are to the listeners, the more impactful the stories are perceived to be.[52]

The more alike the characters are to your buyers, the easier it is for your buyers to create a mental picture of the story. For instance, it is easier for a C-level executive to relate to a narrative that involves another

C-level executive, than one in which the main character is a human resource manager. Robert Cialdini summarizes the scientific research in this area: "The science supports what most sales professionals already know: Testimonials from satisfied customers work best when the satisfied customer and the prospective customer share similar circumstances."[53]

I recommend creating a pallette of stories that you can draw from to match your buyers and their situations. This requires that you invest time in developing them. You can begin by interviewing your past customers. In addition, one of the most efficient ways to quickly develop many high-quality stories is to confer with colleagues about the stories they share. I have found that most organizations have many great stories, but they have never been compiled and put in a central, easy-to-access location. So salespeople only know a small fraction of them. Once you begin collaborating with team members, you will find that the collection of stories you can use in your sales presentation quickly grows.

3. Draw in Listeners with a Compelling Introduction

The way a story begins shapes how it will be perceived by your audience. This is because of the primacy effect described in Chapter 2, the heuristic (mental shortcut) that causes the brain to be more influenced by what is presented first than what is presented later. As a result, the beginning of a story should draw in your buyers because it is what they will use to create their initial judgment about the story. And this early assessment matters, because research shows that it is the lens through which the rest of the story will be viewed.

One of the most famous studies conducted on the primacy effect was led by behavioral scientist Solomon Asch. He asked participants to read a description about a man named John and then give their impressions.[54] Some were shown one description, while others were presented with another. Read the descriptions and evaluate how each shapes your impression of John.

Description 1: "John is intelligent, industrious, impulsive, critical, stubborn, and envious."

Description 2: "John is envious, stubborn, critical, impulsive, industrious, and intelligent."

Not surprisingly, those who read the first description had a much more favorable impression of John than those who read the second. Yet both descriptions are the same—the second simply has the adjectives describing John in reverse order. The primacy effect tells us that because this description begins with a negative word, the perception of John is skewed.

And so it follows that the way you begin your stories, sales presentations, or sales calls matters. So make sure you use the primacy effect in your favor. When it comes to stories, focus on creating a compelling introduction that is so captivating that if you ceased telling the story after delivering it, your buyer's response would be, "Tell me more."

There are many strategies that you can use to make your story introductions engaging. Here are three I recommend:

- **Make the introduction about the buyer:** There is nothing that will grab a buyer's attention more than telling him there is a customer just like him. One example of this is, "You remind me of one of my customers, Bill Smith, the VP of operations at ABC Company. Bill said the same thing you said."
- **Open with a provocative statement:** "This high turnover within your organization is a serious problem, but it can be fixed. For instance, we had a company that came to us with a very similar situation . . ." or "Eighty-nine percent of those who purchase our software report that their operational costs are reduced by at least 22 percent. For example one of our customers . . ."
- **Illustrate how the product or service fulfills one of the buyer's primary buying motivators:** As previously disclosed, there are three primary buying motivators: dominant buying motives, buyer's problems, and the buying requirements. A prospective customer's primary buying motivators are issues that matter to them, and when a story addresses one of them it will instantly be considered significant. There are many ways to accomplish this in the introduction. One example is, "You mentioned that one of your requirements for any solution was being able to have it functional within thirty days. We can definitely meet this requirement. For example, when XYZ Company invested

in our software they had a similar requirement, except they
wanted the software installed within only twenty-one days . . ."

4. Let the Characters Speak

Quote the characters. This is one of the most significant ways you can
breathe life into your stories. When you allow your characters to speak, it
helps you tell the story in a more engaging manner and allows your buyers to more easily "see" the story unfold in their minds. Moreover, dialogue between characters makes the story more engaging. Consider the
difference between the two ways the same event can be described: "John
looked me straight in the eye and said, 'I would never want that'" versus
"John told me he did not want it."

The first option is more active and immediate because the character
is speaking himself. You can feel his emotion, which also produces the
corresponding emotion in you. This will engage your listeners and make
your stories much more influential.

5. Have a Clear Conclusion

Great stories conclude with a bang. Why? Because the way a story ends is
usually how it will be remembered. Acclaimed speech coach Patricia Fripp
summarizes this phenomenon with the phrase "Last words linger."[55]

What's more, the conclusion must answer all the questions raised
within it. If you do not coherently wrap up the narrative, then the listener's brain, which is recreating it, will not allow it to conclude.[56] This will
hinder the story's influence because the listener will be distracted by something that was not addressed. The long-term impact of any story is dependent upon a clear, convincing conclusion.

6. Convey the Singular Point of the Story

What is the point of your story? What new belief or behavior do you want
potential customers to embrace? Every story you tell should be told for the
purpose of conveying a singular takeaway. Remember, as the brain is
mentally re-creating a story it is deciphering what it means. And if you
don't provide your listeners with a clear explanation of what the narrative
means, they will be forced to make one up.

It may seem odd for you to tell another person what a story means, but if you communicate the narrative so the potential customers' brains are able to reconstruct it, then they will be in a very receptive state. Since you are the teller of the story, they will readily embrace what you say it means.

Now that we have reviewed how to construct captivating and productive stories, let's put it all together and look at how to use stories in actual sales presentations. To do this, I will share with you a story that showcases all six components of effective storytelling.

STORY EXAMPLE

Context: Imagine you are a salesperson for a commercial remodeler. Your clients are hotels, resorts, and restaurants. On this sales call, you are talking to a decision maker at a large hotel chain who has many hotels within your territory that need bathtubs replaced. The distinct value that you are focusing on is that your tubs come with a five-year warranty on labor and materials. This is considerably longer than most of your competitors, who only offer one year on labor. After sharing this information, you decide to deploy a story to create an emotional response. Here's what this story could look like.

Story: The fact that most remodelers only guarantee labor for one year presents a real problem for a lot of hotels. For example, we had a customer who, prior to investing in our beautiful bathroom systems, had another remodeler install more than 1,100 fiberglass tubs in her hotels. Two years after the tubs were installed, more than 40 of them had cracks, just from normal use. Remember how we spoke about how fiberglass tubs have the tendency to crack? Well, that's exactly what happened.

The customer called the remodeler and said, "Remember me? About two years ago you installed some tubs for me. Many of them have cracks. What can I do?"

They said, "Well, I don't know. Try calling the manufacturer to see if any are still under warranty."

And that's exactly what she did. She found the manufacturer's information and called them. After finally getting through to someone, the company representative looked up the warranty information for her tubs and said, "You're in luck! Our records show that those tubs have a three-year warranty and you've only had them for a little more than two years. We'll take care of everything!"

She said, "That's great!" and hung up the phone. She told us that a week later she received a delivery. What do you think was sitting on her loading dock? That's right, more than forty tubs!

So she called up the original remodeler and said, "The tubs were under warranty and were sent to me. Can you come out and install them?" They sent over some installers, who visited each of the hotels, ripped out all the cracked tubs, disposed of them, and put the new tubs in. When they were finished, do you think they gave her a bill? Of course they did! That's a big job. My point in sharing this with you is that with this limited, one-year guarantee, if anything goes wrong it's the customer who bears the brunt of the cost. I don't believe that's right. Would you agree?

STORY EXERCISE

There are many types of stories you can create, but let's start with one that can have an immediate impact on your sales presentation—a story about a past customer (commonly referred to as a Third-person Story). These stories are very persuasive because they show the positive results others who have purchased your product or service have experienced. They also project your buyers into the future and demonstrate the outcome they will have when they become a customer.

Think about a past customer who has experienced meaningful outcomes from your product or service and then think through the following areas that will provide an outline for your story:

1. **Problems the customer had before purchasing**
2. **How they decided on your solution** (include any doubts they had and how they overcame them, and choose concerns that many of your prospective customers may also have)
3. **Results after purchasing**

THE SALES TIPPING POINT

The sales presentation is often the tipping point in any sales process; it's what nudges buyers in your direction. By incorporating the five science-based strategies I've shared with you in this chapter, you will be able to communicate in ways that are aligned with how your buyers' brains process information. This will set you up for success and significantly improve the likelihood that they will make a buying decision in your favor.

PART THREE

MERGING SCIENCE
AND SELLING

CHAPTER 10

The Future of Selling

The scientific study of human behavior is flourishing. It's positively transforming the way we work and live in a myriad of ways. For instance, it has been shown to boost retirement savings, increase blood donations, bolster energy conservation, stop youths from joining gangs, and help people lose weight. Even politicians have realized that insights from this science are too important to ignore.

One example of this occurred when social psychologists and behavioral economists were called on by Barack Obama to help him win the presidency.[1] The UK government, NATO, and the U. S. government are also using behavioral science to better serve citizens.[2] In fact, research by the Economic and Social Research Council disclosed that 136 different countries have used behavioral science in some aspect of their public policies.[3] And that's not all—schools, economists, legal organizations, marketers, and businesses are also beginning to use it to advance their causes. Yet nowhere is this science more impactful than in sales.

As we've seen throughout this book, research has shed light on the practical methods that any sales organization can use to improve its results. We now have a rich and growing understanding of the behaviors that promote buying decisions. It's no longer necessary to guess why top producers perform better than average ones.

> Armed with scientific data, we now have the tools to improve any salesperson's performance.

Because of this influx of scientific evidence, there has never been a more exciting time to be in sales. Today, we have an unmatched opportunity: we can literally define the future of our profession. Much like every other discipline that has embraced science, sales can be positively transformed. As salespeople begin basing the way they sell on how the brain is wired to be influenced and make decisions, they will be better equipped to serve buyers in more meaningful and helpful ways, which will fuel sales growth and usher the profession of sales into a new, prosperous era.

Science-based selling is now a reality. But what does that mean for you and the profession of sales? As these strategies begin to permeate selling, what will change? To answer these important questions, I will share with you three major shifts that I predict will occur in the near future.

SHIFT #1: SALES TRUTH WILL TAKE CENTER STAGE

In the first few chapters of this book I laid out the case why you should embrace science as your source of sales truth. What is sales truth? It's how you judge what behaviors you'll utilize when selling. Think about it like this: When you are presented with a new sales strategy, how will you know if it will help you sell more? How you answer this question reveals your sales truth.

For instance, some salespeople determine the behaviors they use when selling by what feels most comfortable to them. Still others sell in the way that they would like to be sold to if they were the buyers. Of course, I'm advocating that you use science as your criteria for deciding how you should sell. And the good news is that this is not a hard process. Once you understand some basic principles, like the ones I have laid out in this book, you will be able to start selling scientifically. The reason this matters is because it will significantly affect how you sell and ultimately determine the very future of selling.

Here's why. In the past, sales truth was almost a nonissue because there was no objective standard to compare it to. Your results were the only way your behaviors were judged. This was highly problematic for three reasons. First, you can't know if your sales behaviors are effective until *after* you see the outcomes they produce. So if you're wrong, by the time you realize it, you're probably out of a job. Second, even if your sales are better than your peers, it does not mean that your sales production is where it could or should be. Third, if your sales are mediocre, how will you know which of your sales behaviors caused the lack of results? Is it all of them, some of them, one of them? Because sales truth used to be subjective, how to sell often boiled down to a treacherous guessing game.

We now have something better. Science offers an alternative that is verifiably effective and has predictable outcomes. And this is why sales truth will be one of the defining issues in the future. It is the foundation for success in selling. When salespeople, organizations, or even an industry begin looking to science as its source of sales truth, sales production increases. Why? Because once you embrace science, you will be much more likely to begin using it when selling. Furthermore, you will start thinking about selling through the lens of how buyers' brains are influenced and formulate buying decisions. This is my goal as a sales trainer: I want you to understand both what to do and why it works, because that is what will fuel your ability to successfully adapt to unique situations and buyers.

What about you? Have you decided on your sales truth? If you have chosen to embrace science—awesome! If not, I would encourage you to reconsider. Ignoring this science is no longer an option. The old sales strategies are not working anymore. The current business environment is increasingly complex, challenging, and competitive, and we all must adapt. As researchers Brad Sagarin and Kevin Mitnick emphasize, "In the marketplace, practitioners live or die by their skill at harnessing the principles of influence. The skilled prosper. The unskilled go out of business."[4]

SHIFT #2: SALES RESEARCH WILL BLOSSOM

As you have seen from the vast number of studies I have already referenced throughout this book, science reveals how to boost influence and sales. However, until now, most of this science has been hidden away in academic journals. Why? Because selling has evaded the scholarly inquiry that other disciplines such as marketing have undergone. For instance, in spite of the fact that virtually every college and business school has courses on marketing, few have any on sales. DePaul University professor Suzanne Fogel and her colleagues commented on the severity of this problem when they wrote, "Take a look at the curricula of the world's top-ranked business schools, and you might come away with the impression that sales is unimportant. Most MBA programs offer no sales-related courses at all, and those that do offer only a single course in sales management. Even at the undergraduate level of business instruction, sales courses are sparse."[5] Sales authorities Jason Jordan and Michelle Vazzana further illuminate, "there are currently fewer than 50 colleges and universities in the United States that offer a major or minor in sales. Compared to finance, manufacturing, or marketing, the discipline of sales is still in its infancy."[6] Sales thought leaders Frank Cespedes and Daniel Weinfurter further explain "of the more than 170,000 students who earn MBAs annually, only a tiny fraction learn anything about sales."[7]

However, this was not always the case. In fact, at one time sales was taught in colleges and the profession was even beginning to look to science for answers. The discipline was rapidly innovating—but then it stopped abruptly. To understand why, we will need to take a brief look at what selling was like in the early part of the twentieth century.

During this period, the study of sales was flourishing. Stanford University's E. K. Strong wrote in 1925 that according to Library of Congress records only one book on sales existed in the year 1869. Yet with each passing decade, more and more books on sales were being published.[8]

	Published	Total
1869	1	1
1870—1880	1	2
1880—1890	3	5
1890—1900	6	11
1900—1910	36	47
1910—1920	220	267
1920—1922	151 (in 3 years)	418

By the early 1900s, sales innovation was booming. The quality of literature and information about the profession was dramatically improving as well. For example, one of the first textbooks on social psychology was authored by William McDougall in 1908.[9] Though social psychology—the study of how human beings are influenced in social settings—was a new discipline, its relevance to selling had caught the attention of the progressive thinkers who were studying the field of selling. One of these visionaries was Harvard University professor Harry Tosdal, whose book *Principles of Personal Selling*, which was published in 1926, quoted McDougall numerous times.[10]

Because selling was being earnestly studied by academics, by the mid-1920s courses in selling were prevalent at universities. As Strong explained, "A few years ago not a course on salesmanship or advertising was given anywhere. Today many of our colleges and universities offer such courses and more and more emphasis is being put upon the training of salesmen."[11] Tosdal echoed this contention when he penned, "Salesmen may take courses in business schools, colleges, universities, or correspondence schools . . . Recognized universities carry courses in salesmanship in their curriculum."[12]

Then something happened that radically shifted the core philosophy of business and, as a result, halted the progression of the study of sales: the Great Depression.

This economic depression began in 1929 and over the ensuing years it decimated the economy. Many businesses closed their doors and those that remained open were forced to go into survival mode. The marketplace was in shambles, and out of necessity, business leaders focused on making decisions that were devoid of any risks and would virtually guarantee profit.

Rather than continuing to use salespeople to drive the awareness of their products, businesses began to rely heavily upon the young discipline of marketing. Surveys would be sent to potential customers asking them what type of products they wanted and how much they were willing to pay. Then, armed with this information, they would create those products that they knew would sell. Though this method restricted growth and innovation, it was the best way to endure the lean years of the Great Depression.

Alfred Sloan, the CEO of General Motors, expressed this shift in philosophy in his 1933 letter to General Motors stockholders. In this letter he announced that GM had invited one million motorists to provide feedback to the company's engineers regarding their likes and dislikes. Sloan wrote:

> To discuss consumer research as a functional activity would give an erroneous impression. In its broad implications it is more in the nature of an OPERATING PHILOSOPHY, which, to be fully effective, must extend through all phases of a business—weighing every action from the standpoint of how it affects the goodwill of the institution, recognizing that the quickest way to profits—and the permanent assurance of such profits—is to serve the customer in the way in which the customer wants to be served.[13]

Sloan's letter represents a vast shift from the previous era, which had been focused on salespeople cultivating interest in a company's products. This change is understandable given the circumstances of the Great Depression. However, the impact that it had upon the discipline of sales still resounds today. As marketing became the driver of business, it also became a business priority and began to be studied in place of sales. Colleges eventually replaced their classes on sales with classes on marketing. Slowly, over the next few decades, marketing evolved into a science, while sales was abandoned by academics and left in the hands of those who had the "gift of gab."

Now that we understand the profession's past, let's talk about its future, which is much brighter. With the new focus on using hard science to define how to sell, I believe that the time is coming when sales will again capture the interest of higher learning institutions as it did prior to the Great Depression. This will spur sales innovation and cause sales to take a giant leap forward. The economic importance of selling is clear, and now that it can be based on predictable science, new research can build on the foundation that *The Science of Selling* has laid.

With this renewed interested in using science to improve sales results, fresh research initiatives will blossom. No longer will companies be willing to base their way of selling on anecdotal evidence. Once they learn how science can transform their sales effectiveness, they will insist on basing their strategies on it. A new trend will emerge. Sales organizations will start to partner with researchers to feed back into academia data regarding the success of the strategies that are being deployed. This research loop will cultivate new insights and will improve positive outcomes for buyers.

What's more, as science continues to demystify sales and make sales teams more predictable and effective, executives will take notice. No longer will they view selling as a mysterious activity. Instead, they will regard it as they do every other part of their business—scientifically. This transparency will spark a renewed focus on sales improvement and again make sales the priority it deserves to be.

In fact, some are even wondering whether the advances in neuroscience and behavioral science will cause the next big innovation in business. Just think what would happen if organizations used science to better identify and meet their customers' needs. It would improve their sales results and have an impressive effect on the economy. Marketing thought leader and vice chairman of OgilvyOne Rory Sutherland agrees. He suggests that discoveries in the scientific understanding of human behavior could possibly lead to a burst of economic growth.[14] He also cites Accenture, which argues that a better understanding of how to change behavior could potentially add 2.6 percent to the world gross domestic product.

What is certain is that science will change sales for the better. As sales professionals are given evidence-based strategies that remove the guesswork from the act of selling, the profession will flourish. This is why I believe that the best days in selling are still ahead.

SHIFT #3: SALES HIRING PRACTICES WILL IMPROVE

One of the most common and costly frustrations for organizations is finding good sales professionals. Yet there is no single activity that will impact a company's sales success more than hiring the right salespeople. Many of the problems surrounding this process are rooted in the way sales leaders make hiring decisions. Often they rely on gut feelings, incomplete interviewing processes, or easily manipulated and inherently flawed personality tests. Because of these unsuccessful practices, research indicates that even the best sales leaders make staffing choices that they later regret.

How often do these bad hires happen? More than you may think. Let's take a look at the data.

A survey of one hundred global companies found that the mis-hire rate was an astounding 80 percent.[15] Sales management experts Andris A. Zoltners, Prabhakant Sinha, and Sally E. Lorimer agree: "Even the most experienced recruiters make mistakes—a 50 percent error rate in hiring salespeople is the norm."[16] As alarming as the amount of poor sales hires is, there is something even worse—what they cost.

Although the estimates vary on the exact financial burden hiring mistakes inflict on companies, all the indicators reveal that it is steep. *Selling Power* reports that hiring the wrong salesperson costs companies $616,000.[17] The Sales Benchmark Index concurs, estimating that a bad sales hire can be a $600,000 expense.[18] The *Wall Street Journal* affirmed that the cost of turnover can easily be several times the annual compensation of the salesperson.[19] Moreover, once you do replace the underperformer, there are still additional costs associated with bringing a new salesperson up to full productivity. For instance, when the *Harvard Business Review* published an in-depth study that surveyed the sales efforts of 1,275 different organizations, it found that the ramp-up time for new salespeople was seven months.[20]

All the statistics on hiring salespeople show that it is a daunting and very costly problem. And this is where science can help.

As I have shared, science has decoded what makes salespeople successful, and has also revealed the core qualities that enable elite levels of performance. Many of these have already been disclosed in this book. At my firm, we have taken this science and put it into a sales-specific hiring system that guides sales leaders in identifying and verifying that interviewees have the skills, knowledge, behaviors, competencies, and character qualities necessary to be successful in the sales position for which they've applied. I call it the Competence Hiring Method®. This unique hiring methodology is easy to learn and is proven to significantly reduce sales mis-hires.

When evaluating sales candidates, you will first need to decide what are the specific essentials of the position, such as education, technical knowledge, and level of experience. Of course, these will vary depending on the type of sales role. But failure to do this is not what causes most poor sales hires. The majority of bad hiring decisions are a consequence of the fact that many sales leaders do not know what they should be looking for in a salesperson. Nevertheless, this can be a thing of the past. There are five essential qualities scientifically linked with high levels of sales performance, regardless of the position a person holds. Here's a look at each, and how they help salespeople succeed:

1. Top Performers Are Intrinsically Motivated

Intrinsic motivation is when someone acts not because of any inducement, but due to an internal desire to perform. There is compelling research that shows salespeople who are intrinsically motivated are far more likely to be successful than those who are not. One reason is because selling is not just something they do for a paycheck—it is who they are. It's personal and something they must excel at. Besides, if salespeople are not intrinsically motivated you will be forced to push them to get better, and once you stop, so will they. As I have already shared, in the current hypercompetitive marketplace, this is a recipe for disaster.

How can you identify whether someone is intrinsically motivated? Begin by asking them questions like these:

- Why are you in sales?
- What do you enjoy most about selling? What do you enjoy least?
- How would you describe someone who is successful at selling?
- In the past, when you have failed to earn a sale, what did you do? How did you respond?
- In your past sales position(s), where did you rank in comparison to your colleagues?
- Outside of the money, how do you stay motivated to sell?
- In your previous position(s), what kind of activities did you engage in that made time fly by so that you lost track of it?

As sales applicants answer these questions, evaluate whether they have a strong desire to be in the profession of sales. Do they enjoy the process of influencing others? Do they have an intense hunger to be great at selling? If not, they probably aren't intrinsically motivated to be a top salesperson. And in today's challenging selling environment, those who are not driven to succeed at sales usually won't.

2. Top Performers Focus on the Perspectives of Others

Many scientific studies have concluded that salespeople who are good at understanding buyers' perspectives are much more likely to be successful. Why? Because this attunement is what fuels the professional nimbleness that allows salespeople to effectively adapt to each unique buyer and situation. When salespeople struggle to understand their potential customers' perspectives, they will also struggle to positively influence them. As Daniel Goleman explains, "It is difficult to have a positive impact on others without first sensing how they feel and understanding their position."[21]

As I shared in Chapter 6, being focused on buyers' perspectives is a hallmark of top salespeople. They want to understand their buyers, so that they can position their company, product, or service in ways that meet those buyers' needs. Without this awareness, salespeople will inadvertently undermine their own selling efforts and behave in ways that extinguish positive influence. This is not a trivial matter, since understanding and adapting to potential customers are vital functions of both positive influence and effective selling.

How do you know if a salesperson is attuned to her buyers? Here are some questions that will help flesh this out:

- Is identifying the perspectives of your potential customers important when selling? Why? How do you do this? Can you give me a real-life example of when you have done this?
- How do you acquire an understanding of what would motivate buyers to purchase from you?
- How do you prepare for a sales call? How do you gather sales intelligence [information about potential clients]?
- Is it important to observe buyers' nonverbal communication? What do you look for?
- Can you share with me a specific time when you noticed your potential customer's perspective shift and you adapted to it?

When you listen to the answers to these questions, what should you focus on? Look for demonstrable evidence that the interviewees are actively thinking about the perspectives of others. Can they share examples of how in previous positions they adapted to a person they were attempting to influence—or did they charge ahead with their own ideas? Do they strive to truly understand their buyers or do they treat everyone the same? Evaluating their past behaviors will help you accurately predict whether they will seek to identify the viewpoints of your potential clients, which will impact both customer loyalty and sales results.

3. Top Performers Possess Integrity

One of the most overlooked yet important characteristic of good salespeople is integrity. Those who experience long-term success in sales are trustworthy, honest, dependable, and honorable. In today's transparent business climate, having salespeople who will do or say anything to earn the sale is just too big a liability and is simply bad for business.

How do you know if someone is a person of integrity? Sometimes spotting that quality is hard. What is far easier is noticing when it's missing. One question that has assisted me in this area comes from Peter Drucker, who stated that when he was interviewing someone and wanted to analyze the character of the person he would ask himself one question: "Would I want one of my sons to work under that person?"[22] I have found that his question helps me crystallize my thoughts about other people. Try it and I think you will be surprised by the instant clarity it provides.

4. Top Performers Embrace a Growth Mindset

As I shared in Chapter 1, a growth mindset, which is the belief that you can improve your sales abilities through your efforts, is a central belief of successful salespeople. Those who don't have a growth mindset believe that selling is an ability that you either have or you don't. As a result, any training or feedback focused on helping them improve is something they take personally—it's as if they are not good enough.

A growth mindset is not only important in sales; it is a characteristic of elite performers in any field. For instance, Leonard Berry and Kent Seltman, in their book *Management Lessons from Mayo Clinic,* state that one of the reasons for the Mayo Clinic's success is that it promotes and incentivizes continual learning. They maintain that it has a culture that "creates strong peer pressure to practice quality medicine. A doctor's skills and knowledge are continually on display. Internally—the peer pressure to keep learning—or leave—is real."[23] To be a top performer it's important to embrace a growth mindset.

That said, I have a confession when it comes to hiring salespeople who do not have a growth mindset—I have done it. But I don't any longer, because every time I hired a salesperson who did not have a growth mindset I regretted the decision. And the many sales leaders with whom I have shared the research on growth mindsets echo my finding. How do you test for a growth mindset? In Chapter 1, I laid out the quiz I use with salespeople. In addition, here are some questions that will help you uncover whether a candidate has a growth mindset:

- Is selling a skill you are born with or can it be developed? Why do you believe that?
- Outside of the training your previous employer provided, what have you done to improve your sales ability? Have you read any articles, blogs, or books, taken courses, or anything else? (If an interviewee says yes, ask which ones and inquire what he learned.)
- If a new salesperson came to you and asked your advice on how to become a competent salesperson, what would you tell her? Why do you believe that?
- What types of sales skills do you think you are weak in? What have you done to improve these skills?
- In your professional life have you ever had a large task or goal that forced you to learn new skills in order to accomplish it? What process did you use to develop the new skills?

When analyzing the answers applicants give you, look for the belief that selling is not a skill you are born with—either you have it or you don't—but something that can be developed with proper training. Moreover, have them demonstrate that they have a growth mindset by sharing how they have implemented it in their own life when attempting to improve in some area. If they cannot share how they have behaved in ways that illustrate a growth mindset, then rest assured that they probably don't have one.

One final thought about having a growth mindset: I have very rarely seen a salesperson achieve heightened levels of performance without it. The reason is that every salesperson desires to improve their sales, make more money, and better serve their customers. However, those with growth mindsets are usually the only ones who seek out the new knowledge and skills necessary to make their goals a reality.

> Every salesperson desires to improve their sales, make more money, and better serve their customers. However, those with growth mindsets are usually the only ones who seek out the new knowledge and skills necessary to make their goals a reality.

5. Top Performers Are Skilled in Interpersonal Communication

Because selling is based on the communication of ideas, the way salespeople communicate matters a lot. Those who have not developed their presentation skills will struggle to compete with those who have. This is because the way something is communicated shapes the interpretation of the ideas. Throughout this book I have provided numerous studies that illuminate this fact, but I can't resist disclosing just one more. This one is unique because it centers on something that none of the other studies I've shared with you have: beer.

When research scientists Leonard Lee, Shane Frederick, and Dan Ariely tested how people evaluated two different types of beers, they found that in a blind taste test people overwhelmingly preferred one of the beers, unless they were told the ingredients.[24] When prior to tasting the beers participants were told that the preferred one contained a few drops of balsamic vinegar, they overwhelmingly chose the other beer as the best tasting. In other words, the way the beers were presented so influenced the participants that it determined which they believed tasted better.

Similarly, the way salespeople communicate will impact how the company, product, or service they represent is perceived. If they are poor communicators, they have a hurdle that must be overcome. But poor sales performance does not afford these salespeople the time necessary to develop their communication skills.

How do you know if interviewees are competent communicators? You can analyze their communication in the following areas:

- **First impression:** Do they give off a positive first impression? Why or why not?
- **Verbal communication:** What do their words say about them? Do they clearly communicate their ideas in a compelling way?
- **Nonverbal communication:** What do their nonverbal cues, such as facial expressions, eye gaze, body movement, body posture, rate of speech, and voice inflections reveal about them and the thoughts they are espousing?

As you scrutinize potential sales hires' communication in each of these areas, it can be helpful to have them deliver a five-minute formal presentation. The topic does not matter, as long as it is one that is familiar to them. You want to focus on their communication skills. If they are stumbling over what to say next, it can distract from their presentation. I recommend having the candidate talk about the product or service they sold in the past, their hobbies, or even a favorite vacation spot. As you observe how they communicate, ask yourself, would I want this person representing me? If not, explore why. If so, ask why as well. This simple exercise will guide you in assessing candidates' communication skills.

Salespeople who meet these five core qualities are much more likely to have exceptional sales results because they have the internal and external traits that will enable them to become elite performers. In contrast, those who do not have even one of these five qualities have a large obstacle to overcome for them to achieve sales greatness. As a result, when you embrace this hiring system, you will grow your ability to identify the right person for a sales position, lower your rate of mis-hires, and improve your organization's overall sales production and efficiency.

YOUR FUTURE SELLING WITH SCIENCE

By now I hope I have convinced you of one fact: understanding and using the scientific principles of influence and decision making can significantly improve sales effectiveness. Throughout this book I have shown you how many of the most common sales strategies are outdated, ineffective, and harmful, because they conflict with the way the brain constructs a buying decision. Yet, perhaps most important, with the fusing of science and selling we also know how we can sell in ways that helps potential purchasers process our sales messages and make wise buying decisions.

What makes this approach to selling so radically different from others? For one thing, it's who I analyzed to create it. Unlike most modern sales systems, I did not survey a bunch of salespeople to find out what they were doing, or simply replicate the way I had sold in the past. Instead, I concentrated on what selling should always be focused on—buyers. Well, more specifically, what science has proven regarding how potential customers formulate buying decisions. Because what the research confirms is that the closer sales strategies are aligned with how the brain is influenced, the more productive they will be.

The Science of Selling also connects the dots between this cutting-edge science and real-world sales situations. It offers a new way of looking at and relating to buyers that is accurate, predictable, and reproducible. No longer must you base how you sell on anecdote or speculation. As this book has revealed, there are practical steps that anyone can take to boost sales success.

My hope is that *The Science of Selling* will make basing sales behaviors on science a normal business practice. It is what the profession of selling has been waiting for. It is what salespeople need to thrive in this challenging selling climate. And the good news is that this future is not far off—this future is *here*.

So now it's your turn. I encourage you to use the science-based strategies in this book to literally sell the way the brain is wired to buy, because when you do you'll become more influential, sell more effectively, and better serve others.

FIVE WAYS YOU CAN IMPROVE YOUR SALES WITH SCIENCE

1. **Book David to speak to your group.** He'll weave humor, stories, and science together in a way that will engage your audience and provide them with proven strategies they can use immediately to sell more.

2. **Have David deliver a sales training workshop or seminar** to take your organization's sales to the next level. His science-backed sales training will guide you in developing the knowledge and skills you need to increase your sales results.

3. **Get Hoffeld Group's sales coaching** to boost your sales production. We are the experts at helping companies improve how they coach their salespeople, and we also provide no-nonsense, highly customized sales coaching that will empower you to attain extraordinary results.

4. **Utilize our sales consulting** to heighten your company's sales effectiveness. We'll thoroughly assess your situation, identify opportunities to significantly increase your sales, and then design a custom solution to make it happen.

5. **Read this book** in your organization and apply it in your selling environment.

   Don't lose sales that should be yours. Contact us today about our proven, science-based selling strategies at

www.HoffeldGroup.com

info@HoffeldGroup.com

ACKNOWLEDGMENTS

The great poet John Donne wrote, "No man is an island." His words ring true as a book of this nature is not based on the research of one person, but on the analysis of the work of an army of men and women on whose shoulders I now stand. First and foremost, I am indebted to the neuroscientists and behavioral scientists who have delved into the inner workings of the human brain and identified the factors that influence behavior. Without their evidence-based findings, this book would have been an impossibility.

I am beholden to progressive sales thought leaders, such as Robert N. McMurry, Dave Stein, and others who sounded the alarms with their insightful critiques of the core problems plaguing the profession of sales. Their ideas deeply impacted me and spurred me on to find science-based answers to the challenges that salespeople face.

Thank you to those sales professionals who made me a better salesperson, particularly those who mentored me early in my career. I can still hear my first sales manager, Paul Winn, telling me, "You can't fly with the eagles, when you hang around with turkeys." Also, I would be remiss to not mention Joey, who listened to my initial presentations and whose influence I still feel to this day.

My literary agent, Leila Campoli, was also instrumental in bringing this book to fruition. She was a great advocate for the book and her insights were a tremendous help throughout the publishing process. I also owe a great debt to Stephanie Bowen, senior editor at TarcherPerigee Books, a division of Penguin Random House. Her enthusiasm for this project was inspiring and her feedback and suggestions elevated the book in every way. I shudder when I think about what it would have looked like without her influence.

My children, Jolene and David, graciously allowed me to focus on this book by keeping their play down to a small roar, "to not disturb Daddy while he is writing." I truly hope that someday, when both of them are older, that they will like the book, learn from it, and be proud of me for writing it.

Without my wife, Sarah's support, I would not have been able to write this book. She never complained as I invested an outrageous amount of time and money into researching and testing the ideas that comprise it. To this day, I am still amazed at how much she believed in me and this project.

I am grateful to NoEl Hoffeld, whose edits throughout the many early drafts of this book and the myriad of research reports that it is based on were indescribably helpful. She tirelessly worked to ensure that my mistakes were never seen by anyone but her. In fact, she has read almost everything I've ever written, and without her influence much of what I have done professionally would never have happened.

Special thanks to Norman Hoffeld, who taught me to speak in public and gave me many opportunities to do so. He was also my foremost example of how one can positively and ethically influence others.

Finally, to those sales professionals who, like me, have been waiting for a book that revealed science-based behaviors they could use to better serve buyers, I wrote this book for you. And now that you have it . . . get out there and sell something.

INTRODUCTION | WHY USE SCIENCE TO SELL

1. "National Occupational Employment and Wage Estimates," U.S. Bureau of Labor Statistics, retrieved July 4, 2016, www.bls.gov/oes/current/oes_nat.htm#41=0000.

2. Barry Trailer and Jim Dickie, "Understanding What Your Sales Manager Is Up Against," *Harvard Business Review* (July–August 2006); *Sales Performance and Optimization Study*, CSO Insights, 2010; *Sales Performance and Optimization: 2013 Key Trends Analysis*, CSO Insights, 2013.

3. Lynette Ryals and Iain Davies, "Do You Really Know Who Your Best Salespeople Are?," *Harvard Business Review* (December 2010).

4. Gregory Berns, "Neuroscientist Reveals How Nonconformists Achieve Success," Emory University Press Release, September 25, 2008, retrieved March 13, 2016, www.whsc.emory.edu/press_releases2.cfm?announcement_id_seq=15766.

5. Dawn R. Deeter-Schmelz and Karen N. Kennedy. "Buyer-Seller Relationships and Information Source in an E-Commerce World," *Journal of Business & Industrial Marketing* 19, no. 3 (2004): 188–201.

6. Benson P. Shapiro and John J. Sviokla, *Seeking Customers* (Boston: Harvard Business Press, 1993), 6.

7. Douglas T. Kenrick, Noah J. Goldstein, and Sanford Braver, eds., *Six Degrees of Social Influence* (Oxford: Oxford University Press, 2012), vii.

8. David G. Myers, *Social Psychology,* 9th ed. (New York: McGraw-Hill International Editions, 2008), 4.

9. "About Neuroscience," *Society for Neuroscience,* retrieved July 6, 2012, http://www.sfn.org/about/about-neuroscience?pagename=whatisneuroscience.

CHAPTER 1 | WHY SALESPEOPLE UNDERPERFORM

1. Lynette Ryals and Iain Davies, "Do You Really Know Who Your Best Salespeople Are?," *Harvard Business Review* (December 2010).

2. Barry Trailer and Jim Dickie, "Understanding What Your Sales Manager Is Up Against," *Harvard Business Review* (July–August 2006); *Sales Performance and Optimization Study,* CSO Insights, 2010; *Sales Performance and Optimization: 2013 Key Trends Analysis*, CSO Insights, 2013.

3. Suzanne Fogel, David Hoffmeister, Richard Rocco, and Daniel P. Struck, "Teaching Sales," *Harvard Business Review* (July–August, 2012), 94.

4. Matthew Dixon and Brent Adamson, *The Challenger Sales* (New York: Portfolio/Penguin, 2011), 51.

5. Peter Drucker, *Management: Tasks, Responsibilities, Practices* (New York: Harper & Row, 1974), 61.

6. K. A. Ericsson, W. G. Chase, and S. Faloon, "Acquisition of a Memory Skill," *Science* 208 (1980): 1181–82; Laura Kray and Michael Haselhuhn, "Implicit Theories of Negotiation Ability and Performance: Longitudinal and Experimental Evidence," *Journal of Personality and*

Social Psychology 93 (2007): 49–64; K. Anders Ericsson, Ralf Th. Krampe, and Clemens Tesch-Romer, "The Role of Deliberate Practice in the Acquisition of Expert Performance," *Psychological Review* 100, no 3 (1993): 363–406; Joseph J. Martochio, "Effects of Conceptions of Ability on Anxiety, Self-efficacy, and Learning in Training," *Journal of Applied Social Psychology* 79 (1994): 819–25.

7.   Lisa S. Blackwell, Kali Trzesniewski, and Carol S. Dweck, "Implicit Theories of Intelligence Predict Achievement Across an Adolescent Transition: A Longitudinal Study and an Intervention," *Child Development* 78 (2007): 246–63; Carol S. Dweck, *Mindset: The New Psychology of Success* (New York: Ballantine Books, 2008).

8.   Carol S. Dweck, C. Chiu, Y. Hong, "Implicit Theories and Their Role in Judgments and Reactions: A World from Two Perspectives," *Psychological Inquiry* 6 (1995): 267–85.

9.   Mark F. Bear, Barry W. Connors, Michael A. Paradiso, *Neuroscience: Exploring the Brain*, 3rd ed. (New York: Lippincott Williams & Wilkins, 2007); Matthew Lieberman, "Intuition: A Social Cognitive Neuroscience Approach," *Psychological Bulletin* 126, no. 1 (2000): 109–37; Pierce J. Howard, *The Owner's Manual for the Brain* (Austin, Tex.: Bard Press, 2006); Larry Squire and Eric Kandel, *Memory: From Mind to Molecules* (New York: Scientific American Library, 2000).

10.   James E. Zull, *The Art of Changing the Brain: Enriching the Practice of Teaching by Exploring the Biology of Learning* (Sterling, Va: Stylus, 2002).

11.   Gerald M. Edelman, *Neural Darwinism: The Theory of Neuronal Group Selection* (New York: Basic Books, 1987).

12.   Eleanor A. Maguire, David G. Gadian, Ingrid S. Johnsrude, Catriona D. Good, John Ashburner, Richard S. Frackowiak, and Christopher D. Firth, "Navigation-Related Structural Change in the Hippocampi of

Taxi Drivers." *Proceedings of the National Academy of Sciences* 97, 8, (2000): 4398–403.

13. K. A. Ericsson, et al. "Acquisition of a Memory Skill."

14. J. Wilding and E. Valentine, *Superior Memory* (Hove, East Sussex, UK: Psychology Press, 1997); J. Wilding and E. Valentine, "Exceptional Memory," in K. Anders Ericsson, Neil Charness, Paul J. Feltovich, and Robert R. Hoffman, eds, *The Cambridge Handbook of Expertise and Expert Performance* (Cambridge: Cambridge University Press, 2006), 539–52; K. L. Higbee, "Novices, Apprentices, and Mnemonists: Acquiring Expertise with the Phonetic Mnemonic," *Applied Cognitive Psychology* 11 (1997): 147–61.

15. K. Anders Ericsson, Roy W. Roring, and Kiruthiga Nandagopal, "Giftedness and Evidence for Reproducibly Superior Performance: An Account Based on the Expert Performance Framework," *High Ability Studies* 18, no. 1 (2007): 5.

16. Ericsson et al., "The Role of Deliberate Practice," 368; Anders Ericsson and Robert Pool, *Peak: Secrets from the New Science of Expertise* (New York: Houghton Mifflin Harcourt, 2016).

17. Betty Edwards, *The New Drawing on the Right Side of the Brain* (New York: Putnam Books, 1999).

18. Ibid., 18, 20.

19. James Kouzes and Barry Posner, *The Leadership Challenge* (San Francisco: Jossey-Bass, 2007), 171.

20. Dave Stein, *The Top 7 Sales Training Pitfalls & 7 Solutions for Sustained Success*, ES Research Group (2012), 3; Dave Stein, *Sales Training: The 120-Day Curse*, ES Research Group (2011), 3; Dixon and Adamson, *The Challenger Sales*, 174.

21.   Adrian Furnaham and Carl Fudge, "The Five Factor Model of
      Personality and Sales Performance," *Journal of Individual Differences*
      29 (2008): 11–16; Steve W. Martin, "Seven Personality Traits of Top
      Salespeople," *Harvard Business Review Blog Network*, June 27, 2011,
      blogs.hbr.org/2011/06/the-seven-personality-traits-o/.

22.   Murray R. Barrick, Michael K. Mount, and Timothy A. Judge,
      "Personality and Performance at the Beginning of the New Millennium:
      What Do We Know and Where Do We Go Next?," *International
      Journal of Selection and Assessment* 9, (March–June 2001): 9–30.

23.   Adam M. Grant, "Rethinking the Extraverted Sales Ideal: The Ambivert
      Advantage," *Psychological Science* 24, no. 6 (June 2013): 1024–30.

24.   Daniel J. Howard, "The Influence of Verbal Responses to Common
      Greetings on Compliance Behavior: The Foot-in-the-Mouth Effect,"
      Journal of Applied Social Psychology 20 (1990): 1185–96.

25.   Ibid., 1185.

CHAPTER 2 | THE TWO METHODS OF SALES INFLUENCE

1.   Norman Miller and Donald T. Campbell, "Recency and Primacy in
      Persuasion as a Function of the Timing of Speeches and Measurements,"
      Journal of Abnormal and Social Psychology 59 (1959): 1–9.

2.   Richard E. Petty and John T. Cacioppo, *Communication and
      Persuasion: Central and Peripheral Routes to Attitude Change* (New
      York: Springer-Verlag, 1986); R. E. Petty and J. T. Cacioppo. "The
      Elaboration Likelihood Model of Persuasion," in L. Berkowitz, ed.,
      Advances in Experimental Social Psychology, vol. 19 (San Diego:
      Academic Press, 1986), 123–205.

3.   Richard Petty, Jeff A. Kasmer, Curt P. Haugtvedt, and John Cacioppo,
      "Source and Message Factors in Persuasion: A Reply to Stiff's Critique of

the Elaboration Likelihood Model," *Communication Monographs* 54 (2004): 233–49; James B. Stiff, "Cognitive Processing of Persuasive Message Cues: A Meta-Analytic Review of the Effects of Supporting Information on Attitudes," *Communication Monographs* 53 (1986): 75–89.

4. Richard Petty and John Cacioppo, *Attitudes and Persuasion: Classic and Contemporary Approaches* (Dubuque, Ia.: William C. Brown Publishing, 1981), 256.

5. Daniel Kahneman, *Thinking, Fast and Slow* (New York: Farrar, Straus and Giroux, 2011), 20.

6. Amy Cuddy, quoted in Julia Hanna, "Power Posing: Fake It Until You Make It," Harvard Business School, *Working Knowledge: Research and Ideas*, September 20, 2010, hbswk.hbs.edu/item/power-posing-fake-it -until-you-make-it.

7. Richard H. Thaler, *Misbehaving: The Making of Behavioral Economics* (New York: W. W. Norton, 2015), 23.

8. Eric J. Johnson, John Hershey, Jacqueline Meszaros, and Howard Kunreuther, "Framing, Probability Distortions, and Insurance Decisions," in Daniel Kahneman and Amos Tversky, eds., *Choices, Values, and Frames* (New York: Cambridge University Press, 2000), 230.

9. Dan Ariely, *Predictably Irrational* (New York: HarperCollins, 2008), xx.

10. Daniel Mochon, "Single-Option Aversion," *Journal of Consumer Research*, 40 (October 2013); "Research Watch," *Harvard Business Review* (October 2013), 30.

11. Joel Huber, John W. Payne, and Christopher Putto, "Adding Asymmetrically Dominated Alternatives: Violations of Regularity and the Similarity Hypothesis," *Journal of Consumer Research* 9 (1982): 90–98.

12. Dan Ariely and Thomas S. Wallsten, "Seeking Subjective Dominance in Multidimensional Space: An Explanation of the Asymmetric Dominance Effect," *Organizational Behavior and Human Decision Processes* 63 (September, 1995): 223; Ian J. Bateman, Alistair Munro, and Gregory L. Poe, "Decoy Effects in Choice Experiments and Contingent Valuation: Asymmetric Dominance," *Land Economics* 84, no. 1 (2008): 115–27.

13. Ariely, *Predictably Irrational*, 4–6.

14. Jonathan K. Frenzen and Harry L. Davis, "Purchasing Behavior in Embedded Markets," *Journal of Consumer Research* 17, no. 1 (1990): 1–12.

15. Jerry M. Burger, Shelley Soroka, Katrina Gonzago, Emily Murphy, and Emily Somervell, "The Effect of Fleeting Attraction on Compliance to Requests," *Personality and Social Psychology Bulletin* 27 (2001): 1578–86; J. S. Seiter, "Ingratiation and Gratuity: The Effect of Complimenting Customers on Tipping Behavior in Restaurants," *Journal of Applied Social Psychology* 37 (2007): 487–85.

16. Sigmund Freud, "Letter to C. G. Jung, December 6, 1906," in E. Jones, *The Life and Work of Sigmund Freud: Years of Maturity, 1901–1919*, vol. 2 (New York: Basic Books, 1955), 435.

17. O. Wiegman, "Two Politicians in a Realistic Experiment: Attraction, Discrepancy, Intensity of Delivery, and Attitude Change," *Journal of Applied Social Psychology* 15 (1985): 673–86.

18. Amy J. C. Cuddy, Matthew Kohut, and John Neffinger, "Connect, Then Lead," *Harvard Business Review* (July–August 2013): 56.

19. D. B. Strohmetz, B. Rind, R. Fisher, and M. Lynn, "Sweetening the Till: The Use of Candy to Increase Restaurant Tipping," *Journal of Applied Social Psychology* 32 (2002): 300–9; D. Kenny and W. Nasby, "Splitting the Reciprocity Correlations," *Journal of Personality and Social Psychology* 38 (1980): 439–48.

20. Edward Ross, *Social Psychology* (New York: Macmillan, 1908), 1.

21. Solomon Asch, "Studies of Independence and Conformity: A Minority of One Against a Unanimous Majority," *Psychological Monographs* 70, (1956).

22. Solomon Asch, "Opinions and Social Pressure," in A. P. Hare, E. F. Borgatta, and R. F. Bales, eds., *Small Groups: Studies in Social Interaction* (New York: Alfred A. Knopf, 1966), 320.

23. Knud S. Larsen, "The Asch Conformity Experiment: Replication and Transhistorical Comparison," *Journal of Social Behavior and Personality* 5 (1990): 163–68; Dana M. Schneider and Michael J. Watkins, "Response Conformity in Recognition Testing," *Psychonomic Bulletin and Review* 3 (1996): 481–85.

24. Gregory S. Berns, Jonathan Chappelow, Caroline F. Zink, Giuseppe Pagnoni, Megan E. Martin-Skurski, and Jim Richards, "Neurobiological Correlates of Social Conformity and Independence During Mental Rotation," *Biological Psychiatry* 58 (2005): 245–53.

25. E. Goodman, "Advertising Hits Zany Levels," *The Herald Journal*, August 11, 2001, A4.

26. Daniel Eisenberg, "It's an Ad, Ad, Ad, Ad World," *Time*, September 2, 2002, 38–41.

27. Steve Martin, "Businesses Are Just Beginning to Understand the Power of 'Social Norms,'" *Harvard Business Review* (October 2012): 25.

28. Michael J. Cody and John S. Seiter, "Compliance Principles in Retail Sales in the United States," in Wilhelmina Wosinska, Robert B. Cialdini, Daniel W. Barrett, and Janusz Reykowski, eds., *The Practice of Social Influence in Multiple Cultures* (Mahwah, N.J.: Erlbaum, 2001), 325–41.

29. R.C.C. Fuller and A. Sheekh-Skeffinton, "Effects of Group Laughter on Responses to Humorous Materials: A Replication and Extension," *Psychological Reports* 35 (1974): 531–34; T. Nosanchuck and J. Lightstone, "Canned Laughter and Public and Private Conformity," *Journal of Personality and Social Psychology* 29 (1974): 153–56.

30. Rod Bond and Peter B. Smith, "Culture and Conformity: A Meta-Analysis of Studies Using Asch's (1952b, 1956) Line Judgment Task," *Psychological Bulletin* 119 (1996): 111–37; D. Abrams, M. S. Wetherell, S. Cochrane, M. A. Hogg, and J. C. Turner, "Knowing What to Think by Knowing Who You Are: Self-categorization and the Nature of Norm Formation, Conformity and Group Polarization," *British Journal of Social Psychology* 29 (1990): 97–119; Nancy P. Gordon, "Never Smokers, Triers and Current Smokers: Three Distinct Target Groups for School-Based Antismoking Programs," *Health Education Quarterly* 13 (1986): 163–79; M. Reed, J. Lange, J. Ketchie, and J. Clapp, "The Relationship Between Social Identity, Normative Information, and College Student Drinking," *Social Influence* 2 (2007): 269–94.

31. Richard Petty, C. Haugtvedt, and S. M. Smith, "Elaboration as a Determinant of Attitude Strength: Creating Attitudes That Are Persistent, Resistant, and Predictive of Behavior," in R. E. Petty and J. A. Krosnick, eds., *Attitude Strength: Antecedents and Consequences* (Mahwah, N.J.: Erlbaum, 1995), 99–130; Richard E. Petty, John T. Cacioppo, Alan J. Strathman, and Joseph R. Priester, "To Think or Not to Think: Exploring Two Routes to Persuasion," in Timothy C. Brock and Melanie C. Green, eds., *Persuasion: Psychological Insights and Perspectives* (Thousand Oaks, Calif.: Sage, 2005), 81–116.

32. Petty and Cacioppo, *Communication and Persuasion.*

33. Petty et al., "Elaboration as a Determinant of Attitude Strength," 99–130; Petty and Cacioppo, *Communication and Persuasion,* 21.

34. Robert H. Gass and John S. Seiter, *Persuasion: Social Influence and Compliance Gaining*, 4th ed. (Boston: Allyn & Bacon, 2011), 35.

Chapter 3 | How to Sell the Way People Buy

1. William Samuelson and Richard Zeckhauser, "Status Quo Bias in Decision Making," *Journal of Risk and Uncertainty* 1 (1988): 7–59.

2. Richard Thaler, *Misbehaving: The Making of Behavioral Economics* (New York: W. W. Norton, 2105), 154.

3. Daniel Kahneman and Amos Tversky, "The Psychology of Preference," *Scientific American* 246 (1982): 160–73.

4. Jacob Getzels, "Problem Finding: A Theoretical Note," *Cognitive Science* 3 (1979).

5. Mark Lindwall, "Why Don't Buyers Want to Meet with Your Salespeople," *Mark Lindwall's Blog*, Forrester Research, September 29, 2014, blogs.forrester.com/mark_lindwall/14-09-29-why_dont_buyers_want_to_meet_with_your_salespeople.

6. John Medina, *Brain Rules* (Seattle: Pear Press, 2008), 71.

7. Brigitte C. Madrian and Dennis F. Shea, "The Power of Suggestion: Inertia in 401(k) Participation and Savings Behavior," *Quarterly Journal of Economics* 116 (2001): 1149–87.

8. Eric J. Johnson and Daniel Goldstein, "Do Defaults Save Lives?," *Science* 302 (2003): 1,338–39.

9. Jonathan Levav and Rui (Juliet) Zhu, "Seeking Freedom Through Variety," *Journal of Consumer Research* 36 (2009): 600–10; Claude H. Miller, Lindsay T. Lane, Leslie M. Deatrick, Alice M. Young, and

Kimberly A. Potts, "Psychological Reactance and Promotional Health Messages: The Effects of Controlling Language, Lexical Concreteness, and the Restoration of Freedom," *Human Communication Research* 33 (2007): 219–40; Sharon S. Brehm and Jack W. Brehm, *Psychological Reactance: A Theory of Freedom and Control* (San Diego: Academic Press, 1981); P. R. Nail, G. MacDonald, and D.A. Levy, "Proposal of a Four-Dimensional Model of Social Response," *Psychological Bulletin* 126 (2000): 454–70.

10. A. Doyne Horsley, "The Unintended Effects of a Posted Sign on Littering Attitudes and Stated Intentions," *Journal of Environmental Education* 19, no. 3 (1988): 10–14; Ralf Hansmann and Roland W. Scholz, "A Two-Step Informational Strategy for Reducing Littering Behavior in a Cinema," *Environment and Behavior* 35, no. 6 (2003): 752–62.

11. Nicolas Guéguen and Alexandre Pascual, "Evocation of Freedom and Compliance: The 'But You Are Free of . . .' Technique," *Current Research in Social Psychology* 5 (2000): 264–70.

12. George A. Akerlof, "The Market for 'Lemons': Quality Uncertainty and the Market Mechanism," *Quarterly Journal of Economics* 84, no. 3 (August 1970): 488–500.

13. Ibid., 489.

14. Amy J. C. Cuddy, Matthew Kohut, and John Neffinger, "Connect, Then Lead," *Harvard Business Review* (July–August 2013): 58.

15. L. Ross and A. Ward, "Psychological Barriers to Dispute Resolution," in M. P. Zanna, ed., *Advances in Experimental Social Psychology*, vol. 27 (San Diego: Academic Press, 1995).

16. Cuddy et al., "Connect, Then Lead," 58.

17. Chanthika Pornpitakpan, "The Persuasiveness of Source Credibility: A Critical Review of Five Decades' Evidence," *Journal of Applied Social Psychology* 34 (2004): 242–81.

18. R. G. Hass, "Effects of Source Characteristics on the Cognitive Processing of Persuasive Messages and Attitude Change," in R. Petty, T. Ostrom, and T. Brock, eds., *Cognitive Responses in Persuasion* (Hillsdale, N.J.: Erlbaum, 1981), 141–72.

19. Peter Aldhous, "Humans Prefer Cockiness to Expertise," *New Scientist*, June 3, 2009, retrieved on March 16, 2016, www.newscientist.com/article/mg20227115.500-humans-prefer-cockiness-to-expertise/.

20. S. Kang, A. Galinsky, L. Kray, and A. Shirako, "Power Affects Performance When the Pressure Is On: Evidence for Low-Power Threat and High-Power Lift," *Personality and Social Psychology Bulletin* 41 (2015); J. D. Creswell, J. M. Dutcher, W.M.P. Klein, P. R. Harris, and J. M. Levine, "Self-Affirmation Improves Problem-Solving under Stress," PLoS ONE 8 (5): e62593. doi:10.1371/journal.pone.0062593.

21. Dana R. Carney, Amy J. C. Cuddy, and Andy J. Yap, "Power Posing: Brief Nonverbal Displays Affect Neuroendocrine Levels and Risk Tolerance," *Psychological Science* 21 (October 2010): 1363–68.

22. Michael Porter, *On Competition* (Boston: Harvard Business School Press, 2008), 88–89.

23. Michael Lynn, "Scarcity Effects on Value: A Quantitative Review of the Commodity Theory Literature," *Psychology and Marketing* 8 (1991): 43–57; Michael Lynn, "Scarcity Effects on Value: Mediated by Assumed Expensiveness," *Journal of Economic Psychology* 10 (1989): 257–74; Michael Lynn and Paulette Bogert, "The Effect of Scarcity on Anticipated Price Appreciation," *Journal of Applied Social Psychology* 26 (1996): 1978–84.

24. Stephen Worchel, Jerry Lee, and Akanbi Adewole, "Effects of Supply and Demand on Ratings of Object Value," *Journal of Personality and Social Psychology* 32, no. 5 (1975): 906–14.

25. "The Prize in Economics 2002—Press Release," Nobelprize.org, retrieved February 14, 2013, http://www.nobelprize.org/nobel_prizes/economic-sciences/laureates/2002/press.html.

26. Daniel Kahneman and Amos Tversky, "The Framing of Decisions and the Psychology of Choice," *Science* 211 (1981): 453–58.

27. Daniel Kahneman and Amos Tversky, "Buyer Theory: An Analysis of Decision Under Risk," *Econometrical* 47 (1979): 263–91; Daniel Kahneman and Amos Tversky, "Advances in Buyer Theory: Cumulative Representation of Uncertainty," *Journal of Risk and Uncertainty* 5 (1992): 297–323.

28. Kahneman and Tversky, "The Framing of Decisions," 453.

29. Melanie B. Tannenbaum, Justin Helper, Rick S. Zimmerman, Lindsey Saul, Samantha Jacobs, Kristina Wilson, and Dolores Albarracín, "Appealing to Fear: A Meta-Analysis of Fear Appeal Effectiveness and Theories," *Psychological Bulletin* 141, no. 6 (2015): 1178–1204.

30. Christopher Trepel, Craig R. Fox, and Russell A. Poldrack, "Buyer Theory on the Brain? Toward a Cognitive Neuroscience of Decision Under Risk," *Cognitive Brain Research* 23 (2005): 39.

31. Ned Welch, "A Marketer's Guide to Behavioral Economics," *McKinsey Quarterly,* February 2010, 3.

32. Howard Leventhal, "Findings and Theory in the Study of Fear Communications," *Advances in Experimental Social Psychology* 5 (1970): 119–86; Howard Leventhal, Robert Singer, and Susan Jones, "Effects of Fear and Specificity of Recommendations Attitudes and Behavior," *Journal of Personality and Social Psychology* 2 (1965): 20–29.

Chapter 4 | Selling to Your Buyers' Emotions

1. Antonio Damasio, *Descartes' Error: Emotion, Reason, and the Human Brain* (New York: Penguin Books, 2005), 193–94.

2. Ibid., 208–10.

3. Daniel Goleman, *Emotional Intelligence* (New York: Random House, 2006), 20.

4. Chip Heath and Dan Heath, *Made to Stick* (New York: Random House, 2008), 275.

5. A. M. Isen and B. Means, "The Influence of Positive Affect on Decision Making Strategy," *Social Cognition* 2 (1983): 28–31; A. L. Stone and C. R. Glass, "Cognitive Distortion of Social Feedback in Depression," *Journal of Social and Clinical Psychology* 4 (1986): 179–88; Antonio Damasio, "In Conversation with David Brooks," interview by David Brooks, July 4, 2009, Aspen Ideas Festival, Aspen, Colorado; A. M. Isen, "The Influence of Positive Affect on Clinical Problem Solving," *Medical Decision Making* (July–September 1991); Alice M. Isen, "Positive Affect," in Tim Dalgleish and Mick J. Power, eds., *Handbook of Cognition and Emotions* (Chichester, England: Wiley, 1999); R. E. Petty, D. W. Schumann, S. A. Richman, and A. J. Strathman, "Positive Mood and Persuasion: Different Roles for Affect Under High- and Low-Elaboration Conditions," *Journal of Personality and Social Psychology* 64 (1993): 5–20; Gordon H. Bower, "Mood Congruity of Social Judgment," in Joseph Forgas, ed., *Emotional and Social Judgments* (Oxford: Pergamon Press, 1991), 31–33.

6. A. M. Isen, "Toward Understanding the Role of Affect in Cognition," in R. S. Wyer and T. K. Srull, eds., *Handbook of Social Cognition*, vol. 3. (Hillsdale, N.J.: Erlbaum, 1984), 179–236.

7. Petty et al., "Positive Mood and Persuasion," 5–20.

8. Scott Magids, Alan Zorfas, and Daniel Leemon, "The New Science of Customer Emotions," *Harvard Business Review* (November 2015): 68.

9. Karen O'Quin and Joel Aronoff, "Humor as a Technique of Social Influence," *Social Psychology Quarterly* 44 (1981): 349–57.

10. Michael Ross and Garth Fletcher, "Attribution and Social Perception," in Gardner Lindzey and Elliot Aronson, eds., *The Handbook of Social Psychology*, 3rd ed. (New York: Random House, 1985).

11. Shai Danziger, Jonathan Levav, and Liora Avnaim-Pesso, "Extraneous Factors in Judicial Decisions," *Proceedings of the National Academy of Sciences* 108, no.17, 6889–92.

12. David G. Myers, *Social Psychology*, 9th ed. (New York: McGraw-Hill International Editions, 2008), 97.

13. Jay A. Conger, "The Necessary Art of Persuasion," *Harvard Business Review* (May–June 1998).

14. Eduardo B. Andrade and Dan Ariely, "The Enduring Impact of Transient Emotions on Decision Making," *Journal of Organizational Behavior and Human Decision Processes* 109 (2009): 1–8.

15. Ross and Fletcher, "Attribution and Social Perception."

16. James M. Dabbs Jr. and Irving L. Janis, "Why Does Eating While Reading Facilitate Opinion Change? An Experimental Inquiry," *Journal of Experimental Social Psychology* 1 (1965): 133–44.

17. Sybil Carrère and John Mordechai Gottman, "Predicting Divorce Among Newlyweds from the First Three Minutes of a Marital Conflict Discussion," *Family Process* 38, no. 3 (1999), 293–301; John Mordechai Gottman and Robert Wayne Levenson, "A Two-Factor Model for Predicting When a Couple Will Divorce: Exploratory

Analyses Using 14-Year Longitudinal Data," *Family Process*, 41, no. 1 (2002): 83–96.

18. Kim Therese Buehlman, John Mordechai Gottman, and Lynn Fainsilver Katz, "How a Couple Views Their Past Predicts Their Future: Predicting Divorce from an Oral History Interview," *Journal of Family Psychology* 5 (1992): 295–318.

19. Albert Mehrabian and Susan R. Ferris, "Inference of Attitudes from Nonverbal Communication in Two Channels," *Journal of Consulting Psychology* 31 (1967): 109–14.

20. J. K. Burgoon, "Nonverbal Signals," in M. L. Knapp and G. R. Miller, eds., *Handbook of Interpersonal Communication* (Beverly Hills, Calif.: Sage Publications, 1985), 344–90.

21. Ellen Langer, "Rethinking the Role of Thought in Social Interaction," in J. H. Harvey, W. J. Ickles, and R. F. Kidd, eds., *New Directions in Attribution Research*, vol. 2 (New York: Wiley, 1978), 35–58; Ellen Langer, "Minding Matters," in L. Berkowitz, ed., *Advances in Experimental Social Psychology*, vol. 22 (New York: Addison-Wesley, 1989), 137–73.

22. Nalini Ambady and Robert Rosenthal, "Half a Minute: Predicting Teacher Evaluations from Thin Slices of Nonverbal Behavior and Physical Attractiveness," *Journal of Personality and Social Psychology* 64, no. 3 (1993): 431–41.

23. Elaine Hatfield, John T. Cacioppo, and Richard L. Rapson, *Emotional Contagion* (Cambridge: Cambridge University Press, 1994), 79.

24. Daniel Goleman, *Social Intelligence* (New York: Bantam Books, 2006), 13.

25. Ibid., 13.

26. Peter Totterdell, Steve Kellett, Katja Teuchmann, and Rob B. Briner, "Evidence of Mood Linkage in Work Groups," *Journal of Personality and Social Psychology* 74 (1998): 1504–15.

27. W. D. Hutchinson, K. D. Davis, A. M. Lozano, and J. O. Dostrovsky, "Pain-Related Neurons in the Human Cingulate Cortex," *Nature-Neuroscience* 2 (1999): 403–5; C. K. Hsee, E. Hatfield, J. G. Carlson, and C. Chemtob, "The Effect of Power on Susceptibility to Emotional Cognition," *Cognition and Emotion* 4 (1990): 327–40; Daniel Goleman, Richard Boyatzis, and Annie McKee, "The Emotional Reality of Teams," *Journal of Organization Excellence* 21 (Spring 2002): 55–65.

28. Howard Friedman and Ronald Riggio,"Effect of Individual Differences in Nonverbal Expressiveness on Transmission of Emotion," *Journal of Nonverbal Behavior* 6 (1981).

29. M. D. Pell, K. Rothermich, P. Liu, S. Paulmann, S. Sethi, and S. Rigoulot, "Preferential Decoding of Emotion from Human Non-Linguistic Vocalizations Versus Speech Prosody," *Biological Psychology* 111 (October 2015): 14–25.

30. Katherine I. Miller, "Compassionate Communication in the Workplace: Exploring Processes of Noticing, Connecting, and Responding," *Journal of Applied Communication Research* 35, no. 3 (August 2007): 223–45.

31. Roland Neumann and Fritz Strack, "'Mood Contagion': The Automatic Transfer of Mood Between Persons," *Journal of Personality and Social Psychology* 79 (2000): 211–13.

32. N. Ambady, D. Laplante, T. Nguyen, R. Rosenthal, N. Chaumeton, and W. Levinson, "Surgeons' Tone of Voice: A Clue to Malpractice History," *Surgery* 132 (2002): 5–9.

33. K. A. Feldman, "Identifying Exemplary Teachers and Teaching: Evidence from Student Ratings," in R. P. Perry and J. C. Smart, eds., *Effective*

Teaching in Higher Education: Research and Practice (New York: Agathon Press, 1997); P. M. Niedenthal, L. W. Barsalou, F. Ric, and S. Krauth-Gruber. "Embodiment in the Acquisition and Use of Emotional Knowledge," in L. F. Barrett, P. M. Niedenthal, and P. Winkielman, eds., *Emotion and Consciousness* (New York: Guilford Press, 2005); D. R. Cruickshank, *Teaching Is Tough* (Upper Saddle River, N.J.: Prentice Hall, 1980); N. L. Gage. "The Generality of Dimensions of Teaching," in P. O. Peterson and H. J. Walberg, eds., *Research and Teaching: Concepts, Findings, and Implications* (Berkeley, Calif.: McCutchan, 1979).

34. Raymond J. Wlodkowski, *Enhancing Adult Motivation to Learn* (San Francisco: Jossey-Bass, 2008), 70.

35. Ellen J. Langer, Arthur Blank, and Benzion Chanowitz, "The Mindlessness of Ostensibly Thoughtful Action: The Role of "Placebic" Information in Interpersonal Interaction," *Journal of Personality and Social Psychology* 36 (1978): 635–42.

36. Anthony Bastardi and Eldar Shafir, "Nonconsequential Reasoning and Its Consequences," *Current Directions in Psychological Science* 9 (2000): 216–19; D. Berlinger, "But Do They Understand?," in V. Richardson-Koehler, ed., *Educator's Handbook: A Research Perspective* (New York: Longman, 1987).

37. F. J. Roethlisberger and W. J. Dickson, *Management and the Worker* (Cambridge, Mass.: Harvard University Press, 1939).

38. Kay-Yut Chen and Marina Krakovsky, *Secrets of the Moneylab: How Behavioral Economics Can Improve Your Business* (New York: Portfolio/Penguin, 2010); M. Morris, J. Nadler, T. Kurtzberg, and L. Thompson, "Schmooze or Lose: Social Friction and Lubrication in Email Negotiations," *Group Dynamics* 6 (2002): 89–100.

39. Norbert Schwarz, Herbert Bless, and Gerd Bohner, "Mood and Persuasion: Affective States Influence the Processing of Persuasive

Communications," in M. P. Zanna, ed., *Advances in Experimental Social Psychology*, vol. 24 (New York: Academic Press, 1991), 161–99.

40. W. Flack, J. Laird, and L. Cavallaro, "Separate and Combined Effects of Facial Expressions and Bodily Postures on Emotional Feelings," *European Journal of Social Psychology* 29 (1999): 203–17; S. E. Duclos, J. Laird, E. Schneider, M. Sexter, L. Stern, and O. Van Lighten, "Emotion-Specific Effects of Facial Expressions and Postures on Emotional Experience," *Journal of Personality and Social Psychology* 57 (1989): 100–8.

41. C. L. Kleinke, T. R. Peterson, and T. R. Rutledge, "Effects of Self-Generated Facial Expressions on Mood," *Journal of Personality and Social Psychology* 74 (1998): 272–79.

42. William James, "The Gospel of Relaxation," in Robert D. Richardson, ed., *The Heart of William James* (Cambridge, Mass.: Harvard University Press, 2010), 131.

43. C. E. Izard, "Facial Expressions and the Regulation of Emotions," *Journal of Personality and Social Psychology* 58 (1990): 487–98.

44. James D. Laird, "Self-Attribution of Emotion: The Effects of Expressive Behavior on the Quality of Emotional Experience," *Journal of Personality and Social Psychology* 29 (1974): 475–86; T. R. McCane and J. A. Anderson, "Emotional Responding Following Experimental Manipulation of Facial Electromyography Activity," *Journal of Personality and Social Psychology* 52 (1987): 759–68; J. T. Cacioppo, D. J. Klein, G. G. Berntson, and E. Hatfield, "The Psychophysiology of Emotion," in M. Lewis and J. M. Haviland-Jones, eds., *Handbook of Emotions* (New York: Guilford Press, 1993), 119–42.

45. Saul Kassin, Steven Fein, and Hazel Rose Markus, *Social Psychology*, 7th ed. (Belmont, Calif.: Wadsworth, 2008), 58.

46. S. Schnall and J. D. Laird. "Keep Smiling: Enduring Effects of Facial Expressions and Postures on Emotional Experience and Memory," *Cognition and Emotion* 17 (2003): 787–97.

47. Robert B. Zajonc, Sheila T. Murphy, and Daniel N. McIntosh, "Brain Temperature and Subjective Emotional Experience," in M. Lewis and J. M. Haviland, eds., *Handbook of Emotions* (New York: Guilford Press, 1993), 209–20.

Chapter 5 | The Science of Asking Powerful Questions

1. Vicki G. Morwitz, Eric Johnson, and David Schmittlein, "Does Measuring Intent Change Behavior?," *Journal of Consumer Research* 20 (1993): 46–61.

2. Anthony G. Greenwald, Catherine G. Carnot, Rebecca Beach, and Barbara Young, "Increasing Voting Behavior by Asking People if They Expect to Vote," *Journal of Applied Psychology* 2 (1987): 315–18.

3. Gaston Godin, Paschal Sheeran, Mark Conner, and Marc Germain, "Asking Questions Changes Behavior: Mere Measurement Effects on Frequency of Blood Donation," *Health Psychology* 27 (March 2008): 179–84.

4. Vicki G. Morwitz et al., "Does Measuring Intent Change Behavior?," 46–61; P. Williams, L. G. Block, and G. J. Fitzsimons, "Simply Asking Questions About Health Behaviors Increases Both Healthy and Unhealthy Behavior," *Social Influence* 1 (2006): 117–27, http://www .tandfonline.com/doi/full/10.1080/15534510600630850; M. Conner, G. Godin, P. Norman, and P. Sheeran, "Using the Question-Behavior Effect to Promote Disease Prevention Behaviors: Two Randomized Controlled Trials," *Health Psychology* 30 (2011): 300–9.

5. Maryanne Garry and Devon L. L. Polaschek, "Imagination and Memory," *Current Directions in Psychological Science* 9 (2000): 6–10;

James E. Driskell, Carolyn Copper, and Aidan Moran, "Does Mental Practice Enhance Performance?," *Journal of Applied Psychology* 79 (1994): 481–92.

6. Pierce J. Howard, *The Owner's Manual for the Brain* (Austin, Tex.: Bard Press, 2006), 497.

7. John Medina, *Brain Rules* (Seattle: Pear Press, 2008), 85.

8. Herbert A. Simon, *Administrative Behavior*, 4th ed. (New York: Simon & Schuster, 1997), 90.

9. Edward M. Hallowell, M.D., *CrazyBusy: Overstretched, Overbooked, and About to Snap!* (New York: Ballantine Books, 2007), 19.

10. Mihaly Csikszentmihalyi, *Good Business* (New York: Penguin Group, 2003), 77.

11. Chanthika Pornpitakpan, "The Persuasiveness of Source Credibility: A Critical Review of Five Decades' Evidence," *Journal of Applied Social Psychology* 34 (2004): 242–81.

12. W. L. Benoit and A. Strathman, "Source Credibility and the Elaboration Likelihood Model," in Robert H. Gass and John S. Seiter, eds., *Readings in Persuasion, Social Influence, and Compliance Gaining* (Boston: Allyn & Bacon, 2004); D. J. O'Keefe, "The Persuasive Effects of Delaying Identification of High- and Low-Credibility Communicators: A Meta-Analytic Review," *Central States Speech Journal* 38 (1987): 63–72; Frances S. Chen, Julia A. Minson, and Zakary L. Tormala, "Tell Me More: The Effects of Expressed Interest on Receptiveness During Dialogue," *Journal of Experimental Social Psychology* 46 (2010): 850–53.

13. Michael T. Bosworth, John R. Holland, and Frank Visgatis, *CustomerCentric Selling* (New York: McGraw-Hill, 2010); Neil

Rackham, *SPIN Selling* (New York: McGraw-Hill, 1988); Dale Carnegie and Associates, Inc., J. Oliver Crom and Michael Crom, *The Sales Advantage* (New York: Simon & Schuster, 2003).

14. Deb Calvert, *DISCOVER Questions Get You Connected* (Morgan Hill, Calif.: Winston Keen James Publishing, 2012).

15. Rackham, *SPIN Selling*, 89.

16. Irwin Altman and Dalmas A. Taylor, *Social Penetration: The Development of Interpersonal Relationships* (New York: Holt Rinehart and Winston, 1973).

17. Chen et al., "Tell Me More," 850–53; Kevin L. Blankenship and Traci Y. Craig, "Rhetorical Question Use and Resistance to Persuasion: An Attitude Strength Analysis," *Journal of Language and Social Psychology* 25 (June 2006): 111–28; Kevin L. Blankenship and Traci Y. Craig, "Language and Persuasion: Tag Questions as Powerless Speech or as Interpreted in Context," *Journal of Experimental Psychology* 43 (2007): 112–18.

18. Chen et al., "Tell Me More," 850–53.

19. Blankenship and Craig, "Language and Persuasion," 112–18; L. A. Hosman and S. A. Siltanen, "Hedges, Tag Questions, Message Processing, and Persuasion," *Journal of Language and Social Psychology* 30 (2011): 341–49; Blankenship and Craig, "Rhetorical Question Use and Resistance to Persuasion," 111–28.

20. Diana I. Tamir and Jason P. Mitchell, "Disclosing Information About the Self Is Intrinsically Rewarding," *Proceedings of the National Academy of Sciences* 109, no. 21: 8,038–43.

Chapter 6 | Why People Buy

1. Mary Parker Follett, "Constructive Conflict," in Henry Metcalf and Lyndall Urwick, eds., *Dynamic Administration: The Collected Papers of Mary Parker Follett* (New York: Harper, 1941), 39–49.

2. David Mayer and Herbert M. Greenberg, "What Makes a Good Salesman?," *Harvard Business Review* (July–August 2006).

3. Erika Rasmusson, "The 10 Traits of Top Salespeople," *Journal of Personal Selling and Sales Management* 20 (2000): 75–87; Bruce K. Pilling and Sevo Eroglu, "An Empirical Examination of the Impact of Salesperson Empathy and Professionalism and Merchandise Salability on Retail Buyers' Evaluations," *Journal of Personal Selling and Sales Management* (Winter 1994); Lucette B. Comer and Tanya Drollinger, "Active Empathetic Listening and Selling Success: A Conceptual Framework," *Journal of Personal Selling & Sales Management* 19 (1999): 15–29.

4. Praveen Aggarwal, Stephen B. Castleberry, Rick Ridnour, and C. David Shepherd, "Salesperson Empathy and Listening: Impact on Relationship Outcomes," *Journal of Marketing Theory and Practice* 13, no. 3 (2005): 16–31.

5. Mark Lindwall, "Why Don't Buyers Want to Meet with Your Salespeople," *Mark Lindwall's Blog*, Forrester Research, September 29, 2014, blogs.forrester.com/mark_lindwall/14-09-29-why_dont_buyers_want_to_meet_with_your_salespeople.

6. D. J. Simons and C. F. Chabris, "Gorillas in Our Midst: Sustained Inattentional Blindness for Dynamic Events," *Perception* 28 (1999): 1059–74.

7. S. B. Most, D. J. Simons, B. J. Scholl, R. Jimenez, E. Clifford, and C. F. Chabris, "How Not to Be Seen: The Contribution of Similarity and

Selective Ignoring to Sustained Inattentional Blindness," *Psychological Science* 12 (2000): 9–17; D. Memmert, "The Effects of Eye Movements, Age, and Expertise on Inattentional Blindness," *Consciousness and Cognition* 15 (2006): 620–27.

8.   Arien Mack and Irvin Rock, *Inattentional Blindness* (Cambridge, Mass.: MIT Press, 1998).

9.   Greg W. Marshall, Daniel J. Goebel, and William C. Moncrief, "Hiring for Success at the Buyer-Seller Interface," *Journal of Business Research* 56 (2003): 247–55; Dawn R. Deeter-Schmelz, Daniel J. Goebel, and Karen Norman Kennedy, "What Are the Characteristics of an Effective Sales Manager? An Exploratory Study Comparing Salesperson and Sales Manager Perspectives," *Journal of Personal Selling and Sales Management* 28 (2008): 7–20; Stephen B. Castleberry and C. David Shepherd, "Effective Interpersonal Listening and Personal Selling," *Journal of Personal Selling and Sales Management* 13 (1993): 35–49; Rosemary P. Ramsey and Ravipreet S. Sohi, "Listening to Your Customers: The Impact of Perceived Salesperson Listening Behavior on Relational Outcomes," *Journal of the Academy of Marketing Science* 25 (1997): 127–37.

10.   Tom Atkinson and Ron Koprowski, "Sales Reps' Biggest Mistakes," *Harvard Business Review* (July 2006).

11.   Francis J. Flynn and Vanessa K. B. Lake, "If You Need Help, Just Ask: Underestimating Compliance with Direct Requests for Help," *Journal of Personality and Social Psychology* 95, no. 1 (2008): 128–43

12.   J. L. Lakin and T. L. Chartrand, "Using Nonconscious Behavioral Mimicry to Create Affiliation and Rapport," *Psychological Science* 14 (2003): 334–39; Marianne LaFrance, "Nonverbal Synchrony and Rapport: Analysis by the Cross-Lag Panel Technique," *Social Psychology Quarterly* 42 (1979): 66–70; Jerry M. Burger, Nicole Messian, Shebani Patel, Alicia del Prado, and Carmen Anderson,

"What a Coincidence! The Effects of Incidental Similarity on Compliance," *Personality and Social Psychology Bulletin* 30 (January 2004): 35–43.

13. R. B. van Baaren, R. W. Holland, B. Steenaert, and A. van Knippenberg, "Mimicry for Money: Behavioral Consequences of Imitation," *Journal of Experimental Social Psychology* 39 (2003): 393–98.

Chapter 7 | Creating Value, Neutralizing Competitors, and Overcoming Objections

1. Myron Rothbart and Pamela Birrell, "Attitude and Perception of Faces," *Journal of Research Personality* 11 (1977): 209–15.

2. John W. Thibaut and Harold H. Kelley, *The Social Psychology of Groups* (New York: Wiley, 1959).

3. Elliot Aronson, Timothy D. Wilson, and Robin M. Akert, *Social Psychology*, 7th ed. (Upper Saddle River, N.J.: Prentice Hall, 2010), 300.

4. Harold H. Kelley and John W. Thibaut, *Interpersonal Relations: A Theory of Interdependence* (New York: Wiley, 1978); Edna B. Foa and Uriel G. Foa, *Resource Theory of Social Exchange* (Morristown, N.J.: General Learning Press, 1975).

5. Elmer Wheeler, *Tested Sentences That Sell* (Englewood, N.J.: Prentice-Hall, 1937).

6. Daniel M. Romero, Roderick I. Swaab, Brian Uzzi, and Adam Galinsky, "Mimicry Is Presidential: Linguistic Style Matching in Presidential Debates and Improved Polling Numbers," *Journal of Personality and Social Psychology* 41 (October 2015): 1311–19; Robin J. Tanner, Rosellina Ferraro, Tanya L. Chartrand, James R. Bettman, and Rick van Baaren, "Of Chameleons and Consumption:

The Impact of Mimicry on Choice and Preferences," *Journal of Consumer Research* 34 (2007): 754–66; William W. Maddux, Elizabeth Mullen, and Adam D. Galinsky, "Chameleons Bake Bigger Pies and Take Bigger Pieces: Strategic Behavioral Mimicry Facilitates Negotiation Outcomes," *Journal of Experimental Social Psychology* 44 (2008): 461–68; Jeremy N. Bailenson and Nick Yee, "Digital Chameleons: Automatic Assimilation of Nonverbal Gestures in Immersive Virtual Environments," *Psychological Science* 16 (2005): 814–19; R. B. van Baaren, R. W. Holland, B. Steenaert, and A. van Knippenberg, "Mimicry for Money: Behavioral Consequences of Imitation," *Journal of Experimental Social Psychology* 39 (2003): 393–98.

7. Robert B. Cialdini and Noah J. Goldstein, "Social Influence: Compliance and Conformity," *Annual Review of Psychology* 55 (2004): 591–621; P. R. Kunz and M. Woolcott, "Season's Greetings: From My Status to Yours," *Social Science Research* 5 (1976): 269–78; R. Cialdini and K. Ascani, "Test of a Concession Procedure for Inducting Verbal, Behavioral, and Future Compliance with a Request to Give Blood," *Journal of Applied Psychology* 61 (1976): 295–300.

8. A. W. Goulder, "The Norm of Reciprocity: A Preliminary Statement," *American Sociological Review* 25 (1960): 161–78.

9. Dennis T. Regan, "Effects of a Favor and Liking on Compliance," *Journal of Experimental Social Psychology* 7 (1971): 627–39.

10. Jill Smolowe, "Contents Require Immediate Attention," *Time*, November 26, 1990, 64.

11. D. B. Strohmetz, B. Rind, R. Fisher, and M. Lynn, "Sweetening the Till: The Use of Candy to Increase Restaurant Tipping," *Journal of Applied Social Psychology* 32 (2002): 300–9.

12. Priya Raghubir, "Free Gift with Purchase: Promoting or Discounting the Brand?," *Journal of Consumer Psychology* 14 (2004), 181–86; Priya

Raghubir, "Framing a Price Bundle: The Case of 'Buy/Get' Offers," *Journal of Product and Brand Management* 14 (2005): 123–28.

13. Varda Liberman, Steven M. Samuels, and Lee Ross, "The Name of the Game: Predictive Power of Reputations Versus Situational Labels in Determining Prisoner's Dilemma Game Moves," *Personality and Social Psychology Bulletin* 30 (2004): 1175–85; R. E. Kraut, "The Effects of Social Labeling on Giving to Charity," *Journal of Experimental Social Psychology* 9 (1973): 551–62; J. K. Beggan and S. T. Allison, "More There Than Meets the Eyes: Support for the Mere-Ownership Effect," *Journal of Consumer Psychology* 6 (1997): 285–97.

14. A. M. Tybout and R. F. Yalch, "The Effect of Experience: A Matter of Salience?," *Journal of Consumer Research* 6 (1980): 406–12.

15. Robert B. Cialdini, Nancy Eisenberg, Beth L. Green, Kelton Rhoads, and Renee Bator, "Undermining the Undermining Effect of Reward on Sustained Interest," *Journal of Applied Social Psychology* 28 (1998): 253–67.

16. W. J. McGuire and D. Papageorgis, "The Relative Efficacy of Various Types of Prior Belief-Defense in Producing Immunity Against Persuasion," *Journal of Abnormal and Social Psychology* 62 (1961): 327–37.

17. William McGuire, "Inducing Resistance to Persuasion: Some Contemporary Approaches," in L. Berkowitz, ed., *Advances in Experimental Social Psychology*, vol. 1 (San Diego, Calif.: Academic Press, 1964), 191–29.

18. Alice H. Eagly and Shelly Chaiken, *The Psychology of Attitudes* (Fort Worth, Tex.: Harcourt Brace Jovanovich, 1993); Bert Pryor and Thomas M. Steinfatt, "The Effects of Initial Belief Level on Inoculation Theory and Its Proposed Mechanisms," *Human Communication Research* 4 (1978): 217–30; L. Killeya and B. Johnson, "Experimental Induction of Biased Systematic Processing: The Directed-Thought Technique," *Personality and Social Psychology Bulletin* 24 (1998): 17–33.

19. G. M. Breen and J. Matusitz, "Preventing Youths from Joining Gangs: How to Apply Inoculation Theory," *Journal of Applied Security Research* 4 (2009): 109–28; M. Pfau, S. Van Bockern, and J. G. Kang, "Use of Inoculation to Promote Resistance to Smoking Initiation Among Adolescents," *Communication Monographs* 59 (1992): 213–30; M. Pfau, H. C. Kenski, M. Nitz, and J. Sorenson, "Efficacy of Inoculation Strategies in Promoting Resistance to Political Attack Messages: Application to Direct Mail," *Communication Monographs* 57 (1990): 25–43.

20. M. Bernard, G. Maio, and J. Olsen, "The Vulnerability of Value to Attack: Inoculation of Values and Value Relevant Attitudes," *Personality and Social Psychology Bulletin* 29 (2003): 63–75.

21. Zakary Tormala and Richard Petty, "What Doesn't Kill Me Makes Me Stronger: The Effects of Resisting Persuasion on Attitude Certainty," *Journal of Personality and Social Psychology* 83 (2002): 1298–313.

Chapter 8 | Closing Redefined: Obtaining Strategic Commitments

1. Karl Duncker, "On Problem-Solving," *Psychological Monographs* 58 (1945).

2. Robert E. Ornstein, *The Evolution of Consciousness: Of Darwin, Freud, and Cranial Fire: The Origins of the Way We Think* (New York: Prentice-Hall, 1991).

3. Jonathan L. Freedman and Scott C. Fraser, "Compliance Without Pressure: The Foot-in-the-Door Technique," *Journal of Personality and Social Psychology* 4 (1966): 195–202.

4. J. M. Burger, "The Foot-in-the-Door Compliance Procedure: A Multiple-Process Analysis and Review," *Personality and Social Psychology Review* 3 (1999): 303–25; James Price Dillard, "The Current Status of

Research on Sequential-Request Compliance Techniques," *Personality and Social Psychology Bulletin* 17 (1991): 283–88.

5. P. Pliner, H. Hart, J. Kohl, and D. Saari, "Compliance Without Pressure: Some Further Data on the Foot-in-the-Door Technique," *Journal of Experimental Social Psychology* 10 (1974): 17–22; Nicolas Guéguen and Céline Jacob, "Fund-Raising on the Web: The Effect of an Electronic Foot-in-the-Door on Donation," *CyberPsychology and Behavior* 4 (2001): 705–9; J. Schwarzwald, A. Bizman, and M. Raz, "The Foot-in-the-Door Paradigm: Effects of Second Request Size on Donation Probability and Donor Generosity," *Personality and Social Psychology Bulletin* 9 (1983): 443–50; A. Lipsitz, K. Kallmeyer, M. Ferguson, and A. Abas, "Counting on Blood Donors: Increasing the Impact of Social Reminder Calls," *Journal of Applied Social Psychology* 19 (1989): 1057–67; R. V. Joule, "Tobacco Deprivation: The Foot-in-the-Door Technique Verses the Low-Ball Technique," *European Journal of Social Psychology* 17 (1978): 361–65.

6. Norbert L. Kerr and Robert J. MacCoun, "The Effects of Jury Size and Polling Method on the Process and Product of Jury Deliberation," *Journal of Personality and Social Psychology* 48 (1985): 349–63.

7. B. R. Schlenker and J. V. Trudeau, "The Impact of Self-Presentations on Private Self-Beliefs: Effects of Prior Self-Beliefs and Misattribution," *Journal of Personality and Social Psychology* 58 (1990): 22–32; B. R. Schlenker, D. Dlugolecki, and K. Doherty, "The Impact of Self-Presentations on Self-Appraisals and Behavior: The Power of Public Commitment," *Journal of Personality and Social Psychology* 20 (1994): 20–33.

8. Edwin A. Locke and Gary P. Latham, "Building a Practically Useful Theory of Goal Setting and Task Motivation: A 35-Year Odyssey," *American Psychologist* 57 (2002): 707.

9. William Grimes, "In War Against No-Shows, Restaurants Get Tougher," *New York Times*, October 15, 1997, www.nytimes

.com/1997/10/15/dining/in-war-against-no-shows-restaurants-get
-tougher.html?pagewanted=all.

10. Dennis T. Regan and Martin Kilduff, "Optimism About Elections:
Dissonance Reduction at the Ballot Box," *Political Psychology* 9 (1988):
101–07.

11. Ibid., 101.

12. R. E. Knox and J. A. Inkster, "Postdecisional Dissonance at Post Time,"
Journal of Personality and Social Psychology 8 (1968): 319–23.

13. Daryl J. Bem, "Self-Perception Theory," in L. Berkowitz, ed., *Advances
in Experimental Social Psychology,* vol. 6 (New York: Academic Press,
1972), 2.

14. Daryl J. Bem, "Self-Perception: An Alternative Interpretation of
Cognitive Dissonance Phenomena," *Psychological Review* 74 (1967):
183–200; R. H. Fazio, "Self-Perception Theory: A Current Perspective,"
in M. P. Zanna, J. Olson, and C. Herman, eds., *Ontario Symposium on
Personality and Social Psychology* (Hillsdale, N.J.: Erlbaum, 1978),
129–50; Schlenker and Trudeau, "The Impact of Self-Presentations on
Private Self-Beliefs," 22–32; A. E. Kelly and R. R. Rodriguez, "Publicly
Committing Oneself to an Identity," *Basic and Applied Social
Psychology* 28 (2006): 185–91.

15. Kassin, Fein, and Markus, *Social Psychology,* 58.

16. Schlenker and Trudeau, "The Impact of Self-Presentations on Private
Self-Beliefs," 22–32.

17. Jonathan L. Freedman and Scott C. Fraser, "Compliance Without
Pressure," 201.

18.   J. K. Beggan and S. T. Allison, "More There Than Meets the Eyes: Support for the Mere-Ownership Effect," *Journal of Consumer Psychology* 6 (1997): 285–297; A. D. Ball and L. H. Tasaki, "The Role and Measurement of Attachment in Consumer Behavior," *Journal of Consumer Psychology* 1 (1992): 155–72.

19.   Mark R. Dadds, Dana H. Bovbjerg, William H. Redd, and Tim R. H. Cutmore, "Imagery in Human Classical Conditioning," *Psychological Bulletin* 122 (1997): 89–103.

20.   James E. Driskell, Carolyn Copper, and Aidan Moran, "Does Mental Practice Enhance Performance?," *Journal of Applied Psychology* 79 (1994): 481–92; Gavan J. Fitzsimons and Sarah G. Moore, "Should We Ask Our Children About Sex, Drugs and Rock & Roll? Potentially Harmful Effects of Asking Questions About Risky Behaviors," *Journal of Consumer Psychology* 18 (2008): 82–95; J. Levav and G. J. Fitzsimons, "When Questions Change Behavior: The Role of Ease of Representation," *Psychological Science* 17 (2006): 207–13.

21.   Kevin L. Blankenship and Traci Y. Craig, "Language and Persuasion: Tag Questions as Powerless Speech or as Interpreted in Context," *Journal of Experimental Psychology* 43 (2007): 112–118; L. A. Hosman and S. A. Siltanen, "Hedges, Tag Questions, Message Processing, and Persuasion," *Journal of Language and Social Psychology* 30 (2011): 341–49.

22.   Robert H. Gass and John S. Seiter, *Persuasion: Social Influence and Compliance Gaining*, 4th ed. (Boston: Allyn & Bacon, 2011), 155.

23.   Dr. Thomas Steenburgh, *Module Note: Personal Selling and Sales Management* (Boston: Harvard Business School Press, 2006), 4.

24.   C. Lee, S. A. Linkenauger, J. Z. Bakdash, J. A. Joy-Gaba, and D. R. Profitt, "Putting Like a Pro: The Role of Positive Cognition in Golf

Performance and Perception," *PLoS ONE* 6, no. 10 (October 2011): e26016, doi:10.1371/journal.pone.0026016.

Chapter 9 | Five Science-Based Sales Presentation Strategies

1. Rachel Young, "Buyer-Centric Sales Presentations That Win," *Rachel Young's Blog*, SiriusDecisions, December 29, 2015, retrieved on March 13, 2016, www.siriusdecisions.com/Blog/2015/December/BuyerCentric -Sales-Presentations-That-Win.aspx.

2. Hillary Chura, "Um, Uh, Like Call in the Speech Coach," *New York Times*, January 11, 2007.

3. Harold Pashler, "Dual-Task Interference in Simple Tasks: Data and Theory," *Psychological Bulletin* 116 (1994): 220–24; John Medina, *Brain Rules* (Seattle: Pear Press, 2008), 130.

4. George A. Miller, "The Magical Number Seven, Plus or Minus Two: Some Limits of Our Capacity for Processing Information," *Psychological Review* 63 (1956): 81–97.

5. Sheena S. Iyengar and Mark R. Lepper, "When Choice Is Demotivating: Can One Desire Too Much of a Good Thing," *Journal of Personality and Social Psychology* 79 (2000): 995–1006.

6. Barry Schwartz, "Self-Determination: The Tyranny of Freedom," *American Psychologist* 55, no. 1 (January 2000): 86.

7. Sheena Iyengar, Wei Jiang, and Gur Huberman, "How Much Choice Is Too Much? Contributions to 401(k) Retirement Plans," in O. S. Mitchell and S. P. Utkus, eds., *Pension Design and Structure: New Lessons from Behavioral Finance* (Oxford: Oxford University Press, 2004), 83–97.

8. Marina Strauss, "In Store Aisles, Less Is More but Customers Can Still Be Particular," *Globe and Mail*, May 18, 2010.

9. C. Janiszewski and D. Uy, "Precision of the Anchor Influences the Amount of Adjustment," *Psychological Science* 19 (2008): 121–27; Amos Tversky and Daniel Kahneman, "Judgment under Uncertainty: Heuristics and Biases," *Science* 185 (1974); John J. Sailors and James E. Heyman, "Compound Anchors and Their Subsequent Effects on Judgment," *American Behavioral Scientists* 55, no. 8 (August 2011): 1035–51.

10. Dan Ariely, George Loewenstein, and Drazen Prelec, "'Coherent Arbitrariness': Stable Demands Curves Without Stable Preferences," *Quarterly Journal of Economics* (February 2003): 73–106.

11. Brian Wansink, Robert J. Kent, and Stephen J. Hoch, "An Anchoring and Adjustment Model of Purchase Quantity Decisions," *Journal of Marketing Research* 35 (1998): 71–81.

12. Ned Welch, "A Marketer's Guide to Behavioral Economics," *McKinsey Quarterly*, February 2010, 4.

13. Ibid., 4.

14. Daniel Kahneman, *Thinking, Fast and Slow* (New York: Farrar, Straus and Giroux, 2011), 125.

15. Gregory B. Northcraft and Margaret A. Neale, "Experts, Amateurs, and Real Estate: An Anchoring-and-Adjustment Perspective on Property Pricing Decisions," *Organizational Behavior and Human Decision Processes* 39 (1987): 84–97.

16. Deepak Malhotra and Max H. Bazerman, *Negotiation Genius* (New York: Bantam Books, 2007), 31.

17. Jerry M. Burger, "Increasing Compliance by Improving the Deal: The That's-Not-All Technique," *Journal of Personality and Social Psychology* 51 (2008): 277–83.

18. J. L. Lakin and T. L. Chartrand, "Using Nonconscious Behavioral Mimicry to Create Affiliation and Rapport," *Psychological Science* 14 (2003): 334–39; R. B. van Baaren, R. W. Holland, K. Kawakami, and A. van Knippenberg, "Mimicry and Prosocial Behavior," *Psychological Science* 15 (2004): 71–74.

19. Jerry M. Burger, Nicole Messian, Shebani Patel, Alicia del Prado, and Carmen Anderson, "What a Coincidence! The Effects of Incidental Similarity on Compliance," *Personality and Social Psychology Bulletin* 30 (January 2004): 35–43; Randy Garner, "What's in a Name? Persuasion Perhaps," *Journal of Consumer Psychology* 15 (2005): 108–16.

20. Douglas T. Kenrick, Steven L. Neuberg, and Robert B. Cialdini, *Social Psychology: Goals in Interaction,* 5th ed. (Boston: Allyn & Bacon, 2010), 117.

21. Elaine Hatfield, John T. Cacioppo, and Richard L. Rapson, *Emotional Contagion* (Cambridge: Cambridge University Press, 1994); R. Newman and F. Strack, "Approach and Avoidance: The Influence of Proprioceptive and Exteroceptive Cues on Encoding of Affective Information," *Journal of Personality and Social Psychology* 79 (2000): 39–48; Daniel Goleman, *Social Intelligence* (New York: Bantam Books, 2006), 25.

22. Michael S. Gazzaniga, Richard B. Ivry, and George R. Mangun, *Cognitive Neuroscience,* 3rd ed. (New York: W. W. Norton, 2009), 618–20.

23. William W. Maddux, Elizabeth Mullen, and Adam D. Galinsky, "Chameleons Bake Bigger Pies and Take Bigger Pieces: Strategic Behavioral Mimicry Facilitates Negotiation Outcomes," *Journal of Experimental Social Psychology* 44 (2008): 461–68.

24. Robin J. Tanner, Rosellina Ferraro, Tanya L. Chartrand, James R. Bettman, and Rick van Baaren, "Of Chameleons and Consumption: The Impact of Mimicry on Choice and Preferences," *Journal of Consumer Research* 34 (2007): 754–66.

25. "Idea Watch: Monkey See, Monkey Buy," *Harvard Business Review* (January–February 2012): 28.

26. Giacomo Rizzolatti and Michael A. Arbib, "Language Within Our Grasp," *Trends in Neurosciences* 21 (1998): 188–94.

27. Sandra Blakeslee, "Cells That Read Minds," *New York Times,* January 10, 2006.

28. Giacomo Rizzolatti and Corrado Sinigaglia, Frances Anderson, trans., *Mirrors in the Brain: How Our Minds Share Actions, Emotions and Experience* (New York: Oxford University Press, 2008); G. Rizzolatti and L. Craighero, "The Mirror-Neuron System," *Annual Review of Neuroscience* 27 (2004): 169–92; Vittorio Gallese, Morton Ann Gernsbacher, Cecilia Heyes, Gregory Hickok, and Marco Iacoboni, "Mirror Neuron Forum," *Perspectives on Psychological Science* 6 (July 2011): 369–407.

29. Derek E. Lyons, "The Rational Continuum of Human Imitation," in Jaime A. Pineda, ed., *Mirror Neuron Systems: The Role of Mirroring Processes in Social Cognition* (New York: Humana Press, 2008), 77.

30. P. M. Niedenthal, L. W. Barsalou, F. Ric, and S. Krauth-Gruber, "Embodiment in the Acquisition and Use of Emotional Knowledge," in L. F. Barrett, P. M. Niedenthal, and P. Winkielman, eds., *Emotion and Consciousness* (New York: Guilford Press, 2005); W. D. Hutchison, K. D. Davis, A. M. Lozano, R. R. Tasker, and J. O. Dostrovsky, "Pain-Related Neurons in the Human Cingulate Cortex," *Nature-Neuroscience* 2 (1999): 403–5.

31.   T. L. Chartrand and J. A. Bargh, "The Chameleon Effect: The Perception-Behavior Link and Social Interaction," *Journal of Personality and Social Psychology* 76 (1999): 893–910.

32.   Michael B. McCaskey, "The Hidden Messages Managers Send," *Harvard Business Review* (November–December 1979).

33.   Marianne LaFrance, "Nonverbal Synchrony and Rapport: Analysis by the Cross-Lag Panel Technique," *Social Psychology Quarterly* 42 (1979): 66–70.

34.   Jeremy N. Bailenson and Nick Yee, "Digital Chameleons: Automatic Assimilation of Nonverbal Gestures in Immersive Virtual Environments," *Psychological Science* 16 (2005): 814–19.

35.   D. Buller, B. LePoire, K. Aune, and S. Eloy, "Social Perceptions as Mediators of the Effect of Speech Rate Similarity on Compliance," *Human Communication Research* 19 (1992): 282–311.

36.   R. B. van Baaren, R. W. Holland, B. Steenaert, and A. van Knippenberg, "Mimicry for Money: Behavioral Consequences of Imitation," *Journal of Experimental Social Psychology* 39 (2003): 393–98.

37.   Medina, *Brain Rules*, 234.

38.   W. E. Hockley, "The Picture Superiority Effect in Associative Recognition," *Memory & Cognition* 36 (2008): 1351–59; G. Stenberg, "Conceptual and Perceptual Factors in the Picture Superiority Effect," *European Journal of Cognitive Psychology* 18 (2006): 813–47.

39.   J. D. Fletcher and Sigmund Tobias, "The Multimedia Principle," in Richard E. Mayer, ed., *The Cambridge Handbook of Multimedia Learning* (New York: Cambridge University Press, 2005), 117–34.

40. Kirsten R. Butcher, "Learning from Text with Diagrams: Promoting Mental Model Development and Inference Generation," *Journal of Educational Psychology* 98 (2006): 182–97.

41. Richard Mayer and Roxana Moreno, *A Cognitive Theory of Multimedia Learning: Implications for Design Principle* (University of California, Santa Barbara: unm.edu/~moreno/pdfs/chi.pdf, accessed January 30, 2009).

42. Medina, *Brain Rules*, 234.

43. Walter R. Fisher, *Human Communication as Narration: Toward a Philosophy of Reason, Value, and Action* (Columbia, S.C.: University of South Carolina, 1987).

44. Ibid., 24.

45. L. Cozolino and S. Sprokay, "Neuroscience and Adult Learning," in Sandra Johnson and Kathleen Taylor, eds., *The Neuroscience of Adult Learning*, New Directions for Adult and Continuing Education, no. 110 (San Francisco: Jossey-Bass, 2006).

46. Jay A. Conger, "The Necessary Art of Persuasion," *Harvard Business Review Onpoint* (Fall 2010): 54.

47. Chip Heath and Dan Heath, *Made to Stick* (New York: Random House, 2008), 242–43.

48. Rolf A. Zwaan and Gabriel A. Radvansky, "Situation Models in Language Comprehension and Memory," *Psychological Bulletin* 123 (1998): 162–85.

49. Greg J. Stephens, Lauren J. Silbert, and Uri Hasson, "Speaker-Listener Neural Coupling Underlies Successful Communication," *Proceedings of*

the National Academy of Science of the United States of America 107, no. 32 (2010): 14425–30.

50.   Zwaan and Radvansky, "Situation Models in Language Comprehension and Memory," 162–85; "Scientists Watch as Listener's Brain Predicts Speaker's Words," *Science Daily*, September 15, 2008.

51.   J. Levav and G. J. Fitzsimons, "When Questions Change Behavior: The Role of Ease of Representation," *Psychological Science* 17 (2006): 207–13; Gavan J. Fitzsimons and Sarah G. Moore, "Should We Ask Our Children About Sex, Drugs and Rock & Roll? Potentially Harmful Effects of Asking Questions About Risky Behaviors," *Journal of Consumer Psychology* 18 (2008): 82–95.

52.   D. Van Knippenberg and H. Wilke, "Prototypicality of Arguments and Conformity to Ingroup Norms" *European Journal of Social Psychology* 22 (1992): 141–55; D. M. Mackie, L. T. Worth, and A. G. Asuncion, "Processing of Persuasive In-Group Messages," *Journal of Personality and Social Psychology* 58 (1990): 812–22.

53.   Robert B. Cialdini, "Harnessing the Science of Persuasion," *Harvard Business Review* (October 2001).

54.   Solomon E. Asch, "Forming Impression of Personality," *Journal of Abnormal and Social Psychology* 41 (1946): 258–90.

55.   *Super Sales Presentations*, Patricia Fripp, DVD (2007; Seminars on DVD).

56.   Nancy Pennington and Reid Hastie, "Explanation-Based Decision Making: Effects of Memory Structure on Judgment," *Journal of Experimental Psychology: Learning, Memory and Cognition* 14 (1988) 521–33.

Chapter 10 | The Future of Selling

1. Roger Dooley, "How Behavioral Science Propelled Obama's Win," *Forbes*, November 19, 2012, retrieved on March 13, 2016, www.forbes.com/sites/rogerdooley/2012/11/19/obama-behavioral/#7fd6bfa3396e; Benedict Carey, "Academic 'Dream Team' Helped Obama's Effort," *New York Times*, November 12, 2012, retrieved on March 13, 2016, www.nytimes.com/2012/11/13/health/dream-team-of-behavioral-scientists-advised-obama-campaign.html?_r=0.

2. "Executive Order: Using Behavioral Science Insights to Better Serve the American People," The White House, Office of the Press Secretary, September 15, 2015, retrieved on March 13, 2016, www.whitehouse.gov/the-press-office/2015/09/15/executive-order-using-behavioral-science-insights-better-serve-american; Noah J. Goldstein, Steve J. Martin, and Robert B. Cialdini, *Yes! 50 Scientifically Proven Ways to Be Persuasive* (New York: Free Press, 2008), xv; Richard Thaler, *Misbehaving: The Making of Behavioral Economics* (New York: W. W. Norton, 2015), 330–45.

3. Mark Whitehead, Rhys Jones, Rachel Howell, Rachel Lilley, and Jessica Pykett, "Nudging All Over the World: Assessing the Global Impact of the Behavioural Sciences on Public Policy," *Economic and Social Research Council*, September 2014, retrieved on March 13, 2016, changingbehaviours.files.wordpress.com/2014/09/nudgedesignfinal.pdf.

4. Brad J. Sagarin and Kevin D. Mitnick, "The Path of Least Resistance," in Douglas T. Kenrick, Noah J. Goldstein, and Sanford L. Braver, eds., *Six Degrees of Social Influence* (Oxford: Oxford Press, 2012), 26.

5. Suzanne Fogel, David Hoffmeister, Richard Rocco, and Daniel P. Strunk, "Teaching Sales," *Harvard Business Review* (July-August 2012): 94.

6. Jason Jordan with Michelle Vazzana, *Cracking the Sales Management Code* (New York: McGraw-Hill, 2012), 9.

7. Frank V. Cespedes and Daniel Weinfurter, "More Universities Need to Teach Sales," *Harvard Business Review*, retrieved May 25, 2016, https://hbr.org/2016/04/more-universities-need-to-teach-sales.

8. Edward K. Strong, *The Psychology of Selling and Advertising* (New York: McGraw-Hill, 1925), 8.

9. William McDougall, *An Introduction to Social Psychology* (London: Methuen, 1908).

10. Harry R. Tosdal, *Principles of Personal Selling* (New York: A. W. Shaw Company, 1926), 76, 86, 91.

11. Strong, *The Psychology of Selling and Advertising*, 8.

12. Tosdal, *Principles of Personal Selling*, 527.

13. Alfred P. Sloan Jr., "Quarterly Dividend Mailing to GM Common Stockholders," General Motors Corporation, September 11, 1933.

14. Rory Sutherland, "The Next Revolution Will Be Psychological, Not Technological," YouTube, February 19, 2013, retrieved on March 13, 2016, www.youtube.com/watch?v=jEVCFS3YEpk.

15. Bradford D. Smart and Greg Alexander, *Topgrading for Sales* (New York: Portfolio/Penguin, 2008), 35.

16. Andris A. Zoltners, Prabhakant Sinha, and Sally E. Lorimer, *Building a Winning Sales Force* (New York: AMACOM, 2009), 130.

17. Scott Fuhr, "Good Hiring Makes Good Cents," *Selling Power* (July/August/September 2012), 20.

18. Smart and Alexander, *Topgrading for Sales*, 5.

19. Joe Light, "More Workers Start to Quit," *Wall Street Journal*, May 25, 2010.

20. Barry Trailer and Jim Dickie, "Understanding What Your Sales Manager Is Up Against," *Harvard Business Review* (July–August 2006).

21. Daniel Goleman, *Working with Emotional Intelligence* (New York: Bantam Books, 2006), 170.

22. Peter F. Drucker with Joseph A. Maciariello, *The Daily Drucker* (New York: Harper Collins, 2004), 107.

23. Leonard L. Berry and Kent D. Seltman, *Management Lessons from Mayo Clinic* (New York: McGraw-Hill, 2008), 61.

24. Leonard Lee, Shane Frederick, and Dan Ariely, "Try It, You'll Like It," *Psychological Science* 17 (2006): 1,054–58.

INDEX

DAVID HOFFELD is the CEO and chief sales trainer at Hoffeld Group, one of the nation's top research-based sales and consulting firms. He is widely regarded as the number one authority on selling with science.

A sought-after sales thought leader and speaker, David has trained and coached salespeople from small and medium businesses to Fortune 500 companies. He's a sales and leadership contributor to *Fast Company* and has been featured in *Fortune, U.S. News and World Report,* the *Wall Street Journal, Harvard Business Review,* CBS Radio, Fox News Radio, and more. David has built a robust and loyal audience as a trusted resource for sales and business leaders. He has received numerous awards from Toastmasters International and is a member of the National Speakers Association, the Association for Talent Development, and the Society for Personality and Social Psychology. David earned a master's degree at Trinity International University and has studied sales at Harvard Business School. To learn more about his work, visit HoffeldGroup.com.